THE TEACHING DELUSION

WHY TEACHING IN OUR SCHOOLS ISN'T GOOD ENOUGH (AND HOW WE CAN MAKE IT BETTER)

BRUCE ROBERTSON

First Published 2020

by John Catt Educational Ltd,
15 Riduna Park, Station Road,
Melton, Woodbridge IP12 1QT

Tel: +44 (0) 1394 389850
Email: enquiries@johncatt.com
Website: www.johncatt.com

Cover photo by NASA on www.unsplash.com

ISBN: 978 1 912906 64 2

Set and designed by John Catt Educational Limited

Praise for
The Teaching Delusion

"This book is indispensable for teachers and school leaders alike. It makes a passionate case for putting learning and teaching at the heart of everything that happens in a school and provides a clear and instantly practical framework for doing this. It is one of the best summaries of key educational research I have read and it has challenged me to think about the most important question in education: what makes great teaching? If you only read one educational book this year, make it this one."

Kelly Fairbairn, Deputy Headteacher
and former Head of English and Literacy, Scottish Borders

"Reading 'The Teaching Delusion' has had an immediate, positive impact on my teaching. The practical skills I have picked up as a class teacher are already making a difference. I am seeing a marked increase in my students' confidence, focus, and knowledge in a very short time."

Derek Huffman, English Teacher,
Berwickshire High School, Scottish Borders

"I have found this book an incredibly interesting and thought provoking look at what is central to both the purpose and practice of the teaching process, and what factors can help to improve it. It challenges teachers to think in its easily readable, personal and conversational style. By bringing together and summarising key ideas from the work of contemporary educational thinkers, the book challenges the reader to explore their own thinking about what makes great teaching or, indeed, poor teaching. An enjoyable, well researched, thought provoking read."

Iain Hughes, Quality Improvement Manager for the South East
Improvement Collaborative; former Headteacher, Waid Academy

For Jamie

'It is far better to grasp the Universe as it really is than to persist in delusion, however satisfying and reassuring.'

Carl Sagan

Contents

Foreword

By Robin Macpherson

Why read this book? There are four reasons.

Firstly, it is incredibly well informed. Bruce not only has substantial experience as a teacher and school leader, he is also very well read. His skill in navigating his way through different debates, showing the range of argument and opinion that exists, makes this plain. He adds his own thinking and reflection to a solid basis of current educational thinking. There's a touch of Hattie here, a bit of Lemov there, and a fair sprinkling of Coe. In fact, as Bruce reminds us, Rob Coe argues that learning is happening when people have to think hard. This book will certainly do that.

Secondly, it is written with clarity and takes very little effort to get through. This is not to say it is reductive - far from it - because Bruce has the commendable skill of taking the complex and making it simple. It is also a book that doesn't need to be read sequentially, as it depends on what your current focus is on. An important caveat is that the book will not necessarily be quick to get through. It takes time to read, because it makes you stop and think. It's the sort of book that you settle down into an armchair to read, and at regular intervals a point is made that causes you to drift off into thought. Before you know it, 15 minutes have passed and you're still on the same paragraph. So take your time and enjoy it; it deserves to be enjoyed.

Thirdly, it is provocative; this much is clear from the title. Yet Bruce hasn't done this for effect, he is very clear about what 'delusion' means in the context of education. It is a strong adjective, but you will be hard pushed to argue that he is using it inaccurately. There are many things about education in the early twenty-first century that are Kafkaesque and Bruce is right to identify and dissect them. My suspicion is that classroom teachers will read this and feel liberated, whereas many school leaders will find good reason to pause and reflect soberly on what they have been doing for the last few years. This is undoubtedly a good thing. Just as David Didau challenged readers to consider that everything they knew about education might be wrong, Bruce is also asking professionals to ask serious questions of themselves. As with David's book, you need to read it with an open mind – and be wary of the Semmelweis Reflex. Orthodoxy is put under the microscope, and, to give an example, on 'student-led learning' Bruce is brave enough to say what many of us are thinking, but few dare say out loud. I can only hope others will feel similarly emboldened by this book.

And finally, I think the Lesson Evaluation Toolkit alone makes this book worth purchasing. It is a great chapter and should open up discussions in schools everywhere about what the core ingredients of great teaching are. Bruce is careful to point out that this is not a check-list, but a framework that schools should produce themselves having distilled the best educational research out there. Imagine if every school did this? Far too many teachers have to wade through CPD that is irrelevant, time-consuming, and expensive. What Bruce maps out is a far better direction of travel. I can see this book being a brilliant addition to reading groups, CPD libraries, and on-line discussions.

I'll admit that there is a fair bit of cognitive bias in what I say here, because Bruce and I share many core beliefs about education. When he writes that "I do not believe that the primary purpose of schools is to prepare students for future study or jobs" I have one hand on the book, and the other punching the air. Like Bruce, I also regret not reading more about the craft of teaching earlier in my teaching career, but also recognise that the literature available today is much more accessible and readily available than in the past. This book is an important addition to the canon.

So my advice is to get a piece of paper and a pencil, and tuck them inside the book. As you go through it, make a note of all the great questions that Bruce asks. For example, what is the purpose of school? Have these questions in your mind when you are next having a discussion with a colleague and throw one or two out to them. See what happens. So much of the best professional learning comes from a simple dialogue over a coffee in the staff room (not on expensive courses in posh hotels). This book is a great conversation starter, and will bring enormous benefit to both the individual reader and to whole school communities. Keep it near to hand; you'll find yourself revisiting it often.

Robin Macpherson

Teacher and author,
What Does This Look Like in the Classroom?

Introduction

There is a lot of great teaching going on in our classrooms and schools.

It is very important that we recognise this from the start. Schools are filled with teachers who are working as hard as they can to teach their students as best they can.

Teachers have one of the most important jobs in the world. For me, there is no question of that. Beyond parents, there are few people in a young person's life who will have a more important influence on their learning, wellbeing and development. When students experience great teaching, not only do they learn and achieve; they never forget it.

Most people don't realise just how complex and demanding the job of a teacher actually is. Because they went to school themselves, they think they do, but they don't. Unless they have worked as a teacher, it is difficult for most people to appreciate just how much there is to it and how challenging it is to do all of it well.

Now, having said all of this, I would like to ask you a question: is the quality of teaching in our schools good enough? Please pause for a moment and think about this.

I recognise you might think this is a controversial question. There is a perception among some teachers that they are always being 'bashed'. School leaders bash them; the media bash them; sometimes, students and parents bash them.

I am not a teacher-basher. First and foremost, I am a teacher myself. It is true that I do a lot less teaching than I used to, but that doesn't mean I don't love teaching or working with teachers. A love of teaching is what drives me, and my working relationship with teachers is as important to me – if not more important – than any other working relationship I have. In my job, I work far more closely, and more often, with teachers than I do with anyone else. So, having said all of this, I hope that you will accept that my intention is not to start bashing teachers.

Back to the question: is the quality of teaching in our schools good enough?

No. It isn't. Please don't throw this book across the room. Stick with me.

While there is a lot of great teaching going on in our classrooms and schools, the reality is that there is also a lot of teaching going on which isn't as good as people think it is, or as good as it needs to be. There are a lot of teachers who aren't teaching to their potential.

When I say this, I am not suggesting that teaching in our schools today is poor (although, being honest, some of it is). I actually think that teaching is as good today as it has ever been. Rather, I am suggesting that it could be better. Good could be very good and great could be even greater. So why isn't this happening?

The answer is not because teachers aren't working hard. Most are. It is not because teachers aren't trying their best. Most are. Instead, a significant reason is that many teachers and school leaders (by whom I mean headteachers, deputy headteachers, heads of department, principal teachers and others with school leadership roles) don't *really* understand what great teaching is. They think they do, but they don't.

A second significant reason is that teachers aren't being supported by their schools to develop and improve their practice. Instead, they are left to this themselves. However, not everyone is managing. Not because they don't want to, but because they don't know how to or believe that they don't have time.

What this means is that many of our students aren't receiving the quality of education that they need and deserve. Too often, the quality of education they receive is determined by the luck of the draw. By this, I mean it is determined by which teachers happen to be teaching them. Usually, students don't get to control this. Whether or not they experience great teaching, good teaching or poor teaching is usually a matter of chance. If you accept this, then I hope you will also accept that this isn't good enough. Everyone involved in education has a duty to do something about this.

So, what can we do? What can we do to help ensure that, regardless of the teachers they have, all students receive a high-quality education? The solution is simple: **we need to improve the quality of our teaching**.

How do we do that? I am glad you asked...

About this book

In this book, we will explore what great teaching is and what it isn't. We will explore effective and ineffective ways for teachers and school leaders to lead improvements to teaching and learning in classrooms, departments and schools. In doing so, we will address 'the teaching delusion'.

'The teaching delusion' is caused by three things. The first is that many teachers and school leaders *think* they know what great teaching is, but really, they don't. The second is that they *think* they know how to improve teaching, but really, they don't. The third is that they *think* teaching is good enough, but really, it isn't. In this book, we will explore how these things can be addressed.

By reading it, you will learn why developing a **shared understanding of what makes great teaching** across a school is so important and how the creation and use of a school *Lesson Evaluation Toolkit* can help achieve this. You will learn what a **professional learning culture** is, why it is so important, and how it can be developed and used to transform teaching practice. As a result, everyone's teaching practice will get better.

This has been the focus of the work I have led in my school and with other schools (primary and secondary) as a deputy headteacher with responsibility for teaching and learning. The significant improvements in teaching quality which have come about as a result have been achieved through a focus on the right things in the right way. In this book, we will explore what the 'right things' are and how, as a teacher or a school leader, you can focus on them in the 'right way'.

The development of a shared understanding of what makes great teaching and a strong professional learning culture are key drivers to improving the quality of teaching in classrooms, departments and schools.

In June 2019, a focus on the right things in the right way led to my school being nominated for a national General Teaching Council for Scotland 'Excellence in Professional Learning Award', which we went on to win. In preparation for the visit from the verification panel, I asked staff to write down what they thought about the teaching and learning improvement work which had been taking place over the past few years. What follows is a sample of what they said:

- 'I used to believe that my teaching was good enough. Now, I want to keep making it better and better.'
- 'Supportive; relentless; positive. An environment which allows you to try out new things.'
- 'Sharing good practice across the school has visibly improved whole-school pedagogy.'
- 'I'm proud that all of the members of my department have taken

part in leading workshops, which has had a positive impact on the experiences of all students, as well as having focused staff on improving teaching and learning.'

- 'When asked to deliver a workshop on formative assessment, I found it really motivating to get my peers' feedback on my approach, which in turn improved my delivery in the classroom.'
- 'My department is genuinely improving its practice week on week on the back of professional learning, e.g. through use of Show-me boards, learning intentions and success criteria.'
- 'Since joining this school, I have been surprised and impressed by the expectation, encouragement and willingness among staff to improve and develop through professional learning.'
- 'There are numerous opportunities in this school to work collaboratively with colleagues, from peer observations to Professional Reading Groups.'
- 'Current educational research is at the centre of the improvement we are making to teaching and learning as a school, as departments and as individuals.'
- 'It is refreshing to work in an environment where teaching and learning for staff and students is discussed openly and naturally.'
- 'Professional learning has now become the "norm" in our school. People regularly chat about and reference educational research. We have a shared understanding of the work of many educational researchers.'
- 'I have learned more about teaching and learning theory in the last nine months than in four years at university.'

Developing a **shared understanding of what makes great teaching** and a **strong professional learning culture** have been key. In Chapter 1, we will ask, 'What makes great teaching?' Thereafter, we will keep returning to this question. In Chapter 7, we will explore what a professional learning culture is. Thereafter, we will discuss how such a culture can be developed and used in your school.

During the verification visit, staff were asked to identify what had made the biggest impact on their professional learning. Time and again, they highlighted the school's *Lesson Evaluation Toolkit*. As a framework to develop a shared understanding of what makes great teaching, they reported that it was hugely successful, bringing focus, support and challenge. Staff talked about how the *Lesson Evaluation Toolkit* had brought people, initiatives and strategy together. They felt a real sense of shared ownership and collective pride: *we* have developed this, *everyone* is using this, and, through its use, teaching and learning in *our* school is getting better and better. The creation and use of a *Lesson Evaluation Toolkit* for your school is a focus of this book from Chapter 8 onwards.

While I recognise that some of the messages in this introduction are challenging, I hope they haven't put you off continuing to read this book. Instead, I hope they have motivated you to read on. This book has a singular aim: to help make teaching better, regardless of how good it is already. It has been written by a teacher for teachers and by a school leader for school leaders.

At times, it will be provocative. This is deliberate: by being provocative, I hope to make you think. As we will go on to discuss, thinking and learning go hand in hand. Learning and enjoyment also go hand in hand. Therefore, I hope you enjoy reading this book.

PART 1.
A shared understanding of what makes great teaching

Chapter 1
What makes great teaching?

What makes great teaching?

Ask 100 teachers: what makes great teaching? How many different answers do you think you will get? Ten? Twenty? Fifty? Is there a 'right' answer to this question?

Try answering it yourself. Take two minutes to write down what you think are the essential features of great teaching. Ask a colleague to do the same, and then take a few minutes to discuss what you have written down.

Did they think the same as you? Did they write something that you hadn't? Did they write something that you disagree with?

I put this question to teachers a lot. The most common answers are:

- 'Having good relationships with your students'
- 'Knowing your students well'
- 'Making the learning fun'
- 'Making the learning interesting'
- 'Engaging students'
- 'Getting students to be active (not passive)'
- 'Letting students lead their own learning'

What do you think about these answers? For you, are these features of great teaching? In this book, we will explore this.

How do we know what makes great teaching?

Ask 100 teachers a different question: if we accept that there is such a thing as great teaching, how do we know what makes great teaching?

What do you think people will say? Again, try it yourself. Take two minutes to write down how you think we know what makes great teaching. Ask a colleague to do the same, and then take a few minutes to discuss what you have written.

So, what did you write? Perhaps you said something like:

- From what I was taught when I trained as a teacher
- From years of experience as a teacher
- From what school leaders tell us
- From what policies and guidelines tell us
- From what students tell us
- From how well students learn
- From how well students attain
- From what research tells us

Of these, which do you think is the most reliable? In this book, we will explore this too.

How good is your teaching?

Here are some further questions for you to think about:

- What is the difference between good teaching and great teaching?
- How good is your teaching?
- How do you know?
- How would you rate the quality of your teaching out of 10?
- How confident are you that your teaching is as good as you think it is?

There is no need to write down answers to these this time, but please do take the time to think about each of these questions. Try to answer them honestly, for yourself. If you feel comfortable doing so, discuss your answers with a colleague.

A need to get better?

If you are a teacher, here are three final questions:

- Does your teaching need to get better?
- Do you want to make your teaching better?
- Do you know how to make your teaching better?

If you aren't a teacher (perhaps because you are a school leader without a teaching remit) or you are a teacher who has a leadership remit, I would also like you to consider the following questions:

- Does teaching in your department or school need to get better?
- Do you want to make teaching in your department or school better?
- Do you know how to make teaching in your department or school better?

If the answer to any of these questions is yes – regardless of how good your teaching or that of your department or school already is – I would encourage you to read on. This is a book for teachers and school leaders who are interested in making teaching better in classrooms, departments and schools, no matter how good it is already.

Finding out how good your teaching is

I believe quite strongly that it does matter that you know how good your teaching is. If we are in the business of making the biggest difference that we can for the students that we teach, then we have to have a clear idea about where our strengths and weaknesses lie, so that we can take action to improve our weaknesses and use our strengths to support the development of our colleagues. If you aren't clear about how good your teaching is, you can't be clear that you are doing the best you can for your students. So how can you know how good your teaching is?

Unlike many professions, in which the effectiveness of professionals can be evaluated relatively quickly and easily, it is far less straightforward to evaluate the effectiveness of teaching. If you are a surgeon performing open heart surgery, your patient living or dying on the operating table offers relatively quick and reliable feedback regarding how successful you were. Getting instant, reliable feedback about the quality of teaching can be trickier.

Exam results and test scores

You might argue that, actually, this *is* straightforward: you can simply look at your students' exam results or test scores. These would let you know how good your teaching is, wouldn't they? Perhaps they would, but perhaps not. For example, it may well have been the case that some students in your class could have gone on to get very similar exam results had they been left to study some or all of the course themselves. Perhaps some of your students were receiving private tuition and it was this which led to strong exam results. Exam results and test scores can tell you something about the effectiveness of teaching (poor exam results and ineffective teaching do often go hand in hand). However, used in isolation, they are generally an unreliable measure of teaching quality.

What's more, by the time your students have sat their exams and received their results, a whole year will have passed since you first started teaching them. You might not even be their teacher anymore. While in-class test results can be obtained more quickly, there remain the same issues with reliability that we discussed for exams.

For all of these reasons, it just isn't sensible for teachers or school leaders to evaluate the quality of teaching based on exam and test results alone.

Feedback from observed lessons

You might argue that you could ask another teacher or school leader to come into one of your lessons, watch you teach and give you feedback on that. That would let you know how good your teaching is, wouldn't it? Well, perhaps, on the assumption that the person watching you teach has an understanding of the principles of high-quality teaching. However, as we will go on to discuss, this is far from certain. Also, it would assume that how you taught in that lesson was the same as how you teach every lesson. However, just because you taught a good (or poor) lesson with another professional watching you doesn't mean that you are a good (or poor) teacher. It just means your teaching was good (or poor) in that particular lesson. You might have taught differently because you knew another professional was watching you, or you might have felt nervous, and this affected your teaching. The feedback from another professional isn't necessarily a reliable indicator of teaching quality.

Student views
You could ask your students what they think about your teaching. That would let you know how good your teaching is, wouldn't it? Again, perhaps, but perhaps not. The usefulness of their views would, in part, rely on them having an understanding about what makes high-quality teaching, which many of them don't have. Their views might also be influenced by factors such as what kind of a day they are having or whether or not they like you. What kind of a day they are having probably has very little to do with you. If they like you, that doesn't necessarily mean that you are an effective teacher; if they don't, that doesn't necessarily mean that you are not an effective teacher – being liked and being an effective teacher are not the same thing. Like exam and test results, and feedback from observed lessons, student views about teaching quality are an unreliable indicator on their own.

So, with all of this in mind, how can you find out how good your teaching is? By the end of this book, you should have a much clearer idea.

Courage

It is important to recognise that to question the quality of your teaching practice takes courage. It is a brave thing to do. It is also the right thing to do. The best teachers and school leaders are the ones who are always questioning what they are doing.

If teachers and school leaders are afraid to question teaching practices and the quality of teaching taking place in their classrooms, departments and schools, they are doing both themselves and their students a disservice. Just because teachers and school leaders are working hard doesn't mean they are working well. Hard work and effective teaching are not the same thing. Neither are hard work and effective leadership.

The very fact that you are reading this book says a lot about you. It suggests that you aren't afraid to question your teaching or leadership practice and that being the best that you can be is important to you. For that, you should be commended.

Poor teaching

While nobody sets out to teach poorly, the reality is that there *is* poor teaching going on in many of our schools. Anyone who tries to argue that poor teaching doesn't exist is deluded. Controversially, I would argue that there is more poor teaching practice taking place in our schools than many teachers and school leaders are comfortable with acknowledging. Sometimes, teachers and school leaders don't recognise that teaching is poor. If we are going to be in any kind of a position to address this in as supportive a way as we can, then we need to understand what poor teaching practice looks like, what good teaching practice looks like and what great teaching practice looks like.

Good teaching

Many teachers and school leaders believe that the quality of teaching in their classroom, department or school is good, and they are satisfied with that. They believe that good teaching is good enough. But it's not. To return to the medical analogy, I don't want a good doctor operating on me: I want a *great* doctor. Why should it be any different with teaching?

There is a lot of good teaching taking place in our schools. Some of it is better than teachers and school leaders think – it is great teaching practice and needs to be recognised and shared. However, there is also a lot of teaching taking place which teachers and school leaders think is good, but actually it isn't. We need to do something about that.

Barriers to great teaching

If we accept that the quality of teaching does indeed vary quite widely in our schools, we can ask why this is the case. Why aren't we seeing great teaching in every classroom in every school, when teachers are working so hard? There are a number of reasons for this, including that many teachers and school leaders:

1. Don't really understand what great teaching is
2. Think they understand what great teaching is and that it is being practised, but they don't, and it isn't
3. Believe that 'good' teaching is good enough
4. Have an idea about what great teaching is, but don't know how to put theory into practice, or aren't supported to do so
5. Don't do anything to share the great teaching practice which is taking place in pockets of the school, allowing it to remain trapped in individual classrooms

So, what can we do to address such barriers? In this book, we will explore this.

A shared understanding?

A few years ago, the local authority which governed the school I was working in carried out a 'school review', the purpose of which was to evaluate the quality of teaching across the school. The review team was made up of six senior members of the local authority, including headteachers, deputy headteachers and quality improvement officers. Over two days, the team observed around 50 lessons. Following each observed lesson, they completed a *pro forma* to record 'strengths' and 'areas for improvement', along with a rating for the lesson: 'excellent', 'very good', 'good', 'satisfactory', 'weak' or 'unsatisfactory'. Most teachers were observed teaching twice, with one member of the review team observing each lesson, but not necessarily the same person observing different lessons taught by the same teacher.

As the deputy headteacher with responsibility for teaching and learning in my school, I felt that I had a good idea about what the review team would report back. I was confident that I knew where teaching practice was typically strong and where it was less so. For me, the review process offered a useful opportunity for this to be validated by an external team.

It therefore came as something of a surprise when, during the feedback process at the end of the review, members of the review team reported that they had observed 'satisfactory' or 'weak' teaching practice in classrooms where I would have told them it was typically 'good' or 'very good'. They also reported 'very good' practice in classrooms in which I would have reported it as 'satisfactory' at best. Not only was this disparity surprising, it was concerning: did this mean that I didn't know my school as well as I thought I did?

As I read through completed *pro formas* in the days that followed, it became apparent that there were multiple instances in which a particular teacher's observed lesson was rated 'very good' by one observer, but 'good', 'satisfactory' or 'weak' by another observer, from a different lesson. While this might have been because the two lessons did, in fact, vary in quality (lesson by lesson, there will always be variations in the quality of any teacher's practice), it was interesting just how many instances of this scenario there were. For me, this begged questions such as:

- What was happening in a 'very good' lesson that led to it being rated 'very good', and in a 'weak' lesson that led to it being rated 'weak'?
- Was there a shared understanding across the review team regarding the criteria for each rating? In other words, was there a shared understanding of what makes great teaching?
- Was the understanding of what members of the review team thought makes great teaching the same as my understanding or the understanding of teachers in my school? In other words, did we all have a shared understanding of what makes great teaching?

Here are two examples of completed *pro formas*:

Example 1

Strengths	Areas for improvement
• Use of ICT • Fun • Relevant activities	• Vary tasks to suit the needs of individual students • There should be different learning intentions for different students

Example 2

Strengths	Areas for improvement
• The demo was good • Positive ethos • Relationship with students	• Get students to lead their learning and take ownership of it • Create more opportunities for group work

Pause for a moment to consider what you think about this feedback.

Collated 'Strengths' and 'Areas for improvement' included the following written comments:

Strengths
- 'Students were on task and motivated'
- 'Students were very well behaved'
- 'Students had lots of opportunities to work co-operatively'
- 'The teacher was enthusiastic'
- 'All responses were valued'
- 'The learning intention was on the board'
- 'The teacher smiled a lot'
- 'Students were clear about what they were being asked to do'
- 'Students were helping each other'
- 'The teacher interacted well with the students'
- 'The teacher acted as the facilitator'
- 'A nice, calm manner'

Areas for improvement
- 'Students need to be allowed to find out things more for themselves'
- 'The lesson was too teacher-led. Reduce the amount of teacher talk'
- 'The lesson wasn't differentiated'
- 'Develop student confidence'
- 'Focus on developing skills'
- 'Be more creative in delivery, e.g. use games'
- 'Students need to be given more choice'
- 'Improve teacher presence'
- 'Improve student engagement'
- 'Make clear how the skills being developed can be applied in other subjects'
- 'Focus on developing soft skills such as teamwork and communication'
- 'Improve the pace of the lesson'

- 'No evidence of learning intentions or success criteria written in jotters'
- 'The learning could have been deepened'
- 'Contextualise learning'

Take a moment to consider this collated feedback and ask yourself:

- For each strength, do I think that this is a feature of great teaching?
- For the areas for improvement, do I think that, in the pursuit of great teaching, these are things on which a teacher should focus?
- How useful do I find the comments as feedback?

One final question: do you think there was a shared understanding of what makes great teaching across this review team?

Now that you have had the opportunity to consider this, I will share some of my thoughts:

- The quality of feedback varied wildly from observer to observer
- Very few of the identified strengths chime with my understanding of what makes great teaching
- Many of the areas identified for improvement are at odds with my understanding of what makes great teaching

In raising these points, I am not trying to argue that 'I am right' and 'they are wrong'. I am not trying to say that I know what makes great teaching and the members of the review team didn't. What I am saying is that my understanding of what makes great teaching was *not the same* as that of members of the review team. This is an issue. Such a disparity means that any 'rating' I assigned to a lesson would be different from that of members of the review team and, more importantly – in fact, much more importantly, because I don't believe that assigning ratings to lessons is important, necessary or productive – the feedback I would give to teachers would be very different.

I have been a member of school review teams myself. On one occasion, I carried out a lesson observation with a headteacher from another school whom I hadn't met before. I remember thinking what a good lesson we had just observed and feeling very positive about it as we left the room – watching good lessons tends to give me a bit of a buzz. It was therefore somewhat disheartening and deflating when, shortly after we had left the classroom, the headteacher said to me: 'Well, that wasn't very good, was it?' Before I'd had a chance to say anything, they continued: 'Poor David. He tries his best, but he just doesn't really have it, does he?'

There is much that we could discuss about this. For example, we could discuss the fact that two senior school leaders, who had been observing the *same* lesson, came out of it with very different views regarding the quality of teaching. We could discuss the fact that this headteacher seemed to believe that a teacher could 'have it' or 'not have it'. In other words, they seemed to be suggesting that some people are able to teach and others aren't. While I do believe that some people have a more natural disposition to teaching than others, I do not believe that some are born to teach and others aren't. I believe that, through a focus on the right things, most people who set their sights on becoming a great teacher have the potential to become one. It may come more easily to some than others, and it will take longer for some than others, but it can be done. However, whether or not someone achieves this will, in part, depend on their understanding of what makes great teaching.

We could also discuss the fact that this headteacher appeared to have used one lesson observation to arrive at an overarching judgement about the quality of this teacher's teaching in more general terms. Or worse, they may have had a preconceived notion and come in having already decided. I do not believe that you can use a single lesson observation to reach a judgement about the quality of a teacher's teaching. However, I do believe that you can use a lesson observation to arrive at a judgement about the quality of teaching *in that lesson*, and that to do so with any sort of reliability would require you to understand what makes great teaching. That is, it would rely on you knowing what you are looking for. This 'what you are looking for' would relate to particular elements of teaching practice. Rather than being about particular things *happening*, it would be about their *quality*.

Being able to arrive at a judgement about the quality of particular elements of teaching practice is far more useful than being able to reach a judgement about the overall quality of a lesson. Where elements of teaching practice are strong, they can be shared and used to support improvements in the practice of others; where they are weaker, they can be improved through feedback and support. Teachers are unlikely to improve particular elements of their teaching practice unless attention is drawn to the fact that they could be improved or need to improve.

Thinking back to the completed *pro formas* from the school review we discussed, the feedback *did* relate to particular elements of teaching practice. How useful this feedback was, however, depended on what was written, which depended on the understanding of the person who had written it of what makes great teaching.

The importance of a shared understanding

A clear and shared understanding of what makes great teaching is essential to improving the quality of teaching in classrooms and schools. Without this, different teachers will teach in different ways – some effectively and some less so. In other words, the quality of teaching across a school will vary widely – some of it great, some poor and most somewhere in between. Different people observing lessons will have different ideas about what they are looking for, and so will give different feedback – some useful and some not. Different people in charge of co-ordinating professional learning will have different ideas about what is important to focus on and what is not, sometimes spending time on things which are worthwhile and sometimes spending time on things which are not. In short: without a shared understanding of what makes great teaching, you might know what you are trying to achieve – great teaching – but you won't know *how* to achieve it.

So, what makes great teaching? We will go on to discuss this in some detail. Before we do, we will turn our attention to the purpose of school.

Chapter 2
The purpose of school

As a teacher or school leader, you will spend most of your professional life working in a school. But have you ever paused to ask yourself: why do we send young people to school? In other words: **what is the purpose of school?**

Think about that question for a moment and then write down your answer. It is important that you do write it down, otherwise there is a risk that you will pretend to yourself that you have thought of an answer, but really, you haven't. Maybe you have thought of a partial answer, but not a complete one. If you were asked to tell someone your answer, you wouldn't be able to do so articulately, because really, you don't have one fully formed.

When you ask students you teach questions, some of them (perhaps *many* of them) will only think of partial answers, and some will not think of any answers at all. It is important that you recognise this and get the students you teach to put their thoughts in writing (but not necessarily on paper, as we will discuss later) or to say them out loud, and to do this as often as you can. Doing so has two big advantages:

1. It encourages students to *think* (they have to, otherwise they won't write or say anything)
2. It allows you to see or hear *what they are thinking*

The capital of Australia

Imagine you are teaching 30 students and you ask the question: 'What is the capital of Australia?'

Imagine, first, that you ask this question and allow the shouting out of answers. A student shouts: 'Sydney', to which you respond, 'No, it's actually Canberra.'

What did that tell you? Very little, other than the fact that one student in the class didn't know the correct answer (and you hope that they now do, because you just told them it – and everyone else, too, because they all listened to you telling that student the correct answer. Didn't they?)

Did any other student in the class know the correct answer? If so, how many? Or did nobody in the class know the correct answer? If they didn't, was everyone's wrong answer the same – did they all think that the correct answer was Sydney? Or did some students think it was Melbourne? It would be useful for you, as the teacher of this class, to have answers to all of these questions. However, doing what you did – letting students shout out and then taking the first incorrect answer and correcting it for the student – didn't let you find out any of that.

You asked the question, 'What is the capital of Australia?' because you thought it was an important or worthwhile question to ask. If you didn't, you probably wouldn't have asked it. But what was the purpose of asking it?

Were you about to start a topic on Australia and wanted to find out what students already knew about the country? Or had you taught a lesson about Australia the day before, which included teaching students the capital of Australia, and you wanted to check that this had been remembered the next day? Or had you taught a lesson about Australia six months ago and wanted to check that, six months on, students remembered the capital? All of these would be good reasons to ask the question, 'What is the capital of Australia?'

It is unlikely that you asked the question because you wanted to check if just one student knew the correct answer. Rather, I imagine you wanted to get a feel for how many students knew the correct answer, and if one or more didn't know it, what they thought it was, and to offer feedback designed to address their mistake. Ideally, I imagine that you wanted to check what *everyone* in the class thought the correct answer was.

When you asked the question, 'What is the capital of Australia?' to your class of 30 students, how many, do you believe, were thinking about an answer? Thirty? Fifteen? One? And how could you know that?

Let's imagine that all 30 students were thinking about an answer, perhaps because, after posing the question, you gave the instruction: 'I want everyone to think about an answer. I'll give you 10 seconds.' And then you stayed silent for 10 seconds, counting down in your head, while holding an assertive stance, casting your gaze around the room to convey to the students that you are watching and expecting everyone to be thinking. You then selected a student and asked: 'Marnie, what did you think?' Marnie said: 'Melbourne', to which you said, 'No, it's actually Canberra.'

Had everyone in the class thought about an answer to your question this time? I suspect more students would have tried to – and had time to – than if you had simply asked the question and then responded to the first answer that was shouted out. You built in 'thinking time' and you didn't allow shouting out – you chose a student to answer the question. But how could you check that everyone had thought about an answer or what it was? This is where getting all students to write down an answer becomes very powerful.

Students don't have to write down much – just a few words – but doing so gets them to *think* about their answer. It minimises the chance of students disengaging to think about something they watched on YouTube last night while they rely on a few of their keener peers to do the thinking instead. It also makes them *commit* to their answer – what they have written down will be what they were thinking. Putting it in writing removes the ambiguity – they've committed to what they wanted to say. Powerfully, it also lets you, as their teacher, *check* that they had thought of an answer, including whether or not it was the correct one. 'I don't know' would be an appropriate answer, because this gives you information about what they do or don't know.

If you get students to write down their answer on a piece of paper (perhaps in their jotter), this is better than not getting them to write something down at all. However, it poses challenges for you, as a teacher, to see what everyone has written, because the chances are that some of their handwriting will be quite small and, logistically, it is difficult for you to move around a room of 30 students to see what is written down on a piece of paper on every desk, particularly if you have given everyone a clear instruction that they have just 10 seconds to do this.

The solution to such challenges is the Show-me board (or mini whiteboard). If every student had been asked to write their answer on a Show-me board and hold it up for you to see, not only would everyone have been expected to *think* about the question you had asked, but you would also be able to see what everyone was thinking. If 20 students thought that the answer was Melbourne, 5 thought it was Canberra and 5 thought it was Sydney, the use of Show-me boards will let you know all of that relatively quickly, which is incredibly powerful.

Teaching in this way not only makes students' thinking visible to you, but potentially to every other student in the room. If students wrote their answer on a Show-me board and held it up, you could start to discuss the range of answers you were seeing, using some of these to make points such as: 'Oh, that's a really interesting answer – please tell us more about that', or 'Ruben, do you mind me reading yours out? Thanks... Who agrees with Ruben? Does anyone disagree? Why?' You might walk around the class and borrow a few Show-me boards with different answers on them and then hold these up one at a time, inviting comments from other students. For example, you might say, 'I saw that a few of you wrote this...' while holding up and reading out what was written. 'What do we think about that?' After some whole-class discussion, you might hold up the next board and repeat the process. Teaching in this way would help generate discussion, help students learn from one another, and help you give specific feedback, including the addressing of misconceptions and misunderstandings. You might conclude by saying something like, 'Okay, well only five of you have got that right today – this is something that, as a class, we will need to come back to.'

But we digress. We will come back to explore pedagogy in later chapters. Back to the question we posed at the start of this chapter: **what is the purpose of school?**

The purpose of school

As with so many questions, there is no definitive answer. It is not a 'right or wrong' question. Rather, it is a question designed to make you *think*. As we have alluded to when discussing the capital of Australia, getting students to think is important. Robert Coe suggests that 'learning happens when people have to think hard'[1]. Getting students to *think* is therefore very important if we are going to help them to *learn*. And, of course, the same is true of adults: adults also learn when they have to think hard. I have asked you to think about what you believe the purpose of school to be and, hopefully, you have now had enough time to think of an answer.

Priorities

Schools are incredibly busy places. Day by day and week by week, teachers and school leaders are expected to manage a vast number of competing priorities. These might come from local and national government or be priorities which schools set themselves. Establishing clarity regarding the purpose of school is important to help determine what the *core business* of your school is, which should help add perspective and balance to the relative importance of all of these 'priorities'. Doing so should help to prioritise the priorities. I often talk about this as 'making the thing *the thing*'.

Core business

This principle can be scaled down from whole-school level to departmental and classroom levels. When considering how important something is to do, ask yourself: is doing this going to support our core business? If the answer is yes, it is likely to be worth investing time in it; if the answer is no, it may not merit any time being spent on it at all.

Purpose

So, what is the purpose of school? Perhaps you answered this question along the lines of one or more of the following:

- For students to get qualifications
- To help students achieve the very best they can

---

1. https://www.ibo.org/globalassets/events/aem/conferences/2015/robert-coe.pdf

- To teach students the knowledge and skills they will need to be successful in the future
- To develop the character, attributes and beliefs of students, so that they will be informed citizens
- To develop students so that they can contribute to society

Arguments can be made for all of these purposes. However, I would argue that each of these is better thought of as a *result* of school – not the *reason* for school. They are *indirect outcomes* of schooling which can be achieved through a more direct focus on the core business of *learning*. **Schools are, first and foremost, about supporting, challenging and inspiring young people to *learn*.**

The importance of learning

If students learn, they will get qualifications, they will achieve, they will develop knowledge and skills, they will develop their character, attributes and beliefs, they will become informed and, as a result, they will be able to contribute to society. All of these outcomes are products of *learning*. The quality of their qualifications, achievements, knowledge, skills and attributes will depend on the quality of their learning. **What students are learning and *how well* they are learning should be the principal focus of everyone who works in a school.**

Learning opens doors and transforms lives[2]. If we accept that schools are, first and foremost, places of learning, then schools are places which transform lives. As a result of going to school, every student's life should become better than if they had not gone to school.

The importance of school

Students come to school from all different kinds of background. Some will have had access to rich learning opportunities at home; some will not. Regardless of students' circumstances, schools have the power to teach students about things they would never have learned, in ways which could never have happened. As a result of going to school, students' lives can go in directions they would never otherwise have gone.

---

2. Robinson, M. (2013) *Trivium 21c*

At primary school, I was taught very little science. Any I was taught, I can barely remember today. However, I do remember my first lesson on my first day of secondary school vividly. It was a science lesson, and Mrs Craig was our teacher. About halfway through the lesson, she took a funny-shaped flask with something in it that looked like water and mixed it with the contents of another funny-shaped flask, which also looked like water. I wasn't expecting much. But then: wow! The stuff that had initially looked like water turned bright yellow the moment it was poured into the other stuff! I will never forget how exciting and amazing I thought that was. I believe that it is this moment which made me fall in love with science, and more specifically, with chemistry. This single school experience had a massive impact on my life. I would never have had this learning experience at home.

In his excellent book *A Short History of Nearly Everything*,[3] Bill Bryson describes the sense of wonder that he experienced on discovering a diagram in a science textbook which showed the Earth's interior as it would look if a large knife were used to cut out and remove a chunk of it. It showed that there were different layers (the crust, the upper and lower mantles, the liquid outer core and the inner core) and that the centre of the Earth was a ball of glowing iron and nickel, as hot as the Sun. He goes on to describe the disappointment he felt when this book (and presumably his teacher) failed to explain how people knew all of this, instead going on to present a lot of information which he found rather dull and which only served to switch him off science. It wasn't until many years later that he came back to science and wrote his book. Schools have the power to impact negatively on learning, too.

Recently, a parent told me that their child was unhappy in their science class because they were 'finding science really boring'. As anyone who has been taught science by a great teacher (or who has read Bill Bryson's *A Short History of Nearly Everything*) knows, science should never be boring. Nor should English literature, maths, history, geography, music, drama, modern studies, languages or any other subject for that matter. In every subject, the student experience should be summed up by '3Es': exciting, engaging and enjoyable. The extent to which this holds true will be determined by the quality of teaching.

---

3. Bryson, B. (2004) *A Short History of Nearly Everything*

Learning for the sake of learning

Despite his poor experience at school, Bill Bryson has an interest in learning about science. He had this interest when he was at school, it's just that his negative experience of science at school quashed that for many years. I use this example to make the point that learning in schools, in its widest sense, is important. We need to be careful about tailoring and specifying learning too early, especially in relation to future jobs and careers. I do not believe that the primary purpose of schools is to prepare students for future study or jobs. If it were, an argument could be made that students should only learn the things that are going to help them do whatever it is they want to do when they leave school. But that would be a misguided argument, not least because what a student wants to do could change before they leave, or five years after they have left. I was once quite angry to hear about a student and their parent being given advice about which subjects the child should study in their fourth year of secondary school. They were told that they shouldn't study history – even though they loved it – because they 'didn't need it' for the career path they wanted to follow when they left school.

I can think of countless examples of students who have gone through school and told me about different subjects they love or which are their favourites, yet they had not gone on to study them in further or higher education, or to take jobs which required that they had studied them. Shakespeare has been of absolutely no use to me in my university studies, through my teacher training, or in my jobs as a teacher and school leader. However, I love Shakespeare's play *Richard III*. I am not even sure why I love it: I just do and it has undoubtedly – though perhaps unquantifiably – enriched my life. To subscribe to a view that learning at school is principally about preparing students for employment is to gloss over the excitement, wonder and enthusiasm which can come from learning for learning's sake.

What should schools be teaching?

Different people have different beliefs about the purpose of school, which means they have different beliefs about what schools should be teaching students. As we will go on to discuss, this is relevant to our exploration of what makes great teaching, because the best way to teach students depends on what we are trying to teach them. The *what* influences the *how*.

Opinion is divided as to whether schools should be focusing on teaching students knowledge or skills. In broad terms, people who believe that schools should focus on teaching students *skills* ('skills people') tend to argue that there is little point in teaching students knowledge, because we live in a technological age where students can just look things up for themselves. Instead, schools should focus on teaching skills (sometimes referred to as '21st century skills', 'soft skills' or 'transferable skills'), such as creativity, critical thinking and problem-solving. On the other side of the debate, people who believe that schools should focus on teaching students *knowledge* ('knowledge people') argue that, while they agree the development of skills is important, knowledge is a prerequisite to skills development, so teaching needs to focus on this in the first instance.

What would you classify yourself as: a 'skills person' or a 'knowledge person'? Deep down, I think I have always been a 'knowledge person', although, until recently, I wouldn't have been able to explain why I thought that teaching knowledge was so important. If someone had challenged me on this and argued a case for the importance of teaching skills, I probably wouldn't have argued too hard with them and might have been convinced by their arguments. Because I believe that skills such as creativity, critical thinking and problem-solving are all important skills to develop, I probably could have been convinced that we should focus teaching in schools on the development of such skills. However, I don't think that anymore. The main reason for this is because I have started to read.

The importance of reading

My beliefs regarding the purpose of school, what should be taught and what makes great teaching have evolved over time. They are quite different today from what they were when I first started teaching, or indeed, even from just a few years ago. The catalyst for my changing views has been my engagement with up-to-date educational literature and research. Professional reading has transformed my understanding of what makes great teaching.

As a teacher at the start of my career, my beliefs were principally informed by:

- What and how I was taught at school myself
- What I was taught at university teacher training
- What the 'Professional Standards' produced by the General Teaching Council for Scotland said
- What Scottish government documentation said
- My experience of what worked well and less well in my own classroom, informed by my self-reflections, student feedback and assessment data

It was not until I became a deputy headteacher that I started to engage with educational literature and research extensively. I really regret not having done this sooner, because my teaching practice would have looked quite different, and much better, had I done so. To some extent, I can't be too hard on myself, because when I first started teaching, there wasn't the rich body of educational literature and research that there is today. Now that it exists, I believe that it is the professional responsibility of every teacher and school leader to engage with it. Failure to do so is failure to commit to developing a robust understanding of what makes great teaching.

Debunking myths

Do you believe that students have different preferred learning styles (auditory, visual and kinaesthetic) and that teachers need to plan teaching to suit each student's preferred style? I used to believe that, because someone in a position of authority once told me so. I don't believe it anymore. Why? Because there is consistency in the literature and research that I have engaged with telling me that it's a load of rubbish[4]. Do you believe that it is important to let students lead their own learning and that a focus on enquiry-based learning approaches should be the focus of teaching and learning? I have lost count of the number of times I have heard teachers, school leaders or senior staff in local government promote such ideas. I used to believe them, but now I

---

4. For example, https://www.theguardian.com/education/2017/mar/13/teachers-neuromyth-learning-styles-scientists-neuroscience-education

would argue strongly against them. Everything I read tells me that, while student-led learning and learning by enquiry have a place in the wide repertoire of teaching practices, that place should be relatively small[5]. There are other teaching practices which research indicates are far more effective to student learning. In Chapter 4, we will explore this further. If I didn't read, I wouldn't feel confident in making this argument.

Recently, I heard of a school leader who had been reading a book which stated there is no evidence that students have different learning styles. So appalled were they by this statement that they said they weren't going to read any more of it. Another school leader attempted to discuss this with them but was met with a frosty response: 'I don't want to hear it – I know what works and what doesn't.' Rather than being prepared to discuss or explore what research says about this, they simply refused to consider it. This is delusion; it is burying your head in the sand.

Making time

When I promote the importance of reading to teachers and school leaders, one of the most common reasons I hear for them not reading is that they don't have time. I understand this. However, I think that something has to be done to address this barrier. If reading really is as important as I am suggesting it is in the pursuit of an understanding of what makes great teaching, teachers and school leaders need to make time for it. This doesn't have to be much time – 20 minutes of reading once every two or three days is significantly better than not reading at all. The key is to get into the habit of doing it and to build it into your daily or weekly routine. One person's routine won't necessarily work for another. You have to find out what works for you. For me, getting up half an hour earlier in the morning has really helped, and I use this extra time for professional reading. For others, perhaps finding time in the evening would be better. Once you get into the habit of reading, so long as you are reading something you can connect with and find interesting, the chances are that you will start to enjoy it. One teacher in my school described the reading they had started to engage in as 'mind-expanding', which I believe it is.

---

5. For example, Christodoulou, D. (2013) *Seven Myths About Education*

Where to start

Twitter is an incredibly useful resource for pointing teachers and school leaders in the direction of powerful educational literature and research. If you aren't using Twitter for this purpose, I would encourage you to consider doing so.

Books and reports are also key. In alphabetical order by title, at the time of writing, my top 10 suggestions for all teachers and school leaders would be:

- *CleverLands* by Lucy Crehan
- *Creating the Schools Our Children Need* by Dylan Wiliam
- *The Learning Rainforest* by Tom Sherrington
- *Practice Perfect* by Doug Lemov
- *Principles of Instruction* by Barak Rosenshine
- *Seven Myths About Education* by Daisy Christodoulou
- *Visible Learning for Teachers* by John Hattie
- *What Does This Look Like in the Classroom?* by Carl Hendrick and Robin Macpherson
- *What Makes Great Teaching? Review of the Underpinning Research* by Robert Coe, Cesare Aloisi, Steve Higgins and Lee Elliot Major
- *Why Don't Students Like School?* by Daniel Willingham

In addition, if you are a school leader, I would recommend that you read:

- *Aligning Professional Learning, Performance Management and Effective Teaching* by Peter Cole
- *Leadership, Capacity Building and School Improvement* by Clive Dimmock

Case study: Professional Reading Library

In my school, we invest in the professional learning of our staff by ensuring that we have a high-quality Professional Reading Library. Once a term, we spend several hundred pounds on recently released educational books, such as those listed above. These are catalogued and made available to staff via a 'sign-in/sign-out' sheet. The library is housed in the staffroom, allowing for easy access. Rather than staff having to invest in their own professional learning, we invest in it for them.

Powerful knowledge and cultural capital

Such reading has played a key role in influencing my beliefs about the purpose of school, what should be taught, and what makes great teaching. Through this reading, I have developed an understanding of the importance of a '**knowledge-rich curriculum**'[6], which I didn't know much about a few years ago. If you'd asked me what this meant then, I would have hazarded a guess that it is about learning things such as the names of capital cities, the symbols of elements in the Periodic Table and key dates in British history. If someone had pushed me and said, 'But students can just look all of that up – we need to focus on teaching skills', I might have been persuaded to go along with them.

I now understand that, while to some extent a knowledge-rich curriculum is about learning these sorts of things, it is about so much more than this. Through reading, I have learned that a knowledge-rich curriculum is about developing '**powerful knowledge**'[7] in students, that is, knowledge which takes them beyond their day-to-day experiences; knowledge which they would be unlikely to have encountered had they not gone to school. The purpose of learning this powerful knowledge is to develop '**cultural capital**'[8], supporting students to play a full and active role in society and to get the most out of life. Not only is such knowledge powerful in itself,

---

6. Wiliam, D. (2018) *Creating the Schools Our Children Need*

7. Young, M. and Lambert, D. (2014) *Knowledge and the Future School*

8. Sherrington, T. (2017) *The Learning Rainforest*

it also underpins the development of important skills such as creativity, critical thinking, and problem-solving.

A knowledge-rich curriculum can play a key role in helping to address social inequalities. Not all students have access to the same knowledge at home. Students from disadvantaged backgrounds typically have access to less knowledge at home than those from more advantaged backgrounds. Through a knowledge-rich curriculum, schools can help redress the balance. By doing so, schools can transform lives. All of this underpins what I now believe to be the purpose of school: *learning*.

Think for yourself

All of this said, I would like to stress how important I think it is for teachers and school leaders to develop their own views regarding the purpose of school, which includes what should be taught and what makes great teaching. If they are to be anything more than anecdotal, these views need to be developed and shaped through reading and discussion, critique and enquiry.

One of the reasons why there isn't a shared understanding as to what makes great teaching among teachers and school leaders in and between schools is that there isn't a consensus regarding the purpose of school which, as we will go on to discuss, influences what is taught and how it is taught. In my experience, teachers and school leaders don't take enough time to reflect on and consider such matters. Often, their views and beliefs lack clarity or haven't been formed at all. How fully formed their views and beliefs are tends to relate to the extent to which they engage with educational literature and research. It comes back to whether or not they have been reading and, crucially, *what* they have been reading. In the pursuit of an understanding of what makes great teaching, reading is key.

What is knowledge? What are skills?

Influencing the debate about whether schools should be teaching students knowledge or skills are differences in people's understanding as to what knowledge is and what skills are. In making sense of this debate, I find two competing conceptualisations useful:

1. Knowledge and skills are one and the same – *skills are just knowledge in action*[9]
2. Knowledge and skills are different but linked – *knowledge underpins the development of skills*[10]

On balance, I prefer the second conceptualisation, which is the one we shall go on to explore in more detail. To do so, we need to consider what the terms 'knowledge' and 'skills' actually mean.

What is knowledge?

In trying to understand what knowledge is, I subscribe to the view that there is value in thinking of knowledge as not being one thing, but rather a spectrum of things. In other words, I find it useful to think of there being different 'types' of knowledge[11]. For the purposes of our discussion, the most useful types to consider are 'declarative knowledge' and 'procedural knowledge'.

Declarative knowledge is knowledge *of facts and concepts*. It can be superficial (like knowing the capital of Australia) or deep (like knowing about the causes of climate change). **Procedural knowledge** is knowledge *of how to do things* (like how to create a bar graph or how to draw a table which summarises the differences between declarative and procedural knowledge, with examples). Figure 2.1 is a table which summarises the differences between declarative and procedural knowledge, with examples.

---

9. Christodoulou, D. (2014) *Seven Myths About Education*
10. Willingham, D. (2010) *Why Don't Students Like School?*
11. https://www.psychologynoteshq.com/metacognition/

Knowledge	Examples
Of facts and concepts (declarative)	The capital of Australia
	The causes of World War II
	The link between greenhouse gases and climate change
	Knowledge about yourself as a learner and factors which can influence your performance
Of how to do things (procedural)	How to create a bar graph
	How to read a map
	How to solve quadratic equations
	How to hit a forehand volley

Figure 2.1: A summary of two different types of knowledge, with examples of each type.

What are skills?

When people talk about skills, they often use terms such as 'soft', '21st century' or 'transferable'. If I'm being honest, I have never found such terms to be particularly useful at supporting an understanding of what we actually mean by 'skills'. Instead, just as I believe there is value in thinking about knowledge as being a spectrum of things, I believe there is value in doing the same for skills. For me, it is useful to think about skills as being of three different types:

1. **Thinking skills** (sometimes referred to as 'higher-order skills')
2. **Practical skills**
3. **Behavioural skills**

Figure 2.2 gives some examples of each type of skill.

	Thinking skills	Practical skills	Behavioural skills
Examples	Problem-solving Critical thinking Creativity	Reading Drawing a bar graph Making a PowerPoint presentation Using a search engine Reading a map	Leadership Teamwork Self-evaluation

Figure 2.2: A suggested classification for types of skill, with examples of each type.

Though there are always exceptions, in broad and general terms:

- **Thinking skills** are *subject specific* and therefore *'non-transferable'*. What I mean by this is that they can be learned within a particular subject but cannot typically be applied across contexts and subject disciplines. They generally rely on subject-specific *declarative knowledge.* For example, it is not possible to think critically about the causes of World War II without knowing what they were – the more you know, the more you can critique. Equally, it is not possible to come up with a creative solution to the issue of disposable plastics without having knowledge of the science which underpins this – the more you know, the more creative you are likely to be.

- **Practical skills** are more *'transferable'*. What I mean by this is that they can be learned and then applied across contexts and subject disciplines. They rely on *procedural knowledge* but not subject-specific declarative knowledge. In other words, procedural skills require knowledge of *how to carry out the skill* but don't necessarily require knowledge of a particular subject (though this will often be beneficial). For example, there is a strong body of evidence to suggest that knowledge of the topic that you are reading about plays a significant role in supporting your understanding of what you are reading[12]. While I argue that the skill of reading is transferable, being able to understand what you are reading relies on subject knowledge – the more subject knowledge you have, the more you

12. Hirsch, E.D. (2016) *Why Knowledge Matters*

will understand what you are reading. Bar graphs can be drawn from tables of data with or without knowing what the data means. To be able to draw a bar graph successfully, you need to know how to draw a bar graph, but you don't need to know anything about the data you are graphing. Therefore, the skill of drawing a graph becomes transferable: if you can do it in maths, you should be able to do it in biology, geography and graphic communication. Similarly, if you know how to make a PowerPoint presentation, so long as you have access to the information you are presenting, you should be able to produce a presentation, regardless of the topic this information relates to. If you have knowledge of the topic you are presenting, your presentation is likely to be higher quality.

- **Behavioural skills** rely on both *declarative* and *procedural knowledge*. Take leadership as an example. If you are going to lead a team tasked with improving the quality of teaching in a department or school, then you need to have declarative knowledge (facts and concepts) of teaching and learning theory. As a leader, you will need to set clear objectives, motivate and delegate. Such skills rely on procedural knowledge (how to do things). This procedural aspect of leadership is transferable. You would be able to transfer these skills to leading a different team – for example, one tasked with developing a new website. However, the declarative aspect is non-transferable. You would have to learn new facts and concepts about developing a new website in order to lead this team successfully – your declarative knowledge of teaching and learning theory is irrelevant.

Figure 2.3 summarises this.

	Thinking skills	Practical skills	Behavioural skills
Examples	Problem-solving, critical thinking, creativity	Reading, drawing a bar graph, making a PowerPoint presentation, using a search engine, reading a map	Leadership, teamwork, self-evaluation
Underpinned by...	Declarative knowledge - *of facts and concepts*	Procedural knowledge - *of how to do things*	Declarative and procedural knowledge - *of facts and concepts, and of how to do things*
Subject specific?	Yes	No	In part
Transferable?	No	Yes	In part

Figure 2.3: A summary of the links between different types of skill and their relationship to knowledge and subject disciplines.

It is important to point out that to think about skills in this way presents things as being more black and white than they actually are. However, thinking in black and white terms is often useful for helping us to make sense of shades of grey. If we are to engage in debates about whether schools should be teaching students knowledge or skills, we need to have a clear understanding of what we are actually talking about. Conceptualisations such as the ones we have just discussed can support this.

An important point to stress before we move on is that, regardless of the type of skill we are talking about, **knowledge always underpins skills development**.

'Knowledge subjects' and 'skills subjects'

I sometimes hear teachers and school leaders talk about different subjects as being 'knowledge-based' (e.g. maths, history, chemistry) or 'skills-based' (e.g. art, home economics, drama), which portrays a misunderstanding of what knowledge is. **All of these subjects are knowledge-based subjects which have skills development features.** Take chemistry as an example. Learning intentions for a secondary school chemistry course for 14-year-old students might include:

- To know what acids and alkalis are
- To understand how to use the pH scale
- To be able to carry out tests to investigate if a chemical is an acid or an alkali

The first two learning intentions relate to knowledge *about things* (declarative knowledge), while the third relates to knowledge *of how to do things* (procedural knowledge), which, ultimately, will underpin the development of a skill such as the ability to carry out the specified tests. Knowledge and skills are both key outcomes of this course.

Take ICT as another example. Learning intentions for a secondary school ICT course for 14-year-old students might include:

- To be able to add references as footnotes in a Word document
- To be able to use conditional formatting in an Excel document
- To know the features of reliable sources of internet information

In this example, the relationship between *how to do things* (procedural knowledge) and *about things* (declarative knowledge) is different compared with the learning intentions for the chemistry course. However, knowledge still underpins all of the learning of this course – it is knowledge-based.

What are attributes?

In the knowledge versus skills debate, it is worth noting arguments for a third classification of what schools should be teaching: *attributes*. Attributes relate to a student's personal qualities in terms of their character and behaviours. They include things like confidence, resilience, positivity, sense of humour, temperament, how they get along with other people, and how they respond to challenging situations.

I would argue that, although they are transferable to different contexts and across subject disciplines, attributes cannot be taught as discrete subjects in themselves. For example, you can't teach someone to be resilient or have a sense of humour through a lesson or via a particular task. Rather, attributes are learned and developed over periods of time, through the development of knowledge or skills.

The relationship between knowledge, skills and attributes

In summary, the terms 'knowledge', 'skills' and 'attributes' serve as useful classifications for what we are aiming to teach students in school. The relationship between them is illustrated in Figure 2.4:

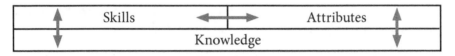

Figure 2.4: The relationship between knowledge, skills and attributes. Knowledge underpins the development of skills and attributes. Skills and attributes can't be developed in the absence of knowledge.

In this conceptualisation, knowledge, skills and attributes are different but intertwined. The lines between them are often blurred. Getting hung up about this is not the point of drawing attention to it. Rather, the point is to emphasise **the importance of knowledge to all learning**. In terms of *what* schools are teaching students, knowledge is key.

Bloom's Taxonomy

In our exploration of the knowledge versus skills debate, Bloom's Taxonomy offers a useful means by which to explore this a little further. The Bloom's Taxonomy pyramid is illustrated in Figure 2.5.

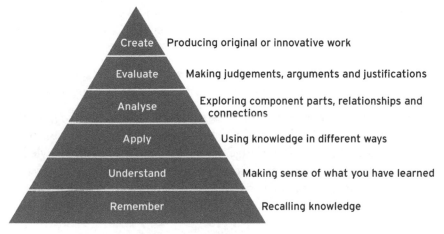

Figure 2.5: Bloom's Taxonomy pyramid[13].

Many teachers and school leaders are aware of Bloom's Taxonomy. However, not all are interpreting it in the same way. This means that not all teachers and school leaders are interpreting it in the *right way,* that is, as it was intended.

In broad terms:

- **'Skills people'** believe and argue that teaching and learning should focus on the higher sections of the pyramid (which get referred to as 'higher-order') and not the lower ones (which get referred to as 'lower-order'). To them, teaching students to 'analyse', 'evaluate' and 'create' is much more important than teaching them to 'remember'. Sometimes they will justify this by saying that it is higher-order skills that employers are looking for and not the ability to remember things. We will discuss this last point further in Chapter 12.

- **'Knowledge people'** also believe that 'higher-order' skills are important. However, they recognise that the development of all of these – analysing, evaluating, creating – relies on having secure 'lower-order' knowledge and understanding. Without secure knowledge and understanding, higher-order thinking skills cannot be developed. They argue that it is therefore essential that

13. Adapted from: https://cdn.vanderbilt.edu/vu-wp0/wp-content/uploads/sites/59/2019/03/27124326/Blooms-Taxonomy-650x366.jpg

teaching and learning has a strong focus on developing knowledge and understanding – not at the expense of skills, but in support of skills development.

So, who is right: 'skills people' or 'knowledge people'? How did Benjamin Bloom intend this pyramid to be interpreted when he developed it?

Bloom's intention was to communicate the idea that *knowledge is the foundation of skills development*, not that it is more important to focus on teaching skills than knowledge[14]. The interpretation of 'knowledge people' is the correct interpretation of Bloom's pyramid. To appreciate this, I find a more simplistic version of this hierarchy more useful:

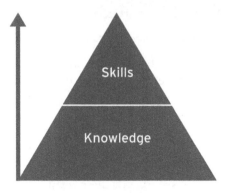

Figure 2.6: A simplified version of Bloom's Taxonomy pyramid. Knowledge underpins skills development.

Presenting the relationship between knowledge and skills as a pyramid can be both helpful and unhelpful. Helpfully, it can support the idea that higher-order cognitive processes build on lower-order cognitive processes. In other words, remembering and understanding are essential prerequisites to be able to apply, analyse, evaluate and create. Unhelpfully, the top of the pyramid can be interpreted as being more important than the bottom; however, without strong foundations, the top of the pyramid would plummet to the ground and crumble. You can have the bottom without the top but not the top without the bottom. The interpretation of the pyramid is as important as the presentation.

---

14. Hendrick, C. and Macpherson, R. (2017) *What Does This Look Like in the Classroom?*

Bloom's Taxonomy in practice

Consider the following questions and ask yourself if you think any question is 'better' than any other. Is there a best question in the list? Is there a worst?

1. Is iron a metal or a non-metal?
2. True or false: we have iron in our bodies.
3. Name a part of our bodies in which you would find iron.
4. Since we have iron in our bodies, why do we not set off metal detectors at airports?

In considering whether or not there is a 'best' or 'worst' question here, many people will pull to mind Bloom's Taxonomy and the associated ideas of lower-order and higher-order. They will then suggest that the questions we ask students can be either lower-order or higher-order and that higher-order questions are better questions to ask than lower-order ones. Based on this logic, Question 4 would be the 'best' question because it is higher-order. But being a higher-order question does not make it a better question. While higher-order questions are likely to be more demanding to answer than lower-order questions because they require students to draw upon prior knowledge (the lower blocks of the pyramid), that doesn't mean that they are better questions to ask. The ability to answer Question 4 is dependent on separate but related knowledge which you may or may not have already learned. In other words, the ability to answer Question 4 depends on the breadth, depth and strength of your knowledge of relevant facts.

Higher-order thinking draws upon and pulls together smaller pieces of knowledge. The ability of a student to interpret, compare, contrast, differentiate, question, appraise, argue, justify, critique and design relies upon the breadth, depth and strength of the knowledge they are drawing upon and pulling together. Just as with the base of the pyramid, the broader, deeper and stronger the knowledge base which students have to draw upon (in other words, the more they know and the better they know it), the better their higher-order skills development is likely to be.

A debate about pedagogy

Just how relevant is this discussion to our exploration of what makes great teaching? The answer is: very much so.

Messages from educational literature and research tell us that the effectiveness of particular pedagogies is influenced by *what it is* that we want students to learn. If we want students to learn knowledge (declarative and procedural) and to develop skills (thinking, practical and behavioural) using this knowledge, there are particular pedagogies which are best for doing that. If we want them to learn to apply this knowledge in creative and open-ended ways, there are alternative pedagogies which are best for doing that. **The best way for students to learn is dependent on what it is that they are learning.**

Getting the pedagogy wrong

In *Leadership, Capacity Building and School Improvement*[15], Clive Dimmock highlights that, in spite of a consistency in educational research about the types of pedagogy which are best for teaching students knowledge, there has been a push in recent years from some policymakers and school leaders for teachers to focus on using pedagogies which are relatively ineffective for this purpose. On the face of it, this seems like madness, which it is. So why is it happening?

There are two reasons. The first is because such people believe it is important for students to develop skills. They are right about that. However, they appear to misunderstand the fact that, in order for students to develop skills of the type they are pushing for (such as creativity, problem-solving, teamwork and leadership), they must first have been taught knowledge. Secondly, they appear to have developed notions that pedagogies which are best for teaching knowledge are old-fashioned, too controlling, stifle creativity and stop students from enjoying school. It is difficult to emphasise just how ill-conceived such notions are.

'Student-led learning'

With these notions has come a push for 'student-led learning' in which students get to choose what they are learning and how they are learning it. Unfortunately, this has more in common with *The Emperor's New*

---

15. Dimmock, C. (2012) *Leadership, Capacity Building and School Improvement*

Clothes than it does with a high-quality education. While student-led learning has an important role to play, its place in the teaching and learning repertoire should be relatively small. When it becomes too big, student learning suffers.

I understand why an emphasis on 'student-led learning' sounds attractive. The language is positive. However, this emphasis is misguided. In part, I believe it has come about as a result of the negative experience which some policymakers and school leaders have had in schools themselves, either as students or professionals. As a reaction to their experiences of *poor teaching*, their solution is to minimise the role of the teacher in the teaching and learning process and maximise the role of students. Accordingly, they advocate the importance of students leading their own learning.

The problem is not so much with the term 'student-led learning' but with what people tend to *mean* by it. If what they mean is *seeking student views* and *using evidence of student learning to inform teaching*, they are right to emphasise the importance of this. However, this is not what they usually mean by 'student-led learning'. Instead, what they usually mean is students *discovering things for themselves, learning by enquiry, problem-based learning*, and *deciding what they are learning and how*. While such approaches can *enrich* learning, they are not usually the best way for students to learn.

Thankfully, not everyone in a position of influence holds such beliefs. There are many who recognise the importance of a focus on knowledge and pedagogies which are best for teaching knowledge. John Hattie[16] captures this with the term 'teacher as activator' (the opposite being 'teacher as facilitator'); Tom Sherrington[17] talks about 'Mode A teaching' (the opposite being 'Mode B teaching'). The term I use is '**Specific Teaching**' (the opposite being '**Non-specific Teaching**').

Specific teaching

In **Specific Teaching**, *specific content* is taught in a *specific way*. There is assessment which assesses *specific knowledge* and *specific skills*, and there

16. Hattie, J. (2009) *Visible Learning*

17. Sherrington, T. (2017) *The Learning Rainforest*

is *specific feedback*. As a result of Specific Teaching, we aim to achieve *specific learning*.

If you want students to learn about the Vikings (that is, to learn *declarative knowledge* about the Vikings), you should teach them about the Vikings using pedagogies which are best for teaching knowledge. Don't teach them about the Vikings by asking them to read about them online or in a textbook – there are better ways. While there is, without question, a place for students to learn about the Vikings (or any other topic) through reading and discovery, ask yourself what the best time and place for students to do that would be. Often, it can be done at home.

If you want to teach students how to filter sand from water (that is, to learn *procedural knowledge* which they can apply as a practical skill), the best way to teach them this is specifically, using a Specific Teaching approach. While it is possible for students to 'discover' how to filter sand from water on their own or collaboratively with peers (perhaps by getting them to look up the index of a textbook to find the appropriate section, read about it and then have a go at doing it through trial and error), I would argue strongly that this is not the best way to teach students filtering. If it isn't the best way to teach it, then why would you teach it in this way? Surely the best way to teach it is to get a teacher with specific knowledge and expertise to teach it to students in a specific way.

All subjects require the teaching of knowledge (declarative or procedural). The best way to do this is *specifically*. Even in subjects where the degree of course content is less prescribed (such as in art and drama), students still need to be taught specific things. To quote Richard Griffiths' character, Hector, in the film adaptation of Alan Bennett's *The History Boys*: 'Knowledge is not general, it is specific'[18]. For the most part, teaching should be specific too.

Specific Teaching is not 'blinkered' teaching; it is not teaching in a bubble. Rather, it is *adaptive* and *responsive*. In Specific Teaching, teachers find out the extent to which what has been taught has been learned and they adapt their teaching accordingly. They seek student views about teaching

---

18. *The History Boys*, film produced by BBC Two Films, DNA Films, UK Film Council (2006)

quality and they respond to these. The learning and views of students are integral to the Specific Teaching approach. In this sense, Specific Teaching is learning-led. This is different from 'student-led learning'. 'Student-led learning' is the pedagogy of Non-specific Teaching.

Non-specific Teaching

Non-specific Teaching is concerned with the *application of learning, exploration* and *discovery*. It involves things like:

- Getting students to prepare and present a talk to their class
- Getting students to create a poster which summarises their learning
- Letting students research a topic of their choosing

In Non-specific Teaching, students have more control over what they are learning and how they are learning it. In this way, they can learn in ways that they couldn't through Specific Teaching. However, a key point to appreciate is that, while students can learn in *different* ways, these are not necessarily *better* ways.

Specific Teaching or Non-specific Teaching?

When considering whether a Specific Teaching or a Non-specific Teaching approach is better, teachers should keep the following principles in mind:

- **Specific Teaching** is generally best for teaching *specific knowledge and skills*
- **Non-specific Teaching** is less effective for teaching specific knowledge and skills but has a key role to play in the *application* of learning and in *enriching* teaching and learning

Specific Teaching can be thought about as the cake; Non-specific Teaching is the icing. Without a cake, there can be no icing. While icing enriches a cake, it isn't necessarily a case of the more the better. Rather, a proportionate amount of icing is what usually makes for the best cakes.

Take the teaching of acids and alkalis as an example. Specific Teaching is best for teaching students about what acids and alkalis are and how the pH scale can be used to identify them. It is also best for teaching students how to solve problems relating to them (such as: 'An unknown chemical has a pH of 8.3 – is it an acid or an alkali?') and how to carry out experiments using them (such as learning how to use pH paper to determine if different chemicals are acids or alkalis). To enrich the learning, students may also be asked to create a YouTube video about what acids and alkalis are, or they may be asked to create a magazine article with the title 'Acids and Alkalis in Your Home'. This is **Non-specific Teaching**. While not essential to the teaching and learning process, it enriches the learning. Students can draw on what they have been taught and apply it in a creative way. Doing so can help to *consolidate* and *demonstrate* their learning.

The balance between Specific Teaching and Non-specific Teaching
Both Specific Teaching and Non-specific Teaching are important. However, they are not equally important. In the interests of maximising student learning, the emphasis should be on Specific Teaching approaches. As a guide, I would suggest that **Specific Teaching typically makes up 80–90%** of teaching and learning time; **Non-specific Teaching should make up 10–20%.**

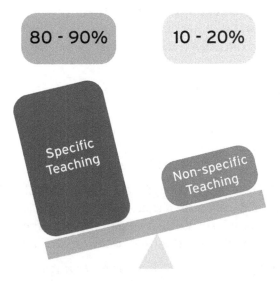

Figure 2.7. The proportion of teaching and learning time that should be spent on Specific Teaching versus Non-specific Teaching approaches in school.

In Chapter 4, we will explore key messages from educational research in relation to teaching. Before we do that, we shall turn our attention to the science of how we learn.

Chapter 3
The science of how we learn

If we are to develop an understanding of what makes great teaching, it is important that we develop an understanding of the science of how we learn. In exploring this, we will discuss seven key areas:

1. Knowledge
2. Memory
3. Thinking
4. Learning
5. Retrieval
6. Understanding
7. Schema

1. Knowledge

In the previous chapter, we discussed the importance of knowledge to all learning. We will not go over the arguments again in this chapter. Rather, we shall simply start by reminding ourselves of the importance of knowledge.

2. Memory

Our brains have two memory compartments: **working memory** and **long-term memory**[19]. Both can hold knowledge in them and one supports the other. They differ in terms of:

- *How long* they can hold knowledge
- *Our awareness* of the knowledge they are holding
- *What they do* with knowledge
- *How much* knowledge they can hold at any particular time

How long they can hold knowledge

Working memory can only hold knowledge for a finite period of time – in the region of 15–30 seconds[20] – unless a conscious effort is made to hold it for longer, such as if you decide to keep thinking about something. Long-term memory, as the name suggests, can hold knowledge for much longer – often indefinitely.

Our awareness of the knowledge they are holding

When knowledge is in working memory, we are aware of it. When knowledge is in long-term memory, we are unaware of it. To appreciate this point, imagine I ask you who the Prime Minister is. Before I did that, you had this knowledge in your long-term memory, but you weren't aware of it. You became aware of it almost immediately when you were asked this question. The knowledge moved from your long-term memory into your working memory.

What they do with knowledge

Working memory uses knowledge to think; long-term memory is a knowledge store. Long-term memory cannot think and working memory cannot store.

How much knowledge they can hold at any particular time

Working memory can only hold a limited number of 'pieces' of knowledge at any one time – around seven, on average[21]. There is no limit

---

19. Willingham, D. (2010) *Why Don't Students Like School?*

20. https://www.theguardian.com/education/2015/sep/16/what-happens-in-your-brain-when-you-make-a-memory

21. Weinstein, Y. and Sumeracki, M. (2019) *Understanding How We Learn*

to the amount of knowledge that long-term memory can store. In other words, the capacity of working memory is small, while the capacity of long-term memory is huge. Figure 3.1 illustrates this relationship.

Working memory   **Long-term memory**

Figure 3.1: The difference in size between working memory and long-term memory. Just as school science textbooks don't do justice to the difference in size between the Earth and the rest of the Solar System (because of the limits that a page presents in terms of how much can fit onto it), this representation doesn't do justice to the difference in size between working memory and long-term memory. Working memory is small; long-term memory is vastly bigger – there is no limit to the amount of knowledge it can store.

3. Thinking

Knowledge is only useful to us if we are required to do something with it. To do something with it, knowledge needs to be brought out of long-term memory and into working memory. Working memory is where thinking happens[22]. Thinking is the interaction of knowledge, from our environment and our long-term memory.

Figure 3.2 illustrates the relationship between memory and thinking.

---

22. Willingham, D. (2010) *Why Don't Students Like School?*

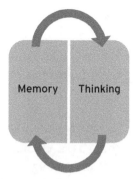

Figure 3.2: The relationship between memory and thinking. The currency of both is knowledge – we learn knowledge and we think with knowledge.

Cognitive Load Theory

Because there is a limit to how much knowledge our working memory can hold at any one time, there is a limit to how much knowledge can interact at any one time. In other words, there is a limit to our *thinking capacity*.

In 'Cognitive Load Theory'[23], the amount of information we are expected to pay attention to and think about at any one time is known as the 'cognitive load'. If this becomes too much for our working memory to process, we get 'cognitive overload'. When in cognitive overload, our working memory stops being able to think.

Fortunately, working memory doesn't need to hold knowledge for very long because it is supported by long-term memory. By storing knowledge and giving working memory access to it, long-term memory frees up working memory space, enabling it to think. A key function of long-term memory is to help prevent working memory from going into cognitive overload. By reducing the load, long-term memory can help you to think.

Learning in schools should focus on getting students to think. However, in order to think, students must first have something to think with. Pre-existing knowledge is what allows students to think. In other words, the ability that students have to think is dependent on what they have already learned. Knowledge that they receive from their environment will mean

---

23. Weinstein, Y. and Sumeracki, M. (2019) *Understanding How We Learn*

nothing to them unless they are able to relate this to knowledge which they already have.

Some educational policymakers and school leaders might try to have you believe otherwise, but long-term memory is essential to thinking.

4. Learning

There isn't a universally agreed definition of what learning is. Kirschner *et al.* have argued that learning is 'a change in long-term memory'[24]. However, as others have pointed out, long-term memory can change as a result of illness or brain injury, so there are limits to the accuracy of defining learning in this way[25]. Also, it isn't immediately obvious what the word 'change' is getting at.

For me, a definition which makes sense is that learning is **the development of long-term memory through the accumulation of knowledge**. I like the word 'development' because it suggests an evolution or a building up; I like the inclusion of 'knowledge' because it helps to get across the importance of knowledge to all forms of learning. Like other definitions, there will be limits to its accuracy, but I think it helps to understand what learning is. It is important to attempt to understand what learning is because learning is the core business of a school. Learning manifests itself as a change in a person's knowledge or understanding *of* something, or in their ability *to do* something.

At a basic level, learning can be thought about as happening when knowledge moves from our *environment*, through our *working memory* and into our *long-term memory*. This perhaps oversimplifies things, but it provides a useful starting point to develop a deeper understanding of what happens in the learning process. We use our senses to take in knowledge from our environment, so long as we have paid attention to this information[26]. When we pay attention, we are able to learn. If we don't pay attention, we can't learn.

24. http://www.danielwillingham.com/daniel-willingham-science-and-education-blog/on-the-definition-of-learning

25. http://www.danielwillingham.com/daniel-willingham-science-and-education-blog/on-metaphor-memory-and-john-king

26. Weinstein, Y. and Sumeracki, M. (2019) *Understanding How We Learn*

When we take in knowledge, it enters our working memory first. Once in working memory, one of two things can happen:

1. The knowledge can be forgotten
2. The knowledge can be learned (or 'memorised')

Figure 3.3 provides a visual summary of this idea. We will build on it over the next few sub-sections.

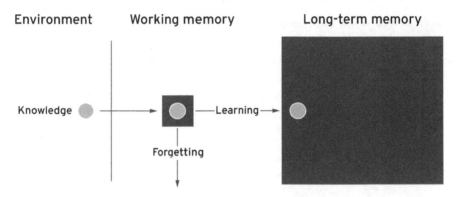

Figure 3.3: A simplified representation of the learning process. We use our senses to take in knowledge from our environment. Having passed through working memory, knowledge can move to long-term memory. Alternatively, it is forgotten.

For the purposes of the discussion which follows, it should be useful to appreciate that 'learning' and 'memory' effectively mean the same thing[27]. From this point on, we will use these terms interchangeably.

5. Retrieval

Knowledge which has been learned can be *retrieved* (or 'recalled' or 'remembered'). Retrieval is the process of bringing knowledge out of long-term memory and into working memory, where it can be thought about. How easily retrieved this knowledge is will depend on how well it has been learned. The better it has been learned, the more easily it can be retrieved[28].

27. Willingham, D. (2010) *Why Don't Students Like School?*

28. http://pdf.retrievalpractice.org/RetrievalPracticeGuide.pdf

Strength of memory

The more students retrieve the same knowledge, the stronger their memory of it becomes. People who become expert on particular topics do so because they are retrieving the same knowledge again and again and again. Think of it like drawing a faint line with a pencil – which is difficult to see – and then going over this line again and again and again. The thicker line represents a stronger memory. Retrieval strengthens memory. In other words, **retrieval strengthens learning**.

Strong and weak knowledge

Knowledge which has been learned well can be considered 'strong knowledge'; knowledge which hasn't been learned well can be considered 'weak knowledge'. Strong knowledge can be more easily retrieved than weak knowledge. It is important that teachers and students understand how weak knowledge can become strong knowledge, so that its retrieval becomes easier.

Strengthening knowledge

Knowledge becomes stronger when it is revisited. This can happen in one of two ways:

1. Someone (such as a teacher) *brings this knowledge to your attention* again
2. You *retrieve* this knowledge from your long-term memory

By way of example, imagine that you are a student and you have been learning about the digestive system in biology. As part of this, you have been taught that insulin is produced by the pancreas. How strong your memory of this knowledge is will be influenced by whether or not you revisit this knowledge, either because your teacher revisits it with you or you revisit it yourself. If you were taught this knowledge in September and the next time you revisit it is in an exam in May through a question which asks you, 'Which organ produces insulin?', your memory of it will probably be weak, so there's a good chance you won't be able to answer the question correctly. However, if you had revisited this memory, in class or at home, then your memory of it would have become stronger. The more you revisited it, the stronger your memory of it would have become, and the more likely you would be to be able to answer the question correctly.

Of the two ways that knowledge can be revisited, in terms of supporting learning, being asked to retrieve it repeatedly is best[29]. What this means for teachers is that the more you ask students to recall particular learning, the better they will learn.

The formative benefits of retrieval

Asking students to retrieve knowledge has an additional benefit to the teaching and learning process. As well as *improving student learning*, getting students to retrieve knowledge *helps teachers to find out what students have learned* (and what they haven't learned). If teachers don't ask students to do this, then they won't be able to find out what students have learned. We will return to this idea in the next chapter.

6. Understanding

Understanding happens when knowledge takes on meaning. When we experience new knowledge, whether or not it has meaning to us will depend on the knowledge we already have. In other words, the more knowledge we have, the more likely we are to understand something new.

The more students know, the more they can understand. The more they understand, the more they can think. The more they can think, the more they can be critical, solve problems, have opinions, be creative and help other people. Knowledge is the key to all of this. Anyone who argues against the importance of knowledge in school doesn't really understand the science of how we learn.

We shall use three examples to explore this further.

Example 1

If someone tells you that a frog is an amphibian, this only makes sense to you if you already have knowledge of what an amphibian is. The more knowledge you have of this, the more this new knowledge will make sense to you. For example, you may have knowledge of the characteristic features of amphibians (such as moist skin) or know examples of other amphibians (like a salamander), to which you can compare this new knowledge. Comparing what you are being told about a frog – that it is

---

29. Hendrick, C. and Macpherson, R. (2017) *What Does This Look Like in the Classroom?*

an amphibian – to your pre-existing knowledge of amphibians helps you to make sense of the new knowledge you are receiving.

If someone were to tell you that snakes are amphibians (which they aren't), you would draw on your knowledge of what amphibians are from your long-term memory and think about this in your working memory. Using your pre-existing knowledge, you would realise that this isn't correct. Without this pre-existing knowledge, you wouldn't be able to do that. The more pre-existing knowledge you have, the more certain you can be that you are right.

Example 2

Imagine that you ask students to identify the metal from a list of chemical symbols:

a. S

b. Ca

c. He

d. N

This is a question about understanding. To answer this question, students need to draw upon different 'pieces' of knowledge. Depending on how much pre-existing knowledge they have, they will attempt to find an answer to this problem in different ways. For example, it might be that a student has learned that Ca is the chemical symbol for calcium (knowledge piece 1) and that calcium is a metal (knowledge piece 2). Drawing on this knowledge, they come to understand that the correct answer is b.

The student may also have knowledge that S, He and N are the chemical symbols for sulfur (knowledge piece 3), helium (knowledge piece 4) and nitrogen (knowledge piece 5), and that all three of these are non-metals (knowledge piece 6). While having this knowledge would not be essential for them to answer the question correctly (because they can do so using knowledge pieces 1 and 2), it would help them to answer it, by allowing them to compare one way of answering with another. Therefore, they can be more confident that they have answered it correctly.

Example 3

Imagine you are given the following chemical equation and asked to explain its relevance to life on Earth:

$$CO_2 + H_2O \longrightarrow C_6H_{12}O_6 + O_2$$

The thinking process which takes place in your working memory will draw upon knowledge from your long term memory. At a basic level, your long-term memory feeds your working memory with the knowledge that what you are looking at are letters, numbers and other symbols. To recognise this, at some point in your life you will have had to have learned what letters, numbers and symbols look like. You will have committed this knowledge to your long-term memory.

Your understanding of what you are seeing beyond this will depend on the reservoir of knowledge you have in your long-term memory. The bigger this reservoir, the broader and deeper your understanding of what you are seeing will be. For example, your long-term memory may be storing some of the following facts:

1. When you see a collection of letters, numbers and symbols arranged in this way, you are looking at a chemical equation
2. The letters represent different chemical elements
3. Carbon has the symbol C
4. Oxygen has the symbol O
5. Hydrogen has the symbol H
6. Letters which are combined with other letters (and with numbers) represent the formulae of compounds
7. Compounds are very different from elements
8. CO_2 is the formula for carbon dioxide
9. H_2O is the formula for water
10. $C_6H_{12}O_6$ is the formula for glucose
11. O_2 is the formula for oxygen
12. The equation is showing that carbon dioxide and water are reacting to produce glucose and oxygen
13. The equation is representing photosynthesis

Many 16-year-old students, on seeing this equation, will instantly be able to tell you that it represents photosynthesis. They will also be able to offer the explanation that the reason it is so important to life on Earth is that it illustrates the production of glucose and oxygen, without which life on Earth wouldn't exist. Their thinking process didn't require them to retrieve individual pieces of knowledge from their long-term memory and to combine these, piece by piece, in their working memory to reach an understanding of what they were seeing. Rather, they would have retrieved *combined knowledge*, which we call **schema**[30].

7. Schema

Knowledge interacts and combines with knowledge in our long-term memories to produce schema[31]. This happens subconsciously. Schema are basically *knowledge constructs*. When retrieving knowledge, whole schema or different pieces of schema can be retrieved. Very helpfully for retrieval, the act of retrieving one piece of a schema allows you to retrieve other parts with it. In other words, making connections between pieces of knowledge supports the retrieval of others.

Knowledge such as '$CO_2 + H_2O \longrightarrow C_6H_{12}O_6 + O_2$ is the equation for photosynthesis' is knowledge which has been built from smaller pieces of knowledge. Rather than having to retrieve individual pieces of knowledge from long-term memory into working memory, one at a time, the student was able to retrieve a schema. As they learn more facts about photosynthesis, they will continue to develop and build this schema. Schema can be linked with other schema to further develop knowledge. For example, this student may combine their photosynthesis schema with their respiration schema so that the knowledge of one supports the knowledge of the other.

Knowledge leads to knowledge

As a final point before we conclude this chapter, it is important to emphasise that, when it comes to knowledge, the principle is: the more we have, the more we can get. I think a snowball rolling down a hill is

---

30. Sherrington, T. (2017) *The Learning Rainforest*
31. Weinstein, Y. and Sumeracki, M. (2019) *Understanding How We Learn*

a useful analogy here: bigger snowballs get bigger more quickly than smaller snowballs. A magnet in a room full of iron nails is another useful analogy: the bigger the magnet, the more nails stick to it. And so it is with knowledge: the more you know, the more you can know. The more schema you have and the more detailed the schema, the more you can make sense of and understand, by building new knowledge into your existing schema. For example, the more facts you know about the history of the 20th century Soviet Union, the more George Orwell's *Animal Farm* will mean to you.

Summary

Figure 3.4 presents a visual summary of the science of how we learn.

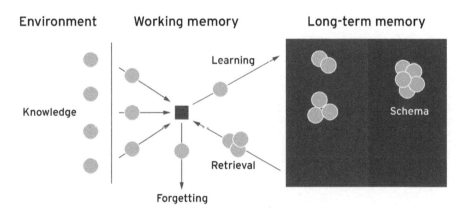

Figure 3.4: A visual summary of the science of how we learn.

As a summary of some of the key concepts we have discussed:

- Learning and thinking are related, but different
- Learning happens in long-term memory; thinking happens in working memory
- Learning and memory are essentially the same thing
- Memory is required for thinking – we can't think without memory
- We tend to memorise what we are thinking about

- Knowledge is the currency of both thinking and learning – both thinking and learning are concerned with the processing of knowledge
- Understanding comes about when knowledge takes on meaning
- The more knowledge we have, the more we can understand
- The more knowledge we have, the more we can learn

In our next chapter, we will build on our exploration of learning to explore key messages from educational literature and research in relation to *teaching*.

Chapter 4
Learning and teaching

Learning in schools

In Chapter 2, I argued that the purpose of school is to support, challenge and inspire students to learn. But learning doesn't just happen in schools – it can happen anywhere, at any time. Learning is lifelong. This means that learning doesn't always require a teacher. In fact, when thought about over the context of a person's life, learning *usually* doesn't require a teacher. Children and adults can learn all by themselves. They do so by playing, reading, talking to people, watching programmes, films and video clips on TV or the internet, going to museums, galleries or the theatre, taking part in sports… the list is endless. If people are able to learn by themselves, why do they need teachers? Do we actually need to be sending young people to school at all?

Of course we do. One reason we need schools is because they are important social institutions – they help young people to learn to interact and engage with other young people, make friends, deal with fallouts and have fun together. However, there is a more important reason we need schools. By giving students the opportunity to work with professional teachers, students' learning can become richer, broader and deeper than it ever could had they not had access to these teachers.

The importance of pedagogy

Learning in schools is different from learning outwith schools, because learning in schools involves students working with professional teachers.

It is the interaction between teachers and students that is the essence of schools. In that sense, schools offer a unique opportunity for students to learn, as they have access to people who are expert in both *what* they are teaching and *how* they teach it. The 'what' is their part of the curriculum and the 'how' is pedagogy.

It is the pedagogical knowledge and skills of a professional teacher which distinguish them from the well-educated 'non-teacher' – for example, someone who has a very good knowledge of physics, but does not understand the principles of how to best teach physics to other people. While knowing their subject well is a key requirement for any teacher, a person with strong subject knowledge doesn't necessarily make a great teacher. Great teachers need to be able to teach other people about their subject. It is not enough for them to know it or be able to do it well themselves. In schools, these 'other people' are children, teenagers and young adults. The best way to teach students to learn is not necessarily the same as the best way to teach adults to learn. Therefore, it is not enough just to be able to teach a subject to other people: you have to be able to teach this subject to *young* people.

It is not normally just one or two young people a teacher is expected to teach. In schools, teachers are usually required to teach a significant number of young people at any one time – perhaps 30 or more in the same class. And all of these young people are different. Some will be motivated to learn, some less so. Some will have an innate interest in the subject being taught, some less so. Some will do everything their teacher asks them to do, first time, and to the best of their ability; some will not. Some will come to lessons knowing quite a bit already about the subject being taught; some won't know as much.

Having so many different students in a class presents tremendous opportunities for teachers. Great teaching takes full advantage of the fact that there are so many students, using this as an opportunity for them to learn from one another and support one another's learning. Every student is valued and the learning of every student matters.

However, having so many different students in the same class can also create tremendous challenges. Overcoming these challenges requires great skill, with success or failure coming down to *how* the teacher teaches. This is why developing expert knowledge and skills in relation to *pedagogy* – the *craft of teaching* – is so important. Dylan Wiliam has gone so far as to argue that, were there to be a metaphorical battle between curriculum (that is, *what* is taught, dependent on subject knowledge) and pedagogy (that is, *how* something is taught, dependent on both subject knowledge and pedagogical knowledge), pedagogy would win every time[32].

The difference teachers can make

John Hattie has suggested that if we were to put a random adult into a class of students and ask them to teach – whether they are qualified as a teacher or not – the chances are they would make a difference, and the class would be better off than they would have been without the adult[33]. However, making a difference isn't enough. It is the *extent* to which a teacher makes a difference that is the most important aspect to consider. While the random adult may add some value, we expect that professional teachers will add considerably more. The value a teacher adds relates to the quality of their teaching. **Put simply: students learn best when they are taught by great teachers.** Poor teachers will add a little value; good teachers will add quite a lot of value; great teachers will add maximum value. It is an uncomfortable truth that when teaching falls short of being great, student learning suffers.

I have taught in schools where examination classes have experienced a year's worth of teaching and not one student has gone on to pass the exam. Pause for a moment to reflect on how you feel about that. There are various reasons why some students might not have been able to pass the exam (perhaps they were studying a course which was too demanding for them, or they were dealing with difficult circumstances in their personal life), but for no student to pass the exam… how do you explain that? The uncomfortable conclusion is that it comes down to the quality of teaching. Just as uncomfortable (but true) is to say that, in terms of passing or failing, the students wouldn't have fared any worse

---

32. Wiliam, D. (2011) *Embedded Formative Assessment*
33. Hattie, J. (2012) *Visible Learning for Teachers*

had they been taught for the year by a random adult with no teaching qualification, or if they hadn't had a teacher at all. While a hard-hitting message, it brings home the reality: the quality of teaching matters.

So, what are the differences between great teaching, good teaching and poor teaching? The answers lie in educational literature and research. It is to some of the key messages from educational literature and research that we will turn next.

Key messages from educational literature and research

In Chapter 2, I emphasised the importance of reading educational literature and research. In this section, I would like to highlight a selection of what are, for me, the key messages which come from this.

While no single piece of research can answer the question, 'What makes great teaching?', combined research messages can help to give us a good idea. When consistent messages start to emerge, it becomes foolish to ignore them.

Robert Coe *et al.*: What makes great teaching?

Having posed the question, 'What makes great teaching?' at the start of Chapter 1, it seems appropriate to turn first to a paper which takes this question as its title. In *What Makes Great Teaching?*[34], Robert Coe *et al.* identify six components, which I will quote directly:

1. **(Pedagogical) content knowledge** (strong evidence of impact on student outcomes)

   The most effective teachers have deep knowledge of the subjects they teach, and when teachers' knowledge falls below a certain level, it is a significant impediment to students' learning. As well as a strong understanding of the material being taught, teachers must also understand the ways students think about the content, be able to evaluate the thinking behind students' own methods, and identify students' common misconceptions.

---

34. Coe, R. *et al.* (2014) *What Makes Great Teaching?*

2. **Quality of instruction** (strong evidence of impact on student outcomes)

   Includes features such as effective questioning and use of assessment by teachers. Specific practices, like reviewing previous learning, providing model responses for students, giving adequate time for practice to embed skills securely, and progressively introducing new learning (scaffolding) are also features of high-quality instruction.

3. **Classroom climate** (moderate evidence of impact on student outcomes)

   Covers quality of interactions between teachers and students, and teacher expectations: the need to create a classroom that is constantly demanding more, but still recognising students' self-worth. It also involves attributing student success to effort rather than ability and valuing resilience to failure (grit).

4. **Classroom management** (moderate evidence of impact on student outcomes)

   A teacher's abilities to make efficient use of lesson time, to co-ordinate classroom resources and space, and to manage students' behaviour with clear rules that are consistently enforced are all relevant to maximising the learning that can take place. These environmental factors are necessary for good learning, rather than its direct features.

5. **Teacher beliefs** (some evidence of impact on student outcomes)

   Why teachers adopt particular practices, the purposes they aim to achieve, their theories about what learning is and how it happens, and their conceptual models of the nature and role of teaching in the learning process all seem to be important.

6. **Professional behaviours** (some evidence of impact on student outcomes)

   Behaviours exhibited by teachers, such as reflecting on and developing professional practice, participation in professional development, supporting colleagues and liaising and communicating with parents.

Coe *et al.* also draw attention to teaching practices which are not proven to be effective and for which there is 'a total lack' of evidence to support their use. Again, I will quote these directly:

1. **Using praise lavishly.** For low-attaining students, praise that is meant to be encouraging and protective can actually convey a message of low expectations. The evidence shows that children whose failure generates sympathy are more likely to attribute failure to lack of ability than those who are presented with rebuke.

2. **Allowing learners to discover key ideas for themselves.** Enthusiasm for 'discovery learning' is not supported by research evidence, which broadly favours direct instruction.

3. **Grouping students by ability.** Evidence on the effects of grouping by ability, by allocating students either to different classes or within-class groups, suggests that it makes very little difference to learning outcomes. It can result in teachers failing to accommodate different needs within an ability group and overplaying differences, going too fast with high-ability groups and too slow with low ones.

4. **Encouraging re-reading and highlighting to memorise key ideas.** Testing yourself, trying to generate answers and deliberately creating intervals between study to allow forgetting are all more effective approaches to memorisation than re-reading or highlighting.

5. **Addressing low confidence and aspirations before teaching content.** Attempts to enhance motivation prior to teaching content are unlikely to succeed – and even if they do, the impact on subsequent learning is close to zero. If the poor motivation of low-attaining students is a logical response to repeated failure, starting to get them to succeed through learning content will improve motivation and confidence.

6. **Presenting information to students in their preferred learning style.** Despite a recent survey showing that over 90% of teachers believe individuals learn better when they receive information in their preferred learning style, the psychological evidence is clear that there are no benefits to this method.

7. **Being active, rather than listening passively, helps you remember.** This claim is commonly presented in the form of a 'learning pyramid', which shows precise percentages of material that will be retained when different levels of activity are employed. These percentages have no empirical basis and are pure fiction.

In separate work, Coe discusses how difficult it is for teachers and school leaders to know the extent to which learning is taking place in a lesson[35]. He argues that we can never really be sure, but that we can use proxies. He distinguishes between 'poor proxies' for learning and better proxies. Poor proxies include:

1. Students are busy doing work, especially written work, such as copying notes

2. Students are keen, paying attention and doing what they are being asked to do

3. Students are receiving attention, including through explanations and feedback

4. The classroom is calm, ordered and under control

5. The curriculum is being covered – that is, appropriate content is being presented to students in some way

6. Some students are giving correct answers to questions (regardless of whether or not they really understood what they were being asked or whether or not they could do this independently)

When I discuss this with teachers and school leaders, they sometimes have difficulty in understanding what Coe means, at least initially. Coe is *not saying* that students being busy, keen, paying attention and doing what they are asked is unimportant – all of these things are important. He is not saying that students shouldn't be getting attention, feedback and explanations, or that classrooms shouldn't be calm, ordered and under control. They should. Rather, he is saying that none of these things indicate that *learning* is taking place. Feedback and explanations do not,

---

35. https://www.ibo.org/globalassets/events/aem/conferences/2015/robert-coe.pdf and http://www.cem.org/attachments/publications/ImprovingEducation2013.pdf

in themselves, lead to learning. Learning depends on the *quality* of these. Learning is unlikely to take place if classrooms aren't calm, ordered and under control. However, learning requires more than this.

In the interests of a focus on *learning*, teachers and school leaders should look for better proxies when evaluating the quality of lessons. With this in mind, Coe suggests that a better proxy for learning is student engagement in activities which get them to *think hard*.

Figure 4.1 illustrates the shift in mindset which we should be trying to achieve in teachers and school leaders, to move away from a focus on 'poor proxies' for learning to better ones.

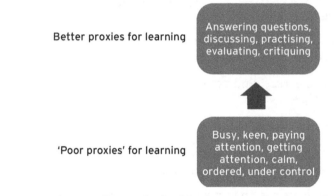

Figure 4.1: When teachers and school leaders are reflecting on the extent to which learning is taking place in lessons, they should move away from a focus on 'poor proxies' for learning to a better one, which is student engagement in activities which get them to think hard.

Dylan Wiliam: Formative assessment

Dylan Wiliam has produced excellent work on the theme of assessment[36]. He suggests that assessment needs to be **frequent, low-stakes** and **formative**.

Frequent means that assessment should be happening all the time. In discussing this, Wiliam draws a distinction between *long-cycle* and *short-cycle* assessment[37]. Long-cycle assessment reviews learning which has

---

36. For example: Wiliam, D. and Leahy, S. (2015) *Embedding Formative Assessment*
37. Wiliam, D. (2018) *Creating the Schools Our Children Need*

taken place over an extended period of time (perhaps a term); short-cycle assessment is an integral feature of day-to-day teaching practice. The five features of short-cycle assessment are:

1. Ensuring that students know what they are meant to be learning
2. Finding out what students have learned
3. Providing feedback that improves student learning
4. Having students help each other learn
5. Developing students' ability to monitor and assess their own learning

Both long-cycle and short-cycle assessment are important. In great teaching, assessment is taking place *minute by minute, lesson by lesson, week by week, month by month* and *topic by topic.*

Low-stakes means that assessment should be carried out in a way that doesn't feel threatening, put students under undue pressure or count for too much. To understand this, consider the following scenarios:

1. The 20-question test paper which students are told to complete in silence and which is taken in by their teacher to correct. Students are given a grade, which is recorded in an electronic log. Based on how they get on, students may move class. This is *high-stakes* assessment.
2. The teacher concludes a lesson by asking all students to answer three questions on a Post-it note, which they put their name on and give to their teacher as they leave the room. The teacher uses green, amber and red highlighter pens to evaluate the quality of student answers, returning them to students the next day. This is *low-stakes* assessment.

Formative means that assessment should be used to give feedback to the teacher *and* students about what has been learned or not learned. The *teacher* can assess learning, students can assess their *own* learning (self-assessment), or students can assess the learning of *peers* (peer assessment). Feedback can come from all three. This feedback can be used by the teacher to influence teaching (that is, to respond to evidence of what has been learned or not learned), and by students to support their learning.

John Hattie: Effect sizes

John Hattie has explored what makes great teaching through his work on 'effect sizes'[38]. Figure 4.2 presents a selection of this work. The numbers shown next to each 'teaching practice' are 'effect sizes'. These relate to the influence of particular teaching practices on student attainment, as informed by meta-analysis of educational research. In short: the larger the number, the larger the effect on student attainment, that is, the more positive influence this teaching practice has.

Teaching practice	Effect Size
Classroom discussion	0.82
Feedback	0.73
Direct instruction	0.60
Spaced (as opposed to mass) practice	0.60
Frequent testing	0.52
Questioning	0.48
Co-operative learning	0.40
Enquiry-based teaching	0.35
Individualised instruction	0.23
Web-based learning	0.18
Within-class grouping	0.18
Problem-based learning	0.12
Student control over learning	0.01

Figure 4.2: A selection of teaching practices with their associated 'effect size', as reported by John Hattie.

Hattie suggests that almost all teaching practices are effective to some extent, because almost all make a positive difference to student learning and therefore attainment. A positive effect on attainment is represented by any number above 0. However, he argues that it is not good enough for a professional teacher to turn up to work thinking, 'I'm doing a good

---

38. https://visible-learning.org/hattie-ranking-influences-effect-sizes-learning-achievement/

job, because I make a difference.' Almost all teaching practices make a difference. Rather, it is the responsibility of the professional teacher to understand which teaching practices make the *biggest* difference to student learning and learn how to use these practices effectively in lessons. Great teaching is about making the biggest difference you can.

Because 'making a difference' isn't good enough, Hattie has assigned an effect size of 0.4 as the key benchmark, which translates as one grade of difference over the course of a year. To maximise attainment, Hattie argues that teachers should **focus teaching and learning time on the teaching practices which make the biggest difference to student attainment,** which means a move away from those with lower effect sizes to those with higher effect sizes.

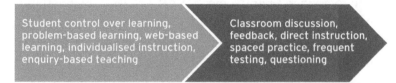

Figure 4.3: A focus on teaching practices which make the biggest difference to student attainment means moving away from teaching practices on the left towards those on the right.

While the messages reported by Hattie should be of great value to teachers and school leaders alike, care is required in interpreting these. At a surface level, specific numbers are being assigned to terms which are very often broad. Teachers and school leaders need to take time to explore key messages and develop a deeper understanding of these.

For example, we have already discussed how Robert Coe has highlighted 'feedback' in itself as a poor proxy for learning. What Hattie's work is suggesting is that *high-quality* feedback has a relatively high effect size. Hattie reports 'homework' as having an effect size of 0.29, but explains that there are marked differences between the effect of homework at primary and secondary school (0.15 and 0.64 respectively) and that the nature of homework makes a difference – homework which asks students to complete non-complex tasks, such as practising questions relating to content covered in lessons, is typically more effective than homework which asks students to engage in higher-level conceptual thinking or project-based tasks[39].

One final important point to highlight from Hattie's work is the significance he places on *all* students' learning in lessons. Hattie argues that it is relatively straightforward to engage a few or some students in thinking and discussion, or to find out about the learning of one or two, but that doing so does not make great teaching. When there is great teaching, teachers are engaging *all* students in thinking and discussion; they are finding out about the learning of *all* students.

Craig Barton: 'I know it works'

Craig Barton has written an excellent book called *How I Wish I'd Taught Maths*. In spite of what its title suggests, this is a book which should be very useful to teachers of any subject. What follows is a quotation which stands out to me from an introductory section of his book[40]:

> If someone had asked me to write a book about maths teaching two years ago… it would have consisted of open-ended tasks and ideas that I have developed over many years and used with thousands of students. It would have been full of me exclaiming how much my students enjoyed these activities, the insights they made, the problem-solving skills they developed, the independent learners they became, and the results they achieved. I would have extolled the benefits of discovery learning, inquiries, projects, puzzles, student-centred learning, and of me as a teacher taking a back seat (I would probably have used the phrase 'the teacher should be the facilitator of learning' more than once). The one noticeable absence from this hypothetical book, of course, would have been any research to back-up my claims. And if someone had pointed out this tiny omission, I would have replied with a patronising smile and explained 'I don't need research, I know it works'.

Framed in the context of his own practice, Barton is summarising the key messages reported by John Hattie. He is also emphasising the importance of teachers and school leaders engaging with educational literature and research.

---

39. Hattie, J. (2009) *Visible Learning*
40. Barton, C. (2018) *How I Wish I'd Taught Maths*

Barak Rosenshine: Principles of Effective Instruction

Through Twitter I discovered the work of Tom Sherrington (author of the excellent *The Learning Rainforest*) and through Tom Sherrington I discovered the work of Barak Rosenshine, author of *Principles of Instruction: Research-Based Strategies That All Teachers Should Know*[41].

Rosenshine's '17 Principles of Effective Instruction' are:

1. Begin a lesson with a short review of previous learning
2. Present new material in small steps with student practice after each step
3. Limit the amount of material students receive at one time
4. Give clear and detailed instructions and explanations
5. Ask a large number of questions and check for understanding
6. Provide a high level of active practice for all students
7. Guide students as they begin to practise
8. Think aloud and model steps
9. Provide models of worked-out problems
10. Ask students to explain what they have learned
11. Check the responses of all students
12. Provide systematic feedback and corrections
13. Use more time to provide explanations
14. Provide many examples
15. Reteach material when necessary
16. Prepare students for independent practice
17. Monitor students when they begin independent practice

At some point in the recent history of schools, the term 'instruction' (or 'direct instruction', as it is commonly called) seems to have assumed negative connotations. Many teachers and school leaders recoil at its very mention. They view it as something archaic, having little or nothing in common with great teaching. They could not be more wrong.

---

41. https://www.aft.org/sites/default/files/periodicals/Rosenshine.pdf

Sadly, such a misconception is relatively widespread. When I lead workshops on teaching and learning with teachers, I usually begin by asking them to identify what they believe to be the key features of great teaching. If I ask this as an open question and get them to write their 'top three features' on Show-me boards, rarely, if ever, does 'direct instruction' appear. If I provide them with a list of features which include 'direct instruction' and ask them to rank these in terms of the effect educational research suggests they have on student learning, the vast majority put direct instruction near the bottom.

It is a travesty that direct instruction has come to be viewed so dimly when its effect on student learning has the potential to be so great. Why has this happened? My view is that it happens because some people mistakenly think that direct instruction means 'lecturing', with the teacher talking and students listening for sustained periods of time. It is true that some teachers do teach like this and that, through a combination of student interest in the subject being taught and the teachers' skills in oratory, these teachers can hold the attention of some students for sustained periods of time. However, this is not direct instruction and it is not great teaching.

Direct teaching is *interactive*. While there is nothing wrong with teachers talking – teachers need to talk in order to teach – if all that is going on in a lesson is that the teacher is talking, then it is not possible for the teacher to assess what students are learning. Look again at Rosenshine's 17 Principles of Effective Instruction and you will see that they include principles such as: 'Ask a large number of questions and check for understanding', 'Provide high levels of active practice for all students', 'Ask students to explain what they have learned', 'Check the responses of all students' and 'Provide systematic feedback and corrections'.

The only thing that direct instruction and lecturing have in common is the need for clarity in what the teacher is saying. Beyond that, they are very different. I actually prefer to refer to direct instruction as 'direct-interactive instruction' to help avoid any misconception that this is about lecturing. Direct-interactive instruction of the type outlined by Rosenshine is a key component of great teaching.

Daniel Willingham: What students think makes a good teacher

It is important to consider the views of students when exploring what makes great teaching. In *Why Don't Students Like School?*[42], Daniel Willingham suggests that when students are asked what makes a good teacher, responses typically fall into three categories:

1. The teacher is a nice person (that they have positive interactions with their students)
2. The teacher is well organised (that they come across as knowing what they are talking about and doing)
3. The teacher makes what they are teaching interesting

This makes a lot of sense. Imagine that you are going for a lesson to learn to play the piano, ski, paint or drive. Whether or not you go back for another lesson will depend, in part, on whether or not you liked the teacher and how good a teacher you thought they were. If you didn't like the teacher, you probably wouldn't go back. If you didn't think they knew what they were talking about, you probably wouldn't go back. If you found the lesson boring or you didn't understand what they were teaching you, you probably wouldn't go back. The only difference between this imaginary scenario and the scenario of students going to school is that in the imaginary scenario you have a *choice* about whether or not you continue with the lessons; students going to school don't usually have this. Until they reach an age where they can choose which subjects they study or to leave school altogether, students *have* to go to lessons, regardless of who their teacher is or how good the teaching is.

Great teaching: The key principles

Having considered a selection of what, to me, are key messages from educational literature and research, we return to the question we asked at the start of Chapter 1: what makes great teaching? In Chapters 5, 9 and 13, we will discuss this in terms of the typical features of high-quality lessons. Before we do, I will summarise what I believe to be the key components.

A description of great teaching

Drawing on and pulling together the key messages from Chapters 2, 3

---

42. Willingham, D. (2010) *Why Don't Students Like School?*

and 4, I suggest that great teaching is **that which typically focuses on teaching knowledge, using pedagogies which are best for teaching knowledge (*direct-interactive instruction* and *formative assessment*), by teachers who have a *strong knowledge of what they are teaching and how students typically think about this*, and who develop *strong relationships* with their students**.

This is the **Specific Teaching** we discussed in Chapter 2.

An important caveat to add to this description of great teaching is that it will always involve more than just this – enquiry-based learning, group work, projects, student presentations and web-based learning all have an important role to play in the kaleidoscope of great teaching. These are examples of the **Non-specific Teaching** approach. **Great teaching is a blend of Specific Teaching and Non-specific Teaching.** However, as we have discussed, the main ingredient of this blend is Specific Teaching.

The extent to which teaching can be deemed to be 'great' is dependent on two factors:

1. The extent to which *all* students are ***learning***
2. The extent to which *all* students ***enjoy*** their learning

One can happen without the other, but in great teaching, there is both.

A model for great teaching
I offer the following model as a visual summary of the answer to the question: what makes great teaching?

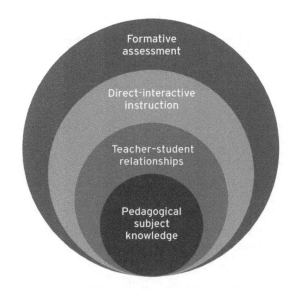

Figure 4.4: A model for the key components of great teaching, as distilled from educational literature and research. A caveat for each component is that they should each be preceded by the words 'strong' or 'high-quality'.

Pedagogical subject knowledge and **teacher–student relationships** are at the core of great teaching. Without high-quality pedagogical subject knowledge (that is, knowledge of the subject you are teaching and how students typically think about this), teachers cannot teach what they are supposed to; without high-quality relationships, students won't engage in the teaching and learning process, and they are unlikely to enjoy the learning. However, high-quality pedagogical subject knowledge and relationships do not, in themselves, lead to great teaching, or indeed to any teaching at all. Great teaching draws upon both, but it requires more.

Direct-interactive instruction is a key component of great teaching. It is concerned with review, explanation, demonstration, modelling, exemplification, interaction, scaffolding, practice, questioning, checking and feedback. While educational literature and research typically refer to 'direct instruction', I argue that inclusion of the term 'interactive' is important to help avoid the misconception that what we are referring to is 'chalk and talk' teaching, which is that in which there is no interaction of any kind.

The principles of direct-interactive instruction overlap with those of the final component of great teaching: **formative assessment**. The purpose of formative assessment is to measure and address the 'teaching–learning gap'. Evidence generated through formative assessment can be used to support both *teaching* (by providing teachers with information about the extent to which what has been taught has been learned) and *learning* (by providing students with feedback based on their responses to assessment tasks). Formative assessment can be used to support students to take responsibility for their learning and to encourage them to support the learning of others.

⌒ℓ⌒

The synergy of high-quality **pedagogical subject knowledge, teacher–student relationships, direct-interactive instruction** and **formative assessment** is the essence of great teaching. In our next chapter, we will explore how these four components influence the pedagogy of high-quality lessons.

Chapter 5
Great teaching - Part 1

What are the key factors that lead to high-quality student learning (and attainment as a result of this learning)? I would argue that there are two:

1. **Great teaching**
2. **Hard work** on the part of students

Our detailed discussion of what makes great teaching is divided into three parts and spread over the course of this book (Chapters 5, 9 and 13). In between these chapters, we will explore how a professional learning culture can be developed and used to transform teaching practice.

Before we begin this discussion, we will touch briefly on the importance of hard work on the part of students.

Hard work on the part of students

Teachers and school leaders can have some influence over how hard students work, but they can't control it. They can – and should – set regular homework which will support student learning (activities which focus on retrieval practice are typically best for that; for example, practice questions and self-quizzing using Knowledge Organisers – see the case study below). They can teach students effective study strategies (again, activities which focus on retrieval practice are typically best). They can make clear their expectations for how much time students should be spending on homework and independent study each week and they can make time outside of class to support them with anything they are finding difficult or don't understand. However, at the end of the day, it is the student who will decide how hard they are going to work.

Parents can also have an influence. There is an increasing body of research suggesting that parental engagement in student learning – even if that involves simply taking an interest – can have a positive impact on student learning[43]. However, like teachers and school leaders, parents can't control how hard students work, either. The only person who can really control how hard a student works is the student themselves.

> ### Case study: Knowledge Organisers
>
> In *Battle Hymn of the Tiger Teachers*, Joe Kirby describes the role that **Knowledge Organisers** can play in supporting students' learning[44]. Knowledge Organisers are documents which set out the knowledge that needs to be learned by students in a particular topic or unit of work. Usually, this knowledge is presented on one or two sides of an A4 sheet, laid out in easy-to-access chunks. This knowledge can be presented in a variety of ways, for example, as facts, definitions, diagrams, images, formulae and equations. A Google search will bring up many examples.
>
> The process of constructing a Knowledge Organiser benefits teachers, because doing so makes you really think about the essential content to be learned, including how challenging it is and whether or not you understand it yourself.
>
> For students and their learning, Knowledge Organisers become powerful when they are used to '**self-quiz**'. Self-quizzing 'gets students to retrieve knowledge from long-term memory which, as we discussed in Chapter 3, is a key aspect of the teaching and learning process. It can take a variety of forms, one of which could be for students to go through the following steps:
>
> 1. **Read** (a short section of the Knowledge Organiser, with a focus on trying to remember it as they read)

43. Campbell, C. (2011) *How to Involve Hard-to-Reach Parents.*

44. Kirby, J. in Birbalsingh, K. (2016) *Battle Hymn of the Tiger Teachers*

2. **Cover** (the Knowledge Organiser)

3. **Write** (what they think they remember from what they just read)

4. **Check** (what they have just written against the uncovered Knowledge Organiser)

5. **Correct** (any mistakes they have made)

6. **Repeat** (the process until they are writing out a short section of the Knowledge Organiser without making a mistake)

Self-quizzing makes for an excellent homework activity, fuelling student learning and reducing teacher workload by removing the need for marking.

The quality of teaching

While teachers and school leaders have limited influence over how hard students choose to work, they can have a great deal of influence over the quality of teaching that students receive. For that reason, while I do believe it is important that teachers and school leaders support, challenge and inspire students to work hard, I believe it is even more important that they work tirelessly to ensure that all students receive the highest quality teaching possible.

Sadly, there are too many examples of the scenario in which a student is working hard and their parents are pushing them to do so, but the quality of teaching they are receiving is failing them. There is no getting away from the fact that the responsibility, in such scenarios, lies with teachers and school leaders. We shouldn't beat about the bush here: some teaching in schools simply isn't good enough.

If teachers and school leaders recognise this and are taking steps to do something about it, then this is just about acceptable. However, if teachers and school leaders don't recognise it and aren't doing something about it, then they are failing the students they came into the job to help.

Case study: The importance of teacher subject knowledge

Sometimes, poor teaching comes about because of a lack of teacher subject knowledge. This can mean that students are taught content poorly or wrongly, or aren't taught the required content at all. I once observed a religious and moral education lesson on the topic of reincarnation. The teacher was explaining to the class that Buddhists believe that, when people die, they are reincarnated and come back as 'something else'. They went on to explain that what people come back as is determined by whether they have lived a good or bad life. When their reincarnated life ends, they are reincarnated again. A student put up their hand and said, 'So are you saying that, if I am bad, I could be reincarnated as a stone?'

'Yes,' replied the teacher.

'And are you saying that the stone will be reincarnated?' said the student.

'Yes,' replied the teacher.

'But how can I be a good or a bad stone?' asked the student.

The teacher paused.

'Well, I guess if someone were to pick you up and throw you through a window,' they replied, 'that would be an example of you being a bad stone.'

Teacher credibility

To some extent, I am sure we can all sympathise with the teacher in this case study. Clearly, they did not have a strong grasp of the subject they were teaching, which was put to the test in an unplanned way when a student asked them a (perfectly sensible) question. Perhaps the teacher answered in the way they did because another professional was in the room and they felt they had to come up with an answer, or perhaps they would have answered in the way they did regardless. However, the key point is *they are the teacher*. Students expect their teachers to know what they are talking about.

In his work on effect sizes, John Hattie highlights 'teacher credibility' as having a high effect (0.9) on student learning[45]. Hattie argues that students are very perceptive about knowing which teachers can make a difference and know their subject well, and which don't. He puts it like this: if a teacher is not perceived as credible, the students just turn off.

Saying it is important that teachers know what they are talking about is not the same as saying teachers need to know *everything* about the subject they are teaching – that would be unreasonable and an unrealistic expectation. However, a certain level of subject expertise is required, because students are always going to ask us questions about what we are teaching, which we should encourage. If we are asked a question we don't know the answer to, there is nothing wrong with telling the student we're not sure but that we will think about it and get back to them. An alternative (and face-saving) strategy would be to say something like, 'That's a good question. We're not going to have time to get into that today, but we will come back to it tomorrow.' In the interim period, you would take steps to find out what the answer is.

Returning to the case study, I think it is probably an extreme example. That said, it is a hard reality that many teachers don't have a solid grasp – or anything close to a solid grasp – of what they are teaching or supposed to be teaching. There is no shame in this if the teacher takes steps to do something about it, to learn about the content they will be teaching and to 'upskill' themselves. Improving your subject knowledge is important professional learning. No one is saying that you need to have a PhD in what you are teaching to be able to teach it successfully. However, you do need to have a sufficiently deep and detailed understanding of the content you are teaching in order to teach it effectively. Not everyone who has such an understanding makes a great teacher, but all great teachers have such an understanding.

Great teachers

Great teaching requires great teachers. Great teachers are people who deliver great teaching, day in, day out. They have *strong pedagogical subject knowledge*, form *strong relationships* with the students they

---

45. https://visible-learning.org/hattie-ranking-influences-effect-sizes-learning-achievement/

teach, and understand the principles of *direct-interactive instruction* and *formative assessment*, which they put into practice in lessons. All of this requires a lot of knowledge and skill. Beyond knowledge and skill, great teachers are people who:

1. Have a **passion** for their subject and for teaching it to students
2. Have a **mindset** that it is their job to **make the biggest difference they can** to the learning of all the students they are teaching
3. **Make time to work with individual students**, both in and out of class, so that students know that their learning is important and that their teacher will give them as much help as they can
4. Have a belief that **evaluating the quality of teaching and learning** in lessons is essential to ensuring high-quality student learning and to the continuous improvement of their teaching practice
5. **Plan lessons** carefully
6. **Communicate** information about student progress clearly with relevant stakeholders (including parents)
7. **Engage in professional learning** which develops their knowledge and skills as a teacher

In a recent lecture I attended by Pak Tee Ng, Associate Professor at the National Institute of Education in Singapore, I was reminded that students will often tell us that they love a subject because they love the teacher. Teachers bring subjects to life and help students to fall in love with subjects. Sometimes it is about the content, but often it is about the teaching. The best curriculum in the world will only lead to high-quality student learning if it is well taught. The curriculum doesn't teach students – only pedagogy can do that. Pedagogy trumps curriculum.

Pedagogy

While deep subject knowledge is a prerequisite for great teaching, as we have discussed, this does not, in itself, lead to great teaching. **Great teaching requires deep knowledge and skills in relation to *pedagogy*.** It is the extent to which someone is expert in pedagogy that is the key distinguishing factor between the non-teacher, the good teacher and the great teacher, all of whom may have expert subject knowledge.

In secondary schools (and, to a lesser extent, primary schools), different teachers teach different subjects – there is no requirement for all teachers to know about the same things, except for pedagogy: knowing about pedagogy is a key requirement for all teachers. Without a shared understanding of pedagogy, different teachers will teach in diverse ways, some effective, some very effective, and some not very effective at all.

No teacher sets out to teach ineffectively, and few are satisfied with teaching to a standard which is 'quite effective'. Most teachers want to teach in a way that is as effective as possible – to make the biggest difference they can to the lives of as many students as possible. But without a shared understanding of pedagogy, some teachers will succeed while others fail. This is not about a lack of hard work or professional commitment. It is not about not caring. It is rarely about a lack of subject knowledge. The distinguishing factors between the great teacher, the good teacher and the poor teacher are knowledge and skills in relation to pedagogy.

When we talk about pedagogy, it is useful to think about two types:

1. **Generic pedagogy** – the principles of teaching practice which span different subjects
2. **Subject-specific pedagogy** – the principles of how best to teach particular topics and concepts within a subject

Both are important and interconnected. The relationship between the two is illustrated in Figure 5.1:

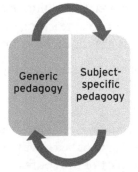

Figure 5.1: Pedagogy can be thought of in both generic and subject-specific terms, which are interconnected. In the pursuit of great teaching, consideration of both is important.

Shown in Figure 5.2 are examples of generic and subject-specific pedagogical knowledge:

Generic pedagogical knowledge	Subject-specific pedagogical knowledge
How to write a good learning intention	How to write a good learning intention relating to the water-cycle
Effective questioning strategies	How to word a set of questions to find out what student understanding of voltage is, including what their misconceptions are
Principles of how to support and challenge all students	How to support a student who is finding it difficult to understand what the word 'equilibrium' means

Figure 5.2: Examples of generic and subject-specific pedagogical knowledge.

Great teaching through high-quality lessons

Great teaching manifests itself through high-quality lessons, day in, day out. It is a blend of Specific Teaching and Non-specific Teaching approaches, with the balance in favour of Specific Teaching. In general, Specific Teaching should account for 80–90% of lesson time.

Having identified the four components of Specific Teaching in the previous chapter (pedagogical subject knowledge, teacher–student relationships, direct-interactive instruction and formative assessment), we will go on to explore how these influence the pedagogy of high-quality lessons, that is, how theory can be put into practice. In doing so, it is appropriate to move away from generic principles of great teaching to a more specific focus on lessons. **High-quality lessons are the delivery units of great teaching.**

Breaking the four components of great teaching down into the specific pedagogy of high-quality lessons, I argue that high-quality lessons are those which typically include:

1. Activities that require students to **recall knowledge** from previous lessons, which may or may not be relevant to this lesson, but which needs to be learned as part of the course

2. Clear communication and use of **learning intentions and success criteria**

3. Activities that allow the teacher to **find out what students know or can do already** (in relation to what is being taught in this lesson)

4. Clear **teacher explanations and demonstrations** which hold student attention

5. Activities that allow students to **put into practice** what they are being taught

6. Appropriate levels of **support and challenge**

7. Use of **questions** to make students think and to check for understanding

8. Activities that get students to **discuss and learn with other students**

9. Clear **feedback** to individual students and to the class about their learning

10. Activities that **evaluate the impact of lessons**

11. Strong **teacher–student relationships**

12. **High expectations and standards** for student behaviour and quality of work

Over the course of three chapters (Chapters 5, 9 and 13), we will explore each of these in detail.

1. Activities that require students to **recall knowledge** from previous lessons, which may or may not be relevant to this lesson, but which needs to be learned as part of the course

The teaching–learning gap

A key understanding for anyone involved in education relates to the '**teaching–learning gap**': that is, the gap between what a teacher teaches and what students learn. The fact is: *what is taught is not necessarily learned*. It doesn't matter how well something has been presented, demonstrated or explained by a teacher; if it hasn't been learned by students, the teaching hasn't been effective. Great teaching is about more than interesting presentations, demonstrations and high-quality explanations.

Accepting this, a key question becomes: how can the gap be bridged?

The first step is to determine the size of the gap. In other words, you need strategies to find out what students have learned – not just one or two students, but all of them. This means that you have to assess student learning regularly. **Assessment** is the key to bridging the teaching–learning gap.

Figure 5.3: Teaching and learning are not the same thing – what is taught is not necessarily learned. In other words, there is usually a gap between what is taught and learned. The key to bridging this gap is assessment.

Assessment

The word 'assessment' often carries baggage. When I talk about the importance of assessment with teachers, it is not uncommon to hear things like, 'But I thought we were trying to get away from having so much assessment!' Comments like this relate to a teacher's understanding of what we mean by assessment, which leads us to a discussion about 'summative' and 'formative' assessment.

Summative and formative assessment

To understand what we mean by 'summative' and 'formative' assessment, it can be useful to draw the following distinction:

- **Summative assessment** assesses student learning of a body of content and reports this learning in the form of a *score (or percentage or grade)*. It 'looks back'.
- **Formative assessment** assesses student learning and uses the information which comes from this to give *feedback to the **student** and **teacher*** about the learning. It 'looks forward'.

Dylan Wiliam has made the point that all assessments have the potential to be used summatively or formatively and that, really, these terms are best thought of with regard to *how the assessment is used*, rather than what the assessment looks like[46]. For example, imagine that your students sit an end-of-topic test which you score out of 40. If all that is done with this is that students are given a score or grade based on how they got on, then the assessment is being used *summatively*. In other words, you are *summing up* what they have learned.

If, in addition to doing that, you use information about how students got on with particular questions to give feedback to them about these, or to adapt your teaching in light of this (perhaps by reteaching certain content because the assessment showed that many students hadn't understood this part of the course), the assessment is being used *formatively* as well. If you hadn't marked the assessment but instead had gone through it adding comments, or had used a green/amber/red system to highlight areas of strength or requiring improvement, you would have been using the assessment *formatively*, but not summatively.

To check your understanding of this, imagine that, at the start of a lesson, you ask students to answer six multiple-choice questions, such as[47]:

> A ball is thrown vertically upwards. The ball reaches its maximum height. Which of the following describes the forces acting on the ball at this instant?

A. There is no vertical force acting on the ball

B. There is only a horizontal force acting on the ball

C. There is an upward force acting on the ball

D. The forces acting on the ball are balanced

E. There is only a downward force acting on the ball

Students are given a few minutes to complete this task individually.

---

46. Wiliam, D. and Leahy, S. (2015) *Embedding Formative Assessment*

47. https://www.sqa.org.uk/pastpapers/papers/instructions/2018/mi_N5_Physics_mi_2018.pdf

Described below are different hypothetical scenarios showing what you might do next. For each one, I would like you to consider the extent to which you think the assessment is being used summatively or formatively.

1. You read through the answers (e.g. 'Question 1 – C; question 2 – B' etc.) and ask students to total their score out of six, before moving on to the next part of the lesson.

2. You read through the answers (e.g. 'Question 1 – C; question 2 – B' etc.), stopping after each question to ask students to indicate if they had answered A, B, C, D or E. You then move on to the next part of the lesson.

3. You read through the answers (e.g. 'Question 1 – C; question 2 – B' etc.), stopping after each question to ask students to indicate if they had answered A, B, C, D or E . You take time to explore why they had chosen a particular answer, using what they say to make teaching points and give feedback about how to improve. You then move on to the next part of the lesson.

Take a moment to consider what you think.

I would argue that scenario one is summative use, two is summative use with some formative use included (the teacher is getting formative information), and three is summative use with more formative use included (both the *teacher* and the *students* are getting formative information).

The extent to which an assessment is used summatively or formatively can be thought of as being on a spectrum, as shown in Figure 5.4:

Summative	Summative-formative	Formative
Scores only	A combination of scores and feedback	Feedback only

Figure 5.4: The assessment spectrum. Rather than thinking about summative and formative assessment as types of assessment, it can be more useful to think about these terms in relation to how an assessment is used. Assessment used summatively is summative assessment; assessment used formatively is formative assessment.

The more an assessment task is used formatively, the more useful it is for supporting teaching and learning. For me, **all assessments should be used formatively.** The only exception to this might be an end-of-course exam. Even then, there is potential for this to be used formatively, if students and teachers are given access to marked papers.

Whenever teaching happens, assessment needs to happen too. If something has been taught, you need to find out if it has been learned. You cannot assume that, because you taught it, students have learned it. If you do, you will end up with a teaching–learning gap. In all likelihood, some students will have learned it and some won't. Depending on the complexities of what was being taught, the chances of every student having learned something perfectly, with no misunderstandings, are pretty slim. Therefore, frequent 'low-stakes' assessment is important to check what has been learned.

Retrieval

Frequent low-stakes assessment is important for another reason. As discussed in Chapter 3, there is an increasing body of research from the field of cognitive science highlighting the importance of getting students to *retrieve* information which has been taught[48]. The act of retrieving information helps to strengthen the memory of it. For this reason, it is important for teachers to build regular retrieval opportunities into lessons (and homework).

For example, you might do this by getting into the habit of starting lessons with short retrieval quizzes, such as:

1. Complete: 'Elements in the Periodic Table are arranged in order of increasing...'
2. True or false: the mass of a neutron is 0
3. Draw a diagram to represent an atom, labelling as much as you can

I recently observed a lesson which began with a PowerPoint slide headed 'Daily Review', on which there were three 'true or false' questions. These were assigned the labels: 'last lesson', 'last week', 'last topic'. The teacher told me that every lesson started with a similar activity. The questions were either true or false, multiple-choice or short response. But every lesson began in exactly the same way. Sometimes the teacher got students to write down their answers on a Post-it note and collected these, to be reviewed after

---

48. Willingham, D. (2010) *Why Don't Students Like School?*

the lesson and for feedback to be given during the next lesson. Sometimes students wrote answers on Show-me boards and held them up for immediate feedback. Sometimes students worked in silence, on their own, to complete these, with a clear two-minute time limit. Sometimes they were given a few minutes to discuss answers with a partner. How Daily Review took place varied from lesson to lesson, but it always took place.

This draws on Barak Rosenshine's idea that '**Daily, Weekly and Monthly Review**' are key elements of great teaching[49]. The difference between the three will typically relate to the number of questions students are expected to answer (with Weekly and Monthly Review being more extensive than Daily Review) and the breadth of content covered (Weekly and Monthly Review will typically cover a broader body of content than Daily Review).

Reviews of this kind support students in retrieving recent and less recent knowledge, strengthening memory. They also provide powerful formative information to teachers about the teaching–learning gap. If teachers collect scores from these, they can track student progress (I would suggest weekly or monthly for this purpose, rather than daily). Alternatively, they can ask students to record these themselves so that they track their own progress. After each review, students can be asked, 'What is it that you are going to do between now and the next review to improve?' This is an example of the 'high challenge, low threat' culture which Mary Myatt identifies as so important in great teaching and great schools[50].

> 2. Clear communication and use of **learning intentions and success criteria**

Learning intentions

In *Practice Perfect*[51], Doug Lemov suggests that the difference between the good teacher and the great teacher is that the good teacher spends approximately 20% of lesson planning time thinking about what the learning intention (and success criteria) for a lesson should be and approximately 80%

---

49. Rosenshine, B. (2012) *Principles of Instruction*

50. Myatt, M. (2016) *High Challenge, Low Threat*

51. Lemov, D. (2012) *Practice Perfect*

of planning time thinking about the activities of the lesson. In the case of the great teacher, the reverse is true: 80% of planning time is spent considering the learning intention (and success criteria) and 20% on the activities. The planned learning should guide the planned activities, not the other way around. In other words, the tail should not wag the dog.

Careful consideration of the learning intention for a lesson is important because it dictates everything that follows. If you aren't clear, as a teacher, what students should be learning in a lesson, then students won't be clear either. Precious learning time will be wasted, because activities won't be focused on a clear learning goal. Students will become busy *doing things*, but not necessarily things which are supporting their learning.

I recently heard about a head of an English department who, as part of a discussion with other heads of department, explained that they didn't believe that having a learning intention for lessons was very important. A colleague challenged them on this and asked: 'So are you saying that you don't think it is important that the teacher has a clear idea about what students should be learning in a lesson?' There was a brief pause, before the head of department replied: 'Well, for subjects like English, which are a bit more nebulous than subjects like maths and science, teachers don't need to be so clear about what students are learning, do they?' I couldn't disagree more (and neither could the head of department who challenged this).

I also recently heard about a headteacher who, as part of a discussion with teachers about learning intentions, argued that they thought you could use the same learning intention for an entire topic. Both of these examples suggest a complete misunderstanding about what learning intentions are and how they can be used to support student learning.

Case study: Misunderstandings about learning intentions

Not all teachers and school leaders are clear about what a good learning intention looks like. Once, as part of a Departmental Review Programme, I observed six science lessons over the course of two days. From these, I saw a learning intention being shared with students in just two lessons, and neither were what I would describe as 'good' learning intentions. On the back of this, I decided to do a piece of work with this department to explore their understanding of what makes a good learning intention.

I asked members of the department to imagine an introductory lesson on atomic structure, to be taught to 13-year-old students, and to consider what the learning intention for such a lesson might be. After a short 'think for yourself and then discuss with a partner' activity, I asked them to consider four possible learning intentions and choose which one they thought best. These were:

Know that atoms are made up of protons, neutrons and electrons

Know about the particles which make up an atom

Name the three types of particle which make up an atom

Be able to draw a labelled diagram of an atom

Multiple-choice activities of this kind are a very powerful formative assessment tool, bringing to the surface people's understandings and misunderstandings. Which one would you pick?

Of the six teachers, two chose option 1, one chose option 3, two chose option 4 and one said that they wouldn't choose any of those options.

Cards on the table: of the options presented, I would have chosen option 2 (which no one in the department chose). Option 2 is a statement which makes clear what students will be *learning about*, which is in keeping with my understanding of what makes a good learning intention. I could also have been persuaded to choose option 4, although, for me, this is more a success criterion, because it relates to how students will *demonstrate* their learning. Similarly, I would say that option 3 is a success criterion statement, not a learning intention. Option 1 is neither a learning intention nor a success criterion: it is a statement of the knowledge which is to be learned (and would be a useful addition to a Knowledge Organiser).

The key point I wish to make is that a shared understanding of what makes a 'good' learning intention did not exist in this department. Discussion among staff followed, which was important, because it gave teachers the opportunity to explain *why* they had made their specific choice. It also allowed teachers the opportunity to learn from each other, which included challenging what someone was saying. However, just as practice does not make perfect (it makes permanent[52]), discussion does not necessarily lead to everyone reaching a 'correct' shared understanding. It is conceivable that, following this discussion, a shared understanding of what a good learning intention looks like could be developed, but it could be a shared *misunderstanding*. This misunderstanding might come about as a result of the persuasive arguments of an individual, or because a tipping point was reached in terms of the number of staff who subscribed to a particular view, and the minority decided that the majority must be right.

In order to ensure that a 'correct' shared understanding is developed, at least one person taking part in the discussion needs to be knowledgeable in relation to what is being discussed. Just as important, they have to be able to influence others, so that misunderstandings are addressed and people learn.

Definition and examples of learning intentions

Learning intentions are statements which summarise the purpose of a lesson in terms of *learning*. A useful acronym is WALT: '<u>W</u>hat we <u>A</u>re <u>L</u>earning <u>T</u>oday'[53].

In writing them, I usually find it useful to include the terms '**know**', '**understand**' or '**be able to**', which helps communicate that the learning will relate to knowledge, understanding or skills, respectively.

Here is an example:

> We are learning about the structure of an atom, specifically to know about:
>
> – The sub-atomic particles which make up atoms

Over the course of several lessons, the class will be learning about the structure of an atom. For that reason, this statement will appear as

---

52. Lemov, D. (2012) *Practice Perfect*
53. Clarke, S. (2014) *Outstanding Formative Assessment*

part of the learning intention in lessons which follow. In this particular lesson, the specific focus is on the sub-atomic particles which make up atoms. The learning intention for the next two lessons might be:

We are learning about the structure of an atom, specifically to understand:

– Nuclide notation

– The electron arrangements of the first 20 elements

Because every lesson is about learning, I would argue strongly that every lesson should have a clear learning intention, whether this be for students to learn something new, to consolidate their learning (through practice or revision) or to demonstrate their learning.

Learning intentions should make clear *what* students will be learning about, not *how* this learning will be achieved (the activities and tasks of the lesson). For example, 'Complete all of the questions on page 45 of your textbook' is not a learning intention – it is a statement about an *activity*. Learning intentions should be about what is to be *learned*.

'Real life' contexts

Relatively often, I hear teachers being told that learning intentions should 'relate to real life wherever possible'. Every time I do, it proves no less baffling to me. We are living in 'real life' – everything that we do and everything that we learn about is real life. I suspect that what people mean is that they believe it is important for learning to be linked to situations to which students can relate. For example, if teaching fractions in maths, students could be taught this in relation to slicing a pizza, because they all know what a pizza is and they can relate to that. Because they have something that they can relate to, the theory goes that this should support their learning. However, this is not necessarily true.

Despite good intentions, 'real life' contexts can sometimes get in the way of student learning. Returning to the example of the pizza, a teacher once told me about a lesson they had taught in this way and which, at the time, they believed to have been a successful lesson. However, two days later, when they were reviewing the learning from the previous lesson, all that some students could tell them about was pizza. Any advice teachers are given about the importance of real life contexts to learning should be treated with caution.

That said, analogies do have a place. When teaching students about electrical charge, current and voltage, I have always found a waterslide analogy to be useful in helping students understand the meaning of these terms. The purpose of the analogy is to help students to develop an understanding – it is not to make the learning more 'relevant' to them. Some students are very capable of understanding what these terms mean without such an analogy, and many students will be interested in what electrical charge, current and voltage are regardless of whether an analogy is used or not. Not using an everyday, 'real life' context won't detract from students' interest in the topic.

Much of what we teach students at school is abstract and unfamiliar. There is nothing wrong with that. Being abstract and unfamiliar does not take way from the importance of learning things or students' interest or enjoyment in learning such things. If we were only to teach students about things that they could relate to in 'real life', their learning would be very narrow, shallow and rather dull. Many students enjoy and are motivated by learning for the sake of learning and it is important to foster that.

Taking chemistry (which is the subject I teach) as a final example, how much of the chemistry I learned as a student, and now teach to others, relates directly to my 'real life'? Very little. Could I live my life without knowing anything about chemistry? Yes, I definitely could – many people do. Instead of being a chemistry teacher, I could have been a maths teacher. However, there is one important point that we are glossing over here: I love chemistry! For me, it is such a wondrous, amazing subject. When I watch a piece of potassium drop into a glass bowl of water and burst into flames, I think, that's incredible! Learning about why this happens has been really interesting to me. What's more, it's not just me who finds it interesting. Just about every student I have ever taught has found this interesting. And here's the other interesting thing: in any given day (other than the days in which I am teaching students about potassium reacting with water), I never really think about potassium. Some people would say that the chemistry of potassium has nothing to do with 'real life'. They are wrong: it has everything to do with 'real life'. Perhaps it has little to do with most people's day-to-day lives, but that doesn't detract from the value of learning about it.

Communicating learning intentions
It is important that learning intentions are clearly communicated with students. Good practice is to do this both verbally and visually. However, saying this is very different from saying that students need to *copy down* the learning intentions (and success criteria) for lessons. Some schools insist that teachers get students to do that, but students learn nothing from doing so and it just wastes valuable learning time.

Revisiting learning intentions
It can be useful to revisit learning intentions during lessons, reminding students of the learning focus. By the end of the lesson, something should have changed: students should know something that they didn't before, they should be able to do something that they couldn't before, or they should have improved at something. **Every lesson should impact on learning; every lesson should count.**

In discussing the importance of every lesson, John Hattie argues that a key mindset for teachers is to see themselves as 'evaluators of impact'[54]. The evidence of what has changed (that is, the evidence of student learning) should relate to success criteria, which is what we will go on to discuss next.

Success criteria

Success criteria relate to the *evidence* you are looking for to determine if students have learned what you intended. A useful acronym is WILF: 'What I am Looking For'[55].

Success criteria can take different forms, including:

- **'I can…' statements**
- **Key features**
- **Exemplars**

---

54. Hattie, J. (2012) *Visible Learning for Teachers*
55. Clarke, S. (2014) *Outstanding Formative Assessment*

The principal purpose of success criteria is to support assessment and feedback. When assessing learning, it isn't enough for a teacher to ask, 'Have you learned this?' and then just to accept yes as an answer. As Doug Lemov describes it, we should 'reject self-report'[56]. There needs to be *evidence* of learning; students need to *prove it*. Success criteria can make clear what that evidence should be. In this way, success criteria become tools to support teacher assessment, peer assessment and self-assessment. Without being clear about what you are looking for, meaningful assessment and feedback is not possible.

'I can...' statements

When success criteria are written as **'I can...'** statements, they include *verbs* which make clear the evidence required to demonstrate learning. Rather than being about 'knowing', 'understanding' or 'being able to' – which is the language of learning intentions – they should be about *what you are looking for* in order for students to demonstrate that they have learned what was intended.

If students can 'state', 'write', 'describe', 'explain' or 'draw', this can evidence learning. Saying that 'I know', 'I understand' or 'I am able to' doesn't evidence learning. While it might be true, it isn't evidence.

To appreciate this, let's return to the learning intention which was used as an example in the previous section:

Learning intention

We are learning about the structure of an atom, specifically to know about:

– The sub-atomic particles which make up atoms

Possible success criteria are:

Success criteria

1. I can *draw* a labelled diagram of an atom, showing the arrangement of the three sub-atomic particles which make it up

2. I can *state* the charge of each of the sub-atomic particles

3. I can *state* the mass of each of the sub-atomic particles

---

56. Lemov, D. (2015) *Teach Like A Champion*

Figure 5.5 includes further examples of possible 'I can…' success criteria for different learning intentions.

Learning Intention (WALT)	Success Criteria (WILF)
Know the main features of an animal cell.	• I can *label a diagram* to show the cell membrane, nucleus and cytoplasm • I can *draw a labelled diagram* to include each of these features
Understand the types of training methods a business uses.	• I can *name* the three main types of training • I can *explain* at least two advantages and two disadvantages of each
Be able to change units of length: metres to centimetres and vice versa.	• Given a length in metres, I can *change* it to centimetres • Given a length in centimetres, I can *change* it to metres, using decimals where necessary

Figure 5.5. Examples of learning intentions with possible success criteria, written as 'I can…' statements.

Occasionally, I hear people argue that success criteria shouldn't be quantified. For example, if success criteria relate to being able to identify advantages and disadvantages of something, teachers shouldn't specify *how many* advantages and disadvantages. The rationale is that, by quantifying, you limit student learning. However, I would argue that, if success criteria are going to be used to assess learning and to guide feedback, they need to be as specific as possible. Sometimes, this will mean quantifying them. The way to get around any issue of 'limiting learning' is to include the phrase 'at least' in front of the quantity (for example, 'I can identify *at least* two advantages and two disadvantages of…').

Key features
Sometimes, rather than writing success criteria as 'I can…' statements, they are better written as '**key features**'. This tends to be when they relate to 'Be able to…' learning intentions. Figure 5.6 gives examples.

Learning Intention (WALT)	Success Criteria (WILF)
Be able to calculate the area of a circle, showing clear working.	When you are completing these calculations, I want to see the following features in your working: • Formula • Substitution • Answer • Units
Be able to swim front crawl with an efficient leg kick.	When doing this, your: • Legs will be straight and toes pointed • Legs will reach a depth of approximately 18 inches and will only create a bubble at the surface • Legs will pass close together • Body position will be flat and will not rotate
Be able to present data in a table.	The key features of this are that: • It has two columns • Each column has an appropriate heading • Each heading has correct units • The data has been entered correctly • It has been drawn with a ruler

Figure 5.6. Examples of learning intentions with possible success criteria, written as 'key features'.

Students can be involved in identifying key features. For example, if you are trying to tease out of students appropriate success criteria for drawing a graph, you might ask them:

- 'What will we be looking for in a very good graph?'
- 'How are we going to decide if a graph is a very good one or not?'
- 'What would a poor graph look like?'
- 'How are we going to make sure our graphs aren't just good, but very good?'

Exemplars

Exemplars can be used to make clear to students what a high-quality piece of work looks like, or what a low-quality piece of work looks like. Students can compare their own work against the exemplars, and can be asked to identify the key features of high-quality work when compared with lower-quality work. In this way, students themselves can start to understand what success criteria should be. Such activities are an excellent means by which to engage students critically and get them to think hard.

Modelling

Regardless of the form success criteria take, teachers should take time to talk them through with students and check that they understand them. Often, there is value in teachers using them to **model** what they are looking for. In doing so, they should explain their thought process and highlight important points. For example, they might use phrases such as:

- 'Pay close attention to *this* – it is something that students often get wrong'
- 'A useful way to remember *this* is…'
- 'Don't forget about *this*…'
- 'Note the capital letter here – it's not lower case'
- 'When you are doing this yourself, I would like you to make sure that you do *this*…'

Confusing learning intentions and success criteria

A common mistake I see teachers make is that they confuse learning intentions and success criteria. In doing so, they confuse themselves and they confuse students.

Consider the following as an example:

Learning intention

Be able to define and describe 'deforestation'

I see this sort of learning intention quite often. In writing it, the teacher has confused the *learning* (which relates to deforestation) with the *evidence* students need to produce to demonstrate their learning. A far better learning intention would be:

Learning intention

Understand what 'deforestation' is

This is focused on *learning.*

Possible success criteria could be:

Success criteria

- I can *write* a definition for 'deforestation'
- I can *describe* three causes of deforestation

These are focused on *evidence* of learning. In checking that students understand what deforestation is, the teacher would be looking to see evidence relating to each success criterion.

3. Activities that allow the teacher to **find out what students know or can do already** (in relation to what is being taught in this lesson)

In an earlier section, we discussed the importance of Daily, Weekly and Monthly Review, all of which are activities designed to promote recall of knowledge. In these activities, the knowledge which is being recalled may or may not be relevant to the lesson being taught that day. In this section, though, the emphasis is on finding out what students know or can do already *in relation to specific content being taught in a particular lesson.*

I once watched a lesson which was, on the face of it, a good one about respiration. The success criteria were:

- I can *write* a word equation for respiration
- I can *identify* the reactants and products of respiration

At the end of the lesson, when the teacher was reviewing learning, almost all students were able to do both of these things. The teacher deemed the lesson a success. However, almost all of the students in the class had been able to do these things before they had come to the lesson, because the science teacher they'd had six months before had taught them. (I found this out by chatting to students after the lesson, almost all of whom told me that they knew how to do all of what had been taught in that lesson already.) Nowhere in the lesson had there been any exploration of what students knew or could do already.

If, as John Hattie suggests, we accept that a key part of a teacher's job is to evaluate their impact on student learning[57], then it is essential that there is assessment within a lesson of what students know or can do already. This process need not be overly complicated or time-consuming.

Imagine the lesson I mentioned on respiration starting with the teacher saying to students, 'Today we are going to be learning about respiration', and following this up with one of the following instructions:

- 'I want you to take two minutes to chat to a partner about what you know about respiration' (the teacher walks around the room and listens in on student conversations)

- 'I want you to take two minutes to write down everything you know about respiration in your jotter'

- 'I want you to take two minutes to work with a partner to write down everything that, between the two of you, you know about respiration'

- 'I want you to write down three things you know about respiration on your Show-me board and then hold it up'

- 'There are three "true or false" statements about respiration on the board. For each of them, I want you to discuss with a partner whether it is true or false, or you don't know'

All of these instructions are designed to make students think and to generate feedback for the teacher about what students already know or don't know, including their misunderstandings. This is formative assessment in action.

Case study: Finding out what students know

Recently, I was having a chat with an English teacher. She described how a 'write down everything you know about...' task in a lesson she had just taught had highlighted, to her surprise, that some students had learned nothing from the lesson she had taught yesterday. Nothing. It was a good example of the importance of finding out the size of the teaching–learning gap (which in this case was huge), which is hidden until students are given recall tasks.

---

57. Hattie, J. (2012) *Visible Learning for Teachers*

'Active assessment' activities

The *Active Assessment* series[58] by Stuart Naylor *et al.* presents a variety of strategies which can be used to get students to think, discuss and generate feedback for the teacher, including in relation to what they know or can do already. The term 'active assessment' is used as a proxy for 'active learning' – the two can be used interchangeably. Before we go on to explore a selection of active learning activities, I would like to address a misconception many people have about what 'active learning' actually is.

Active learning

Recently, I was on holiday in Mexico, relaxing by the poolside. I didn't mean to, but I overheard a conversation between a group of people in the pool who were discussing their children's education at school. 'My son is so gifted,' began one. 'He's so clever. He gets awesome grades, but he really hates school. He hates sitting in the classroom and having to be inactive. He needs to be active. He needs to be allowed to get out of his seat and do things. He doesn't get enough active learning. Girls do well in that environment, but boys don't. Boys need to be up and doing things. It's holding him back.'

There is much that we could chew over in this anecdote. For example, we could discuss the casual gender stereotyping and the ill-informed notions that boys and girls learn differently (they don't), and that boys have to be 'up and doing things' in order to learn (they don't) while girls can learn sitting at desks (they can, but so can boys). However, what I would like to focus on is the all-too-common misunderstanding about what 'active' means in the context of learning, which is shared by many teachers and school leaders.

'Active learning' does not mean students being up, out of their seats and running around a classroom; it relates to students being *actively engaged*. This means that students are *thinking*. If a student is bored or disengaged, it is likely that this is because they are finding the content or activities too easy or too difficult, that there is a lack of support, praise or recognition, that a particular activity has gone on too long or

58. For example, Naylor, S. *et al.* (2004) *Active Assessment in Science*

that there are issues to do with the way the content is being presented. Regardless of which combination of factors is leading to disengagement and boredom, not being 'up and doing things', as an explanation, is usually wide off the mark.

Examples of active assessment activities
Four of my favourite active assessment activities are:

- **True or false**
- **Odd one out**
- **Deliberate mistakes**
- **Concept Cartoons**

True or false
The design of 'true or false' statements will dictate how hard students have to think about them. Compare the following two statements:

1. Snakes are amphibians
2. Snakes and frogs are amphibians

Which requires students to think harder? It is the second one, because it includes more than one thing for them to think about.

Carefully designed true or false statements can target common misunderstandings. For example:

- When you divide a number by another number, it gets smaller
- It takes 365 days for the Sun to go around the Earth

When giving students true or false statements, useful follow-up questions are:

- 'Why?'
- 'Are you sure?'
- 'How sure are you?'

Odd one out
In 'odd one out' activities, sometimes there is a correct answer and sometimes there isn't. Both scenarios have value.

Consider the following example:

Which of these processes do you think is the odd one out, and why?

A. Ice melting

B. Glass breaking

C. Wood burning

D. Water boiling

In the context of a lesson on chemical reactions, a student might argue that the answer is 'C' ('wood burning') because it involves a chemical reaction but the other three don't. Alternatively, a student might choose 'B' ('glass breaking') because the other three involve heat but this one doesn't.

Had students been given a specific context to the problem (perhaps the teacher said, 'This is a problem about chemical reactions'), then there would be a correct answer. Used in this way, the teacher could get information about what students know or don't know in relation to chemical reactions. However, it isn't always necessary to give a context. A teacher might start a lesson with an odd one out activity but not tell students what it relates to. Engagement in the activity gets students to *think* and *discuss*. The teacher can listen to what students say and use this to guide their teaching.

Deliberate mistakes

In this type of activity, students are given something – a paragraph, a table, a graph, a diagram – which has 'deliberate mistakes' in it. This might have been produced by the teacher or it might be an example of real work produced by a student. Students in the class are tasked with finding all of the mistakes. The teacher might tell them how many mistakes there are to find, or they might not.

The mistakes that students identify can be discussed and used to determine 'key features' of a high-quality product. By doing this, teachers are getting students to identify success criteria. Rather than the teacher articulating the key features, deliberate mistakes are used to help students do this themselves.

Concept Cartoons

In 'Concept Cartoons', a character asks a question which other characters in the cartoon comment on. Figure 5.7 gives an example.

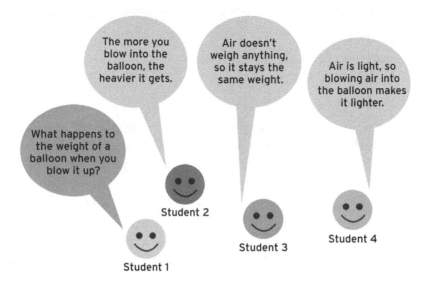

Figure 5.7: An example of a Concept Cartoon.

Students are asked to think about the question posed and what the other characters are saying. They are asked:

- 'Who is right?'
- 'Who is wrong?'
- 'Who is partially right?'
- 'Why?'

Concept Cartoons could be used at the start of a lesson, at the end, or both. Students could be asked to think about their responses individually or to discuss them in a pair or group. They could be asked to write their answers down or to report back as part of a whole-class discussion. As with odd ones out, sometimes there will be a correct answer and sometimes there won't be. What is most important is that there is thinking, discussion and feedback.

Drilling down

Active assessment activities of this kind can be used to drill down into student learning and tease out common misunderstandings. Teachers with good pedagogical subject knowledge are able to do this; teachers with weaker pedagogical subject knowledge are less able.

In *Making Good Progress?*[59], Daisy Christodoulou discusses how **multiple-choice problems** can be used in active assessment. She gives the example of how, in maths, a teacher might give students the following multiple-choice problem:

What is 20% of 300?

A. 30

B. 60

C. 15

D. 6000

The 'distractors' (the wrong answers) have been chosen deliberately by the teacher – they aren't random wrong answers. Rather, they have been chosen because they link to common student misunderstandings, which the teacher is aware of.

The correct answer is B (which I'm sure you have worked out). The distractors have been chosen for the following reasons:

A. To identify students who are good at calculating 10% but unsure how to calculate 20%

B. To identify students who confuse percentages with division

C. To identify students who confuse percentages with multiplication

Knowing which common misunderstanding each distractor is targeting supports the formative information that the teacher receives, which informs the feedback they can give to students.

As a comparison, imagine the distractors had been:

A. 50

B. 60

C. 100

D. 200

---

59. Christodoulou, D. (2016) *Making Good Progress?*

In this case, they have been chosen at random. If a student chooses A, C or D, while this tells the teacher that the student doesn't know how to solve the problem, it won't give them any insight into the student's thinking. Carefully chosen distractors can.

As a related example, imagine a science teacher who is planning to teach a lesson on the water cycle to 10-year-old students. At the start of the lesson, the teacher has planned to use assessment to find out what students know about matter changing from one state to another. They do this by asking some questions:

Teacher: 'What term do we use for a liquid turning into a gas?'

Student: 'Evaporating.'

Teacher: 'So when liquid water turns into gaseous water, is this called "evaporating"?'

Student: 'Yes.'

Teacher: 'Good. And what term do we use for a gas turning into a liquid?'

Student: 'Condensing.'

Teacher: 'Good. Evaporating and condensing are two terms that we are going to be using a lot today.'

Putting the teacher's questioning technique to one side (we will discuss questioning techniques in Chapter 9), for now we can say that, while they might have successfully assessed student knowledge of key terminology needed for the lesson (which is important to do), they haven't done anything to assess the *deeper understanding* which sits below this. When students give us the answers we are looking for to 'surface' questions of this type, we need to be aware that there could be deep-rooted misunderstandings which sit below these. Correct answers to surface questions can hide deeper misunderstandings.

Following this argument, an important question for the teacher to ask students would be something like: 'True or false: water needs to boil in order to turn into a gas.'

Many 10-year-old students will say that this is true. From experience, I know that some teachers of 10-year-old students will also say that this is true. But it is false.

Such a question targets a common misunderstanding that water only changes into a gas when it boils. However, this is wrong. Puddles come and go after a rainy day, but when they 'go', they haven't gone because they boiled – they have gone because they evaporated. The true or false question deliberately targeted this common misunderstanding. Whether or not a teacher planned to ask this question would relate to their pedagogical subject knowledge.

In this chapter, we have started a discussion on the typical pedagogy of high-quality lessons. We shall return to this in Chapter 9. Before we do, we are going to turn our attention to the theme of **professional learning cultures** in schools.

PART 2.

A strong professional learning culture

Chapter 6
Mindsets of teachers and school leaders

Learning schools

When, in Chapter 2, we were discussing the purpose of school, I argued for *learning* to be recognised as the core business of schools, framing this in the context of students. However, learning should be the core business for *everyone* involved in the life of a school – students, teachers, school leaders and support staff. High-quality schools are '**learning schools**', in which the commitment of staff to their own learning is as important as their commitment to the learning of students. When we talk about staff learning, we are talking about 'professional learning'.

If staff aren't committed to professional learning, they are not committed to improvement, because improvement only comes about through learning. Only in a perfect school is there a valid argument that staff don't need to improve the quality of their work. That school does not exist – and it never will.

If we accept the importance of professional learning, what should staff focus their professional learning on? Everything comes back to the learning of students – *what* they are learning and *how well* they are learning it. This means that everything comes back to the quality of teaching they are receiving. 'Learning and teaching'; 'teaching and learning' – I do not believe it matters which comes first because they are interconnected and equally important. However, when it comes to the focus of professional learning, one *is* more important than the other. The focus of professional learning needs to be on *teaching quality*.

Continuous improvement

It takes courage for teachers and school leaders to accept that the quality of teaching in their classrooms and schools could, and should, be improved. By doing so, they are accepting that there may be deficiencies in the quality of teaching practice, which there will be. There is no such thing as the perfect teacher, which means that every teacher's practice has scope to improve. There is nothing personal about this statement. It is about professional practice. It is not about 'teacher-bashing'. It is a reality. We should not feel criticised by it, believing it infers that we are failing because we aren't doing our jobs well enough. That's not what it means at all. Rather, it means that we can always – all of us – do better. This is the mindset of continuous improvement.

Sporting analogies can be helpful. Think about your favourite sport and those who play it at a professional level (and, make no mistake, teachers are professionals too). They are always striving to be better. The professional golfer who scores 60 wishes they hadn't missed the 10-foot putt on the 13th green, which would have meant they scored 59; the 100m sprinter who won the race with a world record-breaking time will go into their next race aiming to run it even faster. And so on.

And so it should be with professional teaching: there is no point at which someone has become the best teacher that they can be and can no longer improve. No matter how good a teacher's teaching is, there is always something they can learn to make their teaching even better.

This is an exciting principle to realise, because the better we get at something, the better outcomes become (in the case of teaching, we are talking about outcomes for students) and the more we tend to enjoy what we are doing. The pursuit of continuous improvement in teaching will be of benefit to both students *and* the teacher teaching them.

Schools transform lives – quite considerably, in many cases, which is why it is so important to be restless and relentless in our pursuit of great teaching, to make it better and better and better. We owe it to the young people we teach and we owe it to ourselves. Knowing that we are teaching to high standards, and that day by day and week by week we are striving to make these standards even better, should bring tremendous professional satisfaction. A commitment to great teaching and continuous improvement is something to be proud of. It is a commitment to making the biggest difference we can in terms of transforming lives.

Experience and expertise

At this point, it is important to emphasise that 'experience' and 'expertise' are not the same thing; nor are they necessarily interconnected. Developing *experience* in teaching is relatively easy – you just turn up to do your job, year on year. Developing *expertise* in teaching is much more challenging, requiring not only a commitment to improving pedagogical *knowledge* but to developing pedagogical *skills* in the classroom, through deliberate practice, self-evaluation and feedback.

In his book *Practice Perfect*[60], Doug Lemov highlights the importance of practice to becoming expert in any field, but crucially, only if practising *the right things*. He cautions that practice does not always make perfect; rather, practice 'makes permanent'. The more someone practises something, the more likely it is that what they are practising will become a habit. However, if someone is practising something which is 'wrong', or isn't adding much value to the area they are trying to improve, then the person is wasting their time. So, practice is important – in fact, essential – but it is practising the right things that is most important.

Professional autonomy

To what extent do you believe that teachers should be professionally autonomous? By this, I refer to teachers' autonomy in relation to what they are teaching and how they are teaching it. In other words: should a teacher be free to teach what they want in a manner of their choosing, or should the 'what' and the 'how' be specified? Please think about this for a moment.

How autonomous are you, as a teacher, in relation to the 'what' and the 'how' of teaching? Do you teach whatever you want, or do you follow a

60. Lemov, D. (2012) *Practice Perfect*

curriculum? Assuming you have a curriculum, do you think it is right that you do? Or do you think it would be better if you could determine the content you teach to students yourself, regardless of the content that other teachers are teaching in your school or another school? In terms of how you teach, how much autonomy do you have? Are there certain teaching practices which you are told must feature in lessons, or are you free to decide which to include and which to exclude? To what extent do you believe a school should specify teaching practices which should be used in lessons?

Regarding the 'what', the idea that the same content is taught to students in the same school isn't usually contentious. Schools tend to have a curriculum. The debate gets a little more interesting when you start to discuss how important it is for students in different schools to be taught the same content. This is where a national curriculum comes in. However, in my experience, the vast majority of teachers and school leaders believe that a national curriculum has merit. They may not agree on what should be included in it, but the idea that different teachers in different schools should be teaching similar content isn't usually contentious either. Teachers accept the accompanying lack of autonomy. So long as they teach the prescribed content, they will have a degree of autonomy in terms of the 'extras' they can bring to it, depending on their subject knowledge and areas of interest.

The debate gets far more interesting when you start to discuss *how* content is taught by teachers. Views as to whether or not pedagogy should be prescribed are far more polarised. On one side, there are teachers who will argue that, as a professional, they should be able to teach how they see fit. On the other side will be those who are more open to some level of specificity.

Consistency

A related but slightly different question is: to what extent do you believe that teaching practice should be consistent across a school? In thinking about this question, it would be helpful to consider examples of what I am getting at. So, in terms of teaching practice in your school, to what extent do you think there should be consistency in relation to each of the following?

- What happens in the first five minutes of a lesson
- The use of the phrase 'learning intention' (as opposed to, for example, 'learning outcome' or 'lesson purpose')
- The font used in PowerPoint presentations and handouts
- Whether or not students put their hand up to answer questions
- The amount of time that should be spent on a lesson plenary
- The use of Specific Teaching and Non-specific Teaching approaches

Similarly, ask yourself:

- Is it okay if some teachers use learning intentions in a school and some don't?
- Is it okay if some lessons have plenaries and some don't?
- Is it okay if some teachers use Specific Teaching and some don't?
- Is it okay if some teachers' lessons are structured around web-based and discovery learning and some aren't?

These are the sorts of questions which schools need to grapple with themselves. Ideally, this grappling should be supported by professional reading, discussion and debate regarding what makes great teaching. While some may swiftly be dismissed as trivial (or not – it's not my place to judge), there are others which will be worthy of more careful consideration.

Perhaps there isn't a need for consistency in terms of the amount of time spent on a lesson plenary (or perhaps there is), but assuming a school decides there isn't, is there a need for consistency in terms of there being a lesson plenary in a lesson at all? If a school decides that there is, is there a need for consistency in terms of what happens during a plenary?

In *When the Adults Change, Everything Changes*[61], Paul Dix argues that if schools are to achieve high standards of student behaviour, there is a need for a consistent approach in terms of how adults respond to poor behaviour. Dix argues that inconsistencies in approach across a school will often, in themselves, lead to poor student behaviours. In other words: inconsistencies can create problems. He makes a case for consistency in

---

61. Dix, P. (2017) *When the Adults Change, Everything Changes*

terms of the language that staff use when addressing issues of poor behaviour, going so far as to recommend scripting conversations, so that staff are saying the same things to students in particular situations.

Dix is making a case for the necessity of consistency in terms of behaviour management. But how necessary is consistency when it comes to considering the way that teachers teach, that is, consistency in terms of the pedagogy?

In my view, when considering questions of this kind, rarely is the answer found at either of the extremes. It is not about absolute consistency; nor is it about a free-for-all across the school. Whenever we push for consistency, to some extent we take away from autonomy; when we allow for autonomy, we lose consistency. Therefore, there is a balance to be struck. We are not – I hope – aiming to produce teachers as robots who do and say exactly as they are told, or are clones of one another, all teaching in exactly the same way, lesson by lesson. But does this mean that we would be happy with a situation whereby teachers are left to their own devices, teaching in ways they see fit, regardless of how they are doing this? Is an 'anything goes' approach okay? I don't think it is. We wouldn't see this kind of ideology in other professions. We expect the practice of doctors, nurses, vets and dentists to be carried out to the very highest of standards, regardless of which doctor, nurse, vet or dentist we go to see. As research points to improved ways of working, we expect that the practices of these professionals will improve. We would not accept a situation whereby, depending on who we go to see, the outcome could be quite different. Is there any good reason why the same principles should not be applied to the teaching profession?

Mindsets of teachers

In my experience, there are four broad categories of teacher mindset:

1. **The moving collaborator:** the teacher who is committed to improving their teaching practice, including through learning with other teachers, and who sees themselves as having an important role in helping to improve the practice of others. These are the teachers who want to keep on making their teaching better and work with other teachers to achieve this. They are the teachers

who see the quality of teaching across the school, as a whole, as an important consideration, and not just the quality of teaching in their own classroom. Professional learning impacts on their practice. Regardless of their current standard, their teaching keeps on getting better.

2. **The moving individualist:** the teacher who is committed to improving their teaching practice but who likes to work by themselves to achieve this. They don't see themselves as having a role in improving the practice of others. These are the teachers who want to keep on making their teaching better, but who would prefer to do this on their own terms. While the quality of teaching in their own classroom is important to them, they don't consider the quality of teaching across the school as an area with which they should be concerned. Professional learning impacts on their practice. Regardless of their current standard, their teaching keeps on getting better.

3. **The static collaborator:** the teacher who is committed to improving their own teaching, including through collaboration with other teachers, but for one or more reasons, it isn't improving. They are trying to improve their practice, but despite this, nothing is really changing. They are teachers who see the quality of teaching across the school, as a whole, as an important consideration, and not just the quality of teaching in their own classroom. Their teaching practice may be high quality, but it may not be. Regardless of the quality, it is not improving.

4. **The static individualist:** the teacher who is content with the quality of teaching in their classroom and who would like to be left alone to get on and teach. They don't believe there is a need to improve the quality of their teaching, because it is good enough already. They don't see a need to collaborate with other teachers and they don't view the quality of teaching across the school as an area with which they should be concerned. Their teaching practice may be high quality, but it may not be. Regardless of the quality, it is not improving.

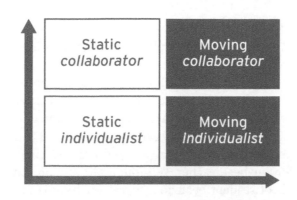

Figure 6.1: Categories of teacher mindset. We want all teachers to be 'moving' (that is, improving), not 'static'. Preferably, we want them to be collaborating as they move, so they can learn from and with other teachers.

To which category would you say you typically belong? Is your practice static or is it moving? If it is moving, how fast is it moving? Is this movement being achieved by yourself, or are you collaborating with other teachers? If you are collaborating, is your collaboration also helping other teachers to move?

In reality, you may find yourself somewhere between two of these mindset categories, or perhaps you find that you move between categories, depending on particular circumstances. Mindsets can and will shift in different directions.

Perhaps you were once a Moving Individualist but now you are a Moving Collaborator; perhaps you were once a Moving Collaborator but now you are a Static Individualist.

Which category do you think we should be aiming to be in? For me, the mindset of the Moving Collaborator is the one we should be trying to develop and maintain in all teachers and school leaders. This is the mindset of continuous improvement and working together to achieve better outcomes for students. It is the mindset of teachers who work in a *learning school*. Understanding how to influence such mindsets is a key consideration for teachers and school leaders who want to be a part of such a school.

Mindsets of school leaders

School leaders have a key role to play in the development of a *learning school*. However, in my experience, there are many school leaders – and I include headteachers in this – who believe that teachers should be left to get on with the teaching while school leaders deal with 'the other things'. But what 'other things' are more important than a focus on the continuous improvement of teaching? Health and safety? Yes, that is certainly important. Ensuring a safe and orderly school should be a key priority for any headteacher. Without a safe and orderly school with high standards of student behaviour, great teaching is unlikely to take place in very many classrooms. However, for the most part, on a day-to-day basis, so long as the school is being well led and managed, and has effective behaviour management systems in place, health and safety should generally take care of itself.

So, what else is important? A headteacher's job used to be about bells, buses and behaviour[62], but in the 21st century, this has all changed. The headteacher is the lead professional – the lead learner. If the headteacher isn't demonstrating, through their words and actions, that learning is the core business of the school, and that the continuous improvement of teaching and learning is the number one priority, how can others be expected to believe this?

In *Leadership, Capacity Building and School Improvement*[63], Clive Dimmock pulls together evidence from literature and research to present the 'top 10 leadership behaviours' for the most effective headteachers, these being:

1. Promoting and actively participating in teacher learning and development

2. Encouraging the use of data and research evidence – especially analysing student progress and achievement data – to inform teaching and teacher development

3. Planning, co-ordinating and evaluating teaching and the curriculum

---

62. Dimmock, C. (2012) *Leadership, Capacity Building and School Improvement*
63. Dimmock, C. (2012) *Leadership, Capacity Building and School Improvement*

4. Expanding the curriculum to secure wider student engagement and improving assessment procedures

5. Establishing goals and expectations

6. Sharing leadership

7. Encouraging collaborative enquiry among leaders and teachers

8. Providing and strategising the allocation of resources, including deployment of personnel

9. Ensuring an orderly and supportive environment

10. Developing a learning-centred culture

Count how many times the importance of focusing on learning, teaching and teacher development comes up. 'Promoting and actively participating in teacher learning and development' is at the very top of this list. It is at the top of the list because it is the most important action of a high-performing headteacher.

Just as I would argue that there are static and moving teachers, so I would argue that there are static and moving schools. Whether or not a school is static or moving is determined by the quality of school leadership. Educational research is consistent in its message that, in terms of having an impact on student outcomes, the quality of leadership in a school is second only to the quality of teaching[64]. Further, it is the leadership of the headteacher which is the most significant factor.

Like teachers, headteachers and other school leaders need to consider their mindsets in relation to teaching and learning improvement. The reality is that too many headteachers pay lip service to a teaching and learning improvement agenda. Occasionally, they talk about it, but there is no real focus or consistency to what they are saying. Occasionally, they drop into lessons or carry out lesson observations, but very little happens as a result. Often, teachers are just told that they are doing a good job. These lesson observations focus on quality assurance and ticking boxes, rather than being about professional learning and continuous improvement.

Some headteachers have never observed the teaching of some of the teachers who are teaching in their school: they employed them based on

---

64. Barber, M. *et al.* (2010) *Capturing the Leadership Premium*

an interview and have left them to get on with it ever since. A teacher in their school could be the best in the world or they could be very poor, but unless a parent phones in or a student comes to tell them about it, the headteacher works on a principle of trust – trusting that it is good enough. Trust is important, but there is a fine line between trust and burying your head in the sand.

Some headteachers do think that the continuous improvement of teaching and learning should be a high priority, but they are too busy with other work to spend any time doing anything about it. In this case, they really need to be questioning what they are spending their time on, asking themselves: does this need to be done and could someone else do it?

The most effective headteachers are those who understand that schools are incredibly busy places, that time is precious and that there is a vast array of competing initiatives and priorities, but that in spite of this, the continuous improvement of teaching and learning must be the central driver. They understand that **the development of a *learning school* is key**. They foster and encourage the mindset of the Moving Collaborator in all of their staff.

Everything I have said in this section about headteachers can be brought down to the level of deputy headteacher, principal teacher or head of department. If you are a leader of any kind, here are 10 key questions I would like you to consider:

1. Do you believe that learning is the core business of your school (or department)?
2. Do you believe that teaching quality has a direct impact on the quality of student learning and achievement?
3. Do you accept that there are variations in the quality of teaching practice across your school (or department)?
4. Do you accept that a mindset of the Moving Collaborator is the right one for your school (or department)?
5. Do you agree that the continuous improvement of teaching and learning should be the principal focus of professional learning in your school (or department)?

6. Do you agree that teachers in your school (or department) have the capacity to support the professional learning of other teachers?

7. What role do you currently play in supporting the improvement of teaching practice in your school (or department)?

8. To what extent do teachers and school leaders in your school (or department) know what research says about effective teaching?

9. To what extent are teachers in your school (or department) making use of teaching practices which research suggests are the most effective?

10. What is the one thing that you could start to do, or do differently, which would make a positive impact on teaching practice across your school (or department)?

All of these questions are important for you to think about and discuss with others. However, the last one is key: just as improvements don't come about without learning, they also don't come about by doing things the same way. If you decide things need to improve, then you need to start doing things differently to bring about improvement.

✧

Having got this far, you clearly believe continuous improvement is important. Key to continuous improvement in classrooms, departments and schools is a strong **professional learning culture**. This is the theme we will explore in our next chapter.

Chapter 7
Professional learning culture

Key to the development of great teaching in classrooms and schools is the strength of a school's **professional learning culture**. *Learning schools* are schools which have a strong professional learning culture.

In schools with such a culture, professional learning is understood to be as important a consideration as student learning. Teachers and school leaders understand that professional learning and student learning are interconnected: where there is high-quality professional learning, improved student learning follows. Figure 7.1 illustrates this relationship.

Figure 7.1: The relationship between professional learning and student learning. High-quality professional learning leads to improved student learning. In the absence of professional learning, student learning will not improve.

In this chapter, we will explore what we mean by a 'professional learning culture' and start a discussion about how such a culture can be developed. In later chapters, we will drill down to explore specific features of this. We will begin our discussion with an exploration of what the word 'culture' means.

Culture

Cultures are about people. When we talk about the **culture** of a school, we are referring to the idea that *this is what we do here*. In other words, we are referring to the behaviours of the people who work in the school. When behaviours become routine, they become *habits*. Rather than thinking, 'I must remember to do that', people just do it. The behaviour has become a part of the way that the school works. Habits are the essence of culture.

Climate

The behaviours of people are influenced by **climate**. By climate, I mean *how it feels* to work here. Climate is about ethos and the environment in which people work. Climate isn't a physical thing – it doesn't relate directly to the quality of the building or the resources available in it. The most important influences on climate are the *interactions between people* who are working in the organisation. Positive interactions typically lead to a positive climate; negative interactions lead to the opposite.

On the one hand, climate is invisible, because it is about *feel*. On the other hand, climate is very visible through the behaviours and actions of staff. In that sense, culture is a visible manifestation of climate. Ensuring a positive climate is essential to ensuring a positive culture.

In schools with a positive climate:
1. Teachers are supported and encouraged to 'take risks'
2. There are high levels of trust (balanced with appropriate accountability)
3. There is mutual respect between teachers, students and school leaders
4. There are high standards of conduct from students and staff
5. Working practices are grounded in collegiality (which is different from consensus – it means that the views of people are sought, listened to and considered)

6. There is recognition of effort and high standards of work (which comes across as sincere, rather than tokenistic or over the top)

7. Staff and students are made to feel valued and appreciated

8. People are prioritised over paperwork

9. There is a sense of 'team' – we are all in this together, we all have a vested interest in success and we can all play a role in helping to support, challenge and learn from each other

10. There is collective pride

Mindsets

In the previous chapter, we talked a lot about **mindsets**. Mindsets influence the climate and the culture of a school. Positive mindsets typically lead to positive climates and cultures; negative mindsets lead to negative climates and cultures. Figure 7.2 illustrates the relationship between culture, climate and mindsets.

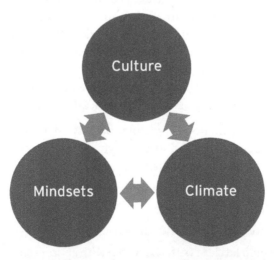

Figure 7.2: The relationship between culture, climate and mindsets.

Culture, climate and mindsets feed off and influence one another. If there are problems with one, it is usually a result of a problem with one or both of the others. If we accept that the development of culture (specifically, a *professional learning culture*) is key to the development of great teaching in classrooms and schools, then understanding the link between culture, climate and mindsets is an important prerequisite to understanding how great teaching can be developed.

Professional learning

Having discussed what we mean by the word 'culture', it makes sense to turn our attention to what we mean by the term 'professional learning'.

At a basic level, 'professional learning' means exactly what it suggests: the *learning of professionals*. In the context of our discussions, this means the learning of teachers and school leaders. However, what is it that teachers and school leaders should be learning and what activities would best support this? In relation to these questions, the term 'professional learning' is less clear.

A definition of professional learning

In *Aligning Professional Learning, Performance Management and Effective Teaching*[65], Peter Cole helps us make sense of the 'what' and 'how' of professional learning. In this paper, he defines professional learning as:

> The formal and informal learning experiences undertaken by teachers and school leaders that improve their individual professional practice and the school's collective effectiveness as measured by improved student engagement and learning outcomes.

With this definition, Cole is arguing that professional learning is learning which impacts positively on 'professional practice'. For teachers, this means *teaching practice*; for leaders, this means *leadership*. **Teaching and leadership should be the key focus of professional learning in schools.**

This is an important point to emphasise. Too often, the focus of professional learning in schools is on learning which is not directly concerned with teaching and leadership. While there will always be a need for learning to go beyond these areas (for example, in relation to policy and legislation, covering topics such as health and safety or child protection), it is imperative that a focus on teaching and leadership is maintained.

---

65. Cole, P. (2012) *Aligning Professional Learning, Performance Management and Effective Teaching*

Building capacity

Through a focus on developing the quality of teaching and leadership, professional learning builds **capacity**. When we talk about capacity, we are referring to *professional knowledge and skills*. **The purpose of professional learning in schools should be to develop the capacity of teachers and school leaders**, in other words, to develop knowledge and skills in relation to teaching and leadership. Figure 7.3 illustrates this point.

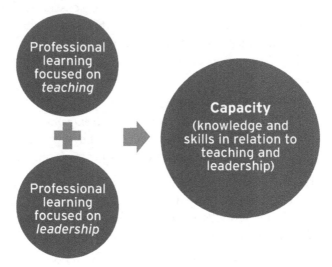

Figure 7.3: In the drive towards great teaching across a school, professional learning needs to focus on developing capacity (professional knowledge and skills) through a focus on teaching and leadership quality.

The stronger the professional learning culture of a school, the more capacity it will develop. In the pursuit of great teaching in every classroom, every day, schools need to focus on developing their professional learning culture in order to build staff capacity.

The impact of professional learning

Professional learning, in itself, has limited value. To be able to say that staff in your school engage in professional learning is one thing, but to say that staff in your school engage in professional learning which is *making a positive impact on teaching and learning* is quite another. To be able to say that staff in your school engage in professional learning which is making a positive impact on teaching and learning in *every classroom* across your school is the ultimate goal.

Ineffective professional learning

Achieving impact is not easy. Educational research tells us that, all too often, professional learning is ineffective, in that it fails to make a significant impact in the classroom[66]. In other words, too often, professional learning fails to make any difference to teaching practice. Understanding why – and how this can be addressed – should be a key consideration for all teachers and school leaders.

Peter Cole has discussed why there is often poor transference from professional learning to improvements in teaching practice and student outcomes. He highlights nine reasons[67]:

1. Professional learning activities aren't linked closely enough with effective teaching practice, but instead focus on policy and procedures

2. There is no agreement across the school about what constitutes effective teaching

3. Professional learning activities lack focus and are fragmented, with little or no follow-up

4. Professional learning activities don't engage teachers, that is, they don't get them to *think* and to *discuss*

5. Professional learning activities highlight practices which could improve teaching and learning, but don't explain or exemplify how

6. School leaders don't convey the message, through their words and actions, that they think professional learning is important

7. Teachers aren't supported to implement improved practices

8. Teachers believe that their professional learning is a private affair and don't see other teachers as having a role in supporting

---

66. For example: Hargreaves, A. and Fullan, M. (2012) *Professional Capital*

67. Cole, P. (2012) *Aligning Professional Learning, Performance Management and Effective Teaching*

their professional learning, or see themselves as having a role in supporting the professional learning of others

9. Teachers aren't held accountable for the implementation of practices which are in line with the school's 'instructional model' (which this book refers to as a *Lesson Evaluation Toolkit*)

If school leaders are to lead the development of a professional learning culture which will bring out transformations in teaching practice and student outcomes, then they need to consider how each of these points can be addressed.

Types of professional learning activities

When we talk about professional learning, many teachers don't understand what sort of activities constitute this, and far less what types of professional learning are most effective. Often, when they hear the term 'professional learning', they think: 'courses'.

Courses

External courses offer relatively weak professional learning[68]. While teachers who go on courses might enjoy their day out of school and the opportunity which comes with this to network with other professionals, which is important, the impact:cost ratio is usually very low. To send a member of staff on an external course typically costs hundreds of pounds. Unless they are encouraged to disseminate what they have learned with other staff, the impact of the course on teacher professional learning is limited to the staff who attended the course. Even if they do disseminate information, staff on the receiving end of this tend to learn very little.

Powerful professional learning

Far richer and more cost-effective professional learning is high-quality in-school professional learning. This can take many forms, which are summarised in the Professional Learning Model presented in Figure 7.4.

---

68. Forde, C. in J. O'Brien (2016) *School Leadership*

Read	Observe	Practice	Get feedback	Participate	Share
• Books • Research • Blogs • Twitter	• Other teachers • Other professionals (e.g. Support for Learning, Pastoral)	• Trying things out • Self-evaluate	• From peers • From school leaders • From students • From assessment evidence	• In discussions • In workshops • In working groups • In collaborative planning	• Your learning • Good practice

Figure 7.4: A suggested in-school Professional Learning Model for departments and schools.

The professional learning activities captured in this Professional Learning Model are not only cost-effective, they are effective. By this, I mean they are effective in terms of their potential to build teaching and leadership capacity in teachers and school leaders. On their own, each should have an impact. However, it is when each of the components of the Professional Learning Model are combined that transformations to teaching practice in classrooms and schools start to occur. The synergy of the different components produces powerful professional learning. In later chapters, we will explore these components in more detail.

The power of collaboration

Professional learning can be an individual activity or it can be collaborative. Generally, it is far more powerful when staff learn with and from one another, rather than alone. While staff are able to learn alone, isolated professional learning usually leads to disjointed professional learning, with different teachers developing their teaching practice in different ways – some effectively and some less so. In *learning schools*, the culture is one of collaboration, not isolation. **Collaborative professional learning is key to the development of a strong professional learning culture.**

Developing a shared understanding

For a shared understanding of great teaching to develop across a school, staff need to learn together. By learning together, pedagogical principles take on a common meaning, as opposed to meaning one thing to one person and a different thing to another. Discussions support staff to refine their learning, reconsidering and reconceptualising it in ways they might not have had they not discussed it.

In a school where professional learning is collaborative, the professional learning of teachers is de-privatised. Teachers don't read, learn and keep information to themselves. Instead, they discuss what they have been reading and their learning from this. They observe other teachers teaching and they invite other professionals to watch them teach. They plan and evaluate lessons together. They use meeting time to discuss pedagogy and to share practice. In doing so, pockets of good practice spread and become hives of good practice. Collaboration is the hallmark of a *learning school.*

Leading professional learning

A high-quality in-school professional learning programme will not come about by itself. Rather, there needs to be leadership of such a programme. Accordingly, school leaders should establish a '**Teaching and Learning Improvement Group**', the remit of which is to plan, co-ordinate and evaluate the school's professional learning programme.

Teaching and Learning Improvement Group

A Teaching and Learning Improvement Group should be an open community – every member of staff should have the opportunity to join. It should meet regularly (about once a month) and be empowered to make strategic decisions. In the interests of transparency and good communication, the minutes from meetings should be shared with all staff.

The Teaching and Learning Improvement Group should use a Professional Learning Model (such as the one presented in this chapter) to guide their planning of professional learning initiatives. Such initiatives might include:

1. A Professional Reading Group
2. Systems for teachers to share learning with each other
3. Peer Observation Programmes
4. A staff-led, in-school workshop programme

Depending on the size of the group, there may be value in establishing sub-groups which lead different initiatives. A key benefit of creating sub-groups is that it creates more leadership opportunities for staff, which helps to develop leadership capacity.

Case study: A Professional Reading Group

In my school we have established a Professional Reading Group which is having a tremendous impact on teaching practice across the whole school. The group is led by a middle leader and has around 10 teacher participants (out of a teaching staff of 40). The choice of book is up to group members, but the focus is always on books which are going to help staff learn more about teaching and learning.

We invest in a copy of a book for each member of the group. This is important, because members are investing their time in being a part of the group. Once they have finished the book, group members can either keep it or donate it to our staff Professional Learning Library, which is what most of them do.

The group meets once a fortnight. At these meetings, there is discussion about the section of the book the group has been reading over the past two weeks. Usually, this is around 40 pages. Group members are encouraged to come to meetings with examples of things they have found particularly interesting or which have resonated with them. Key quotations are shared with other members of staff via a 'Learning from Reading' noticeboard in the staffroom.

The Professional Reading Group plays an integral part in the professional learning culture of our school. Prior to its existence, very few staff engaged in regular professional reading. Staff understanding of what makes great teaching was inconsistent and, in many cases, misguided. While most staff were well-read in terms of national policy, this had resulted in a very narrow understanding of what high-quality teaching looks like. This is no longer the case. Professional reading has played a key role in expanding minds, motivating staff and improving teaching quality across our school. To quote one member of the group: 'The Professional Reading Group is a genuine highlight of my job. It has made me a better teacher.'

If you don't have a Professional Reading Group in your school, set one up. It doesn't need to be the headteacher who does this – anyone can. My advice is, just get on and do it! You might be surprised by just how many staff have a genuine desire to get involved.

Professional learning versus performance management

The key to improving teaching and learning in schools is high-quality professional learning. High-quality professional learning supports all teachers to become good and good teachers to become great. So long as teachers want to improve and are prepared to work with peers and school leaders to improve, professional learning should always be the preferred option to performance management.

That said, performance management does have a place and sometimes needs to be used. The time to use it is either when:

1. A poor teacher is refusing to engage in professional learning to improve their teaching
2. Professional learning is failing to have any significant impact on the practice of a poor teacher

While nobody ever wants to go down the performance management route, occasionally, in the interests of our students, this is what needs to be done.

The professional learning culture in your department or school

How strong is the professional learning culture in your department or school?

Because the strength of a professional learning culture is fundamental to the improvement of teaching and learning, if you are a middle or senior leader I encourage you to make use of the evaluation tool below to help you evaluate the strength of this culture in your department or school. This will be most powerful if you do it collaboratively, with your team.

Evaluating the strength of your culture

Use a green/amber/red or 0–10 system to evaluate the strength of your school or departmental professional learning culture against the features listed.

	Key features of a teaching- and learning-focused professional learning culture	Evaluation
1	There is a shared understanding of what makes great teaching.	
2	There is a mindset of continuous improvement.	
3	There is a positive climate for learning.	
4	Learning (for everyone) is the core business.	
5	The continuous improvement of teaching and learning is the number one priority.	
6	Teachers collaborate with other teachers to improve their teaching.	
7	Teachers and school leaders learn from professional reading.	
8	Learning from professional reading is shared and discussed.	
9	Teaching practices from across the school are shared, discussed and evaluated.	
10	Teachers have access to a high-quality in-school workshop programme, led by staff.	
11	Teachers regularly watch each other teach.	
12	Teachers receive high-quality feedback on their teaching from other professionals.	
13	Teachers seek feedback on their teaching from students.	
14	Coaching and mentoring approaches are used to support the development of teachers.	
15	Teachers self-evaluate the quality of teaching in lessons.	
16	Teachers are empowered to try things out and take risks.	
17	Assessment evidence is used to evaluate the extent to which what is taught is learned.	
18	Teachers analyse performance data relating to student attainment and progress.	
19	Individual and whole-school improvement planning focuses on teaching and learning.	
20	Teachers maintain teaching-focused Professional Learning Plans*.	

As we conclude this chapter, I hope I have been successful in persuading you that the strength of your professional learning culture is the key factor in determining the extent to which teaching and learning in your department or school can improve. Assuming I have, I will also assume that you are interested in developing the professional learning culture in your department or school. The evaluation tool above should have supported you to think about this. However, with so much to think about, a logical question is: where do I start? My answer to this is: create a *Lesson Evaluation Toolkit*.

In the next chapter, we will explore what a *Lesson Evaluation Toolkit* is and how you can go about creating one.

---

* We will discuss Professional Learning Plans in Chapter 12.

Chapter 8
Lesson Evaluation Toolkit

Where do we start?

When I discuss teaching and learning improvement in schools with teachers or school leaders, I am usually asked the same question: 'Where do we start?' My answer is always the same: **start by creating a school** *Lesson Evaluation Toolkit.*

In this chapter, we will explore what a *Lesson Evaluation Toolkit* is, why I believe creating one for your school is so important and how you can go about doing so. In the chapters which follow, we will explore how your *Lesson Evaluation Toolkit* can be used to transform teaching practice in your own classroom and department, and across your school.

Lesson Evaluation Toolkit

A *Lesson Evaluation Toolkit* is a framework which makes clear the typical features of high-quality lessons, as determined by a school. It is a version of the 'instructional model' which Peter Cole[69] highlights as key to ensuring that professional learning makes an impact on teaching practice.

Figure 8.1 presents an example.

---

69. Cole, P. (2012) *Aligning Professional Learning, Performance Management and Effective Teaching*

Lesson Evaluation Toolkit: typical features of high-quality lessons		
Elements	Illustrations	Notes
Structural features		
Daily Review (including Weekly & Monthly Review)	• Low-stakes assessment, promoting recall from everyone. • Includes material required for the lesson, recent and less recent material.	
Learning intentions	• Set out precise learning goals ('Know…' 'Understand…' 'Be able to…'). • Clearly communicated (verbally and visually, if possible) in student friendly language. • Revisited during lesson and in plenary.	

Success criteria	• Clear communication of what you are looking for/what success looks like, e.g.:
	  • 'I can…' statements
	  • Key features
	  • Exemplars
	• Used to support feedback and student self-evaluation.	

Presentation of content	• Clear presentation, including explanations and visuals which stimulate interest. • Checking what students know or can do already. • Interactive – includes frequent checks for understanding. • Repeating and summarising key points.	

Lesson Evaluation Toolkit: typical features of high-quality lessons		
Elements	Illustrations	Notes
Structural features		
Practice	• Guided, supported, then independent. • Co-operative learning opportunities. • Over-learning – lots of opportunities to master content. • Teacher circulating class.	
Plenary	• Revisits the learning intention and success criteria. • Reinforces the main learning points of the lesson. • Gathers further evidence about what has been learned, was difficult, or not learned (e.g. via Exit Tickets*). • Summarises next steps.	
Key principles		

Challenge & support	• Availability and use of support resources, e.g.:
	  • Knowledge Organisers
	  • Checklists and scaffolds
	  • Peer teaching
	• Choices within activities, with differing levels of challenge.
	• Balance of familiar and less familiar content.	

---

* 'Exit Tickets' are Post-it notes which students complete and give to their teacher before leaving a lesson

Lesson Evaluation Toolkit: typical features of high-quality lessons		
Elements	Illustrations	Notes
Key principles		
Making students think & checking for understanding	• Strategies to make everyone think and their learning visible, e.g.: • **Questioning**: pose, pause, pounce, bounce • **Discussion** (e.g. chat to a partner, think-pair-share) • **Active assessment activities** (e.g. true/false, multiple-choice) • **Show-me boards**	
Feedback	• Clear and precise. • Recognises positives and points to next steps – 'what' and 'how'. • Links to success criteria (e.g. 'I can' statements, key features or exemplars). • Individual and whole-class messages. • Time available for students to take on board feedback and improve (maybe via homework).	
Learning environment		
Relationships	• Knowing students well. • Positive and professional interactions. • Recognition of positives, particularly effort.	
High Expectations	• High expectations of effort, behaviour and quality of work. • Target/goal setting (e.g. personal bests). • Encouragement.	

Lesson Evaluation Toolkit: typical features of high-quality lessons		
Elements	Illustrations	Notes
Learning environment		
Management	• Calm, ordered, under control. • Effective use of time, space and resources. • Appropriate pace.	
Behaviour	• Students are on task, engaged, interested, motivated. • Poor student behaviours are dealt with promptly and in as low-level a way as possible.	

Figure 8.1: An example of a Lesson Evaluation Toolkit, setting out the typical features of high-quality lessons, as determined by a school. Note: this is an example only – it is not a definitive or 'best' version.

'Elements'

In the left-hand column of the example *Lesson Evaluation Toolkit* shown in Figure 8.1, typical 'elements' of a high-quality lesson are detailed. The elements of a lesson are the parts which come together, interact and, through this interaction, determine the quality of teaching and learning.

In the example shown, some elements relate to the structure of a lesson (e.g. 'Daily Review', 'presentation of content' and 'plenary'), some to *key principles* which weave through the structure (e.g. 'challenge and support' and 'feedback') and some to the *learning environment* (e.g. 'relationships' and 'high expectations'). They have been arranged into three sections to reflect this.

'Illustrations'

To support teachers and school leaders to think about *quality* and *effective use*, next to each element are brief 'illustrations'. These are designed to support **critical reflection** and **discussion**, like when a teacher self-evaluates a lesson or is discussing it with another professional who observed the lesson. These illustrations help to guide thinking and conversations.

'Notes'

The right-hand column of the *Lesson Evaluation Toolkit* has space for notes. When a teacher self-evaluates a lesson against the elements and illustrations of the *Lesson Evaluation Toolkit*, this section can be used to summarise their thoughts. Similarly, if another professional observes a lesson, they can use this section to make notes, which can support discussion and feedback.

Illustrative purposes

I want to stress that the example *Lesson Evaluation Toolkit* presented in Figure 8.1 is for illustrative purposes only – **it is not being presented as a definitive or 'best' framework. It is just an example**.

This is because there is no such thing as a definitive or 'best' version of a *Lesson Evaluation Toolkit*. Rather, the example presented is one which teachers and school leaders in a particular school have developed together, based on their shared understanding of what makes great teaching, informed by key messages from literature and research. It represents a shared understanding of the features of high-quality lessons in that school at that time. As this understanding develops through continued engagement with educational literature and research, the elements and illustrations of the *Lesson Evaluation Toolkit* will evolve.

What a Lesson Evaluation Toolkit is and what it isn't

In a podcast conversation with Craig Barton[70] (author of *How I Wish I'd Taught Maths*[71]), Tom Sherrington (author of *The Learning Rainforest*[72]) discusses the theme of professional autonomy, which we explored in Chapter 6. Sherrington makes the point that, in the interests of ensuring that all students have access to high-quality teaching (regardless of who their teacher is), there is a professional duty for teachers and school leaders to ensure that the pedagogy of lessons across a school is high quality. An 'anything goes' approach to teaching is never okay. I agree with that fully.

---

70. Can be accessed at: http://www.mrbartonmaths.com/blog/tom-sherrington-rosenshines-principles-in-action/

71. Barton, C. (2018) *How I Wish I'd Taught Maths*

72. Sherrington, T. (2017) *The Learning Rainforest*

At the same time, Sherrington says that he hopes school leaders will resist the temptation to turn messages from educational research into checklists. Rightly, he makes the point that we do not want to create a culture in schools where teachers 'go through the motions', constrained in their teaching by the use of a prescriptive framework. Nor do we want to create a culture in which school leaders use such a framework to 'check up' on teachers, for example, during lesson observations. Again, I agree with him fully.

Accepting this, you might reasonably ask: isn't a *Lesson Evaluation Toolkit* just this sort of checklist? No, it absolutely isn't. We shall go on to explore why.

Purpose

The key purpose of a school *Lesson Evaluation Toolkit* is to **direct the attention of teachers and school leaders to features of a lesson which, typically, combine to produce high-quality teaching**. It highlights, summarises and signposts. It is not telling teachers how they *must* teach. Rather, it invites teachers to think about particular aspects of teaching practice; for example, as they plan lessons, when they self-evaluate after teaching, or when they are discussing lessons with other members of staff. It is the pivotal role of the *Lesson Evaluation Toolkit* in self-evaluation which has led to its name.

'Checklists' versus 'tick-lists'

To help understand what a *Lesson Evaluation Toolkit* is and what it isn't, it is useful to draw a distinction between 'checklists' and 'tick-lists'. Checklists *support you to remember things*, which is a key purpose of a *Lesson Evaluation Toolkit*; tick-lists are about *ticking things off*: *this* was there; *that* wasn't. Tick-lists are about checking up and auditing. They are superficial and tend to be negatively received by teachers. As a result, their impact on teaching practice is usually very low or non-existent.

Therefore, while it could be argued that a *Lesson Evaluation Toolkit* is a type of checklist, it should never be used as a tick-list. Because people often equate the term 'checklist' with 'tick-list', to avoid the negative connotations associated, I suggest that a *Lesson Evaluation Toolkit* is better thought about as an *aide-mémoire*.

Making mental checklists visible

We form checklists in our heads all the time. When planning lessons or thinking over lessons we have taught, we tend to refer to mental checklists. As the checklists in our heads evolve, for example as a result of professional reading and discussion, we think to ourselves: 'I must remember to start doing that.' However, for one reason or another, over time we forget about things. Months or years down the line, we remember them and think: 'I must start doing that again – I don't know why I stopped.' A *Lesson Evaluation Toolkit* helps make mental checklists visible. It also **helps to ensure that different teachers are thinking about the same pedagogy.** In the absence of a framework which provides common reminders, teachers will often think about very different things in their planning and self-evaluation. But, as we have discussed, educational research tells us that there are particular pedagogies which there would be value in all teachers thinking about, regardless of the subject they are teaching. A *Lesson Evaluation Toolkit* helps to support teachers to think about the same important things.

If 'Daily Review' has been included as an element in a school's *Lesson Evaluation Toolkit*, it has been included because the school believes it to be a *typical* feature of high-quality teaching. It would be up to a teacher to decide whether or not Daily Review is included in any particular lesson. If a teacher were never to include Daily Review in any of their lessons, that would be an issue which could be discussed with the teacher, because through their *Lesson Evaluation Toolkit*, the school has clearly identified that Daily Review should be a typical feature of lessons. However, this is different from specifying that Daily Review must be an integral feature of *all* lessons.

Summarising messages from educational literature and research

Despite the emphasis I have placed on the importance of professional reading to the development of great teaching in classrooms and schools, we must recognise that, realistically, not all teachers and school leaders are going to engage in such reading. What's more, among those who do, different people will read different things. This is, of course, as it should be and is a good thing. The more teachers and school leaders read, and the more widely they read, the better they will understand what makes great teaching.

However, with so much to learn and think about, there can be value in distilling the key messages from educational literature and research in a way that supports teachers to draw on these in planning, evaluation and discussion. This can also support those who aren't engaging in professional reading. A *Lesson Evaluation Toolkit* is such a distillation, presenting key messages in an accessible and easy-to-refer-to format. As a means to overcome the challenge of developing a shared understanding of what makes great teaching across a department and a school, a *Lesson Evaluation Toolkit* has the potential to be a very powerful resource.

Common principles

A push for a shared understanding of what great teaching is and what the typical features of high-quality lessons are is not the same thing as a push for every teacher to teach in exactly the same way. However, there *are* common principles. If you know what these are, you can learn how to put these into practice and develop them; if you don't know what they are, then this is unlikely. A *Lesson Evaluation Toolkit* sets out these principles.

Some school leaders will argue that, in the interests of achieving consistency across a department or school, it is essential that all lessons have the same structure and include the same features. This is misguided. What all school leaders and teachers should be interested in is achieving consistency *in terms of high-quality teaching practices*, not in terms of all lessons having the same structure and features. This is an important distinction to appreciate, especially as the effectiveness of these elements is not ensured by simply doing them.

Think about quality and effective use

A *Lesson Evaluation Toolkit* draws attention to the typical features of high-quality lessons. However, it does not tell you about the *actual quality* of these features as they play out in a lesson. For example, by including 'learning intention' as an element, a *Lesson Evaluation Toolkit* reminds teachers and school leaders that, typically, a high-quality lesson will include a learning intention. The illustration can offer guidance regarding what a good learning intention looks like and how these might be used to support learning. However, just because there is a learning intention in a lesson doesn't mean it is a *high-quality* learning intention; just because it was used doesn't mean it was used well. **Quality** and **effective use** are the most important considerations.

If a teacher or school leader were to reflect on a lesson they have taught or observed using the *Lesson Evaluation Toolkit* and simply tick off a learning intention as 'being there', they are using the *Lesson Evaluation Toolkit* as a tick-list. That is not its purpose. Rather, what a *Lesson Evaluation Toolkit* does is remind teachers and school leaders that, typically, a high-quality lesson will have a learning intention. The teacher or school leader will have to draw on their pedagogical knowledge and understanding to *evaluate the quality* of this and the *effectiveness of its use*. In this book, Chapters 5, 9 and 13 are about supporting the development of pedagogical knowledge and understanding.

Art, science and magic

Is great teaching an art or a science? Personally, I don't believe it is one or the other. Rather, I think it sits somewhere in between. Briefly, we shall explore why.

Art?

As anyone who has ever visited an art gallery knows, just about anything can be described as 'art'. However, whether or not something is described as *great art* is in the eye of the beholder – it is a matter of opinion. What you think is great art might not be my idea of great art, and vice versa. Does the same idea hold true in teaching? In other words, is great teaching something which is in the eye of the beholder – is it a matter of opinion?

No, it very definitely is not. As we have discussed, educational literature and research tell us that *not all teaching is great teaching*. There are very definite practices which are associated with great teaching and very definite practices which are not. There is nothing subjective about that. Accordingly, while great teaching does have a lot in common with art, for example, in terms of the scope for creativity, imagination and flair available to teachers, to think about teaching as being an art isn't quite right.

Science?

How much does great teaching have in common with science?

Science is concerned with finding answers. It deals with systems, structures, rules, principles and laws. There are things which hold true and things which don't. In one sense, then, great teaching does have something in common with science: from educational literature and research, we know that there *are* certain principles associated with great teaching. However, great teaching involves an awful lot more than the application of these principles. This is what separates it from science. In science, you know that if you apply the right principles you will get a particular result. In teaching, things are much more nuanced and less certain than that. There is a *craft* to teaching which goes beyond science and has more in common with art. It is difficult to capture exactly what that craft is, but when you see it in action, you know it is there.

Magic

Sir John Jones describes great teaching as being like 'magic'[73]. I agree with him. When you watch great teaching, there is something magical about what is going on. Great teaching has the 'wow' factor. Unfortunately, this can't be bottled and sold. Instead, it has to be learned.

A *Lesson Evaluation Toolkit* can support this learning. While it can never create the magic of great teaching – only great teachers can do that – it can support its development. Through its use, a *Lesson Evaluation Toolkit* can help make the quality of teaching in classrooms and schools significantly better than it would be without. Used regularly and in the right way, it can help to bring about transformations in teaching practice.

Tight–loose

To borrow a phrase used by Michael Fullan, a *Lesson Evaluation Toolkit* aims to strike a 'tight–loose'[74] balance: tight, in that it sets out the typical features of high-quality lessons; loose, in that how these features look in lessons is up to teachers. Fullan has said, 'Tell people what to do, not how

---

73. Jones, J. (2009) *The Magic-Weaving Business*
74. Fullan, M. (2011) *The Six Secrets of Change*

to do it'[75]. I agree with this principle. A *Lesson Evaluation Toolkit* offers limitless scope for variation, creativity and professional autonomy. It helps to support the perfect balance between art and science.

'We already have a framework to support teaching and learning'

Many schools already have something similar to a *Lesson Evaluation Toolkit* in place. Perhaps yours has. You might not refer to it as a '*Lesson Evaluation Toolkit*', but you believe that what you have is effectively the same thing. But is it?

In thinking about this, I would like you to reflect on five questions:

1. How was it put together?
2. To what extent is it informed by key messages from educational literature and research?
3. To what extent do all staff understand it?
4. To what extent are all staff using it?
5. When was it last updated?

The potential that a *Lesson Evaluation Toolkit* (or its equivalent) has to transform teaching practice in classrooms across your school is dependent on the answers to these questions. For it to have maximum impact, there are five criteria:

1. *All* teachers and school leaders need to have been **involved in its development**
2. The *elements and illustrations* which make it up need to have **clear links to key messages from educational literature and research**
3. *All* teachers and school leaders need to **understand what is meant by each of the elements and illustrations**
4. *All* teachers and school leaders need to **make regular use of it**
5. It should be **updated every two to three years**

Where schools don't have a *Lesson Evaluation Toolkit* in place, they need to develop one. Where they do, but where it fails to meet the five-point

---

75. Fullan, M. (2008) *What's Worth Fighting for in Headship?*

criteria set out above, it should be recreated or updated. The potential for a *Lesson Evaluation Toolkit* to have a positive impact on teaching practice in your classroom, department or school is determined by how closely its use and development matches these criteria.

Shared ownership

In my experience, where schools do have frameworks of this kind in place, too often they have been put together by an individual (such as the headteacher) or a small group of individuals, meaning there is no sense of **shared ownership** over it. As a result, others feel detached from it and see it as just another thing being 'imposed' on them.

It is essential that staff feel that they 'own' their *Lesson Evaluation Toolkit*. One of the best ways for people to own something is for them to be involved in creating it. At the very least, staff need to feel that their voice has been sought and listened to during the process. One of the worst things a school can do is take a *Lesson Evaluation Toolkit* from another school and claim it as their own. It doesn't matter how good the other school's *Lesson Evaluation Toolkit* is; bringing it into your school in this way will lead to it being resented and rejected by staff. I have seen schools try to do this – it doesn't work.

Links to educational literature and research

Too often as well, the relationship between what is included in a school's *Lesson Evaluation Toolkit* and key messages from educational literature and research is weak. For example, when I look at frameworks that schools have produced, I often see the typical features of high-quality lessons highlighted as being things like:

- 'Open questions (not closed questions)'
- 'Higher-order questions (not lower-order questions)'
- 'Carousel activities'
- 'Group work'

I am not aware of any educational research which says that asking 'open questions' is better than asking 'closed questions' or that 'higher-order' questions are better questions to ask than 'lower-order' questions. Rather, all of these have an important role to play. Similarly, I am not aware of any educational research which says that 'carousel activities' and 'group work' are typical features of high-quality lessons. Their usefulness depends on what is being taught. When schools create or update their *Lesson Evaluation Toolkit*, taking key messages from educational literature and research into account is crucial.

Case study: Evaluating teaching quality in Scottish schools

In Scotland, Education Scotland (a branch of the Scottish government) has produced a document called *How Good Is Our School?*[76], the purpose of which is to support internal self-evaluation and external inspection. Within this, there is a relatively short section titled 'Quality of teaching'. In the context of our discussion about the importance of a focus on pedagogy in schools, it is worth pointing out that, of the 20,000+ words in this document, roughly 200 of them (1%) are concerned with pedagogy. Significantly more space is given to areas such as 'Personalised support', 'Family learning', 'Partnerships' and 'Increasing creativity and employability'. The proportion of space given to such areas risks distracting schools from a focus on pedagogy.

Included are illustrations to support 'national benchmarking'. The illustration for 'very good' 'Quality of teaching' states:

> Our teaching is underpinned by our shared school vision and values. We use a wide range of learning environments and creative teaching approaches. Learning is enriched and supported by our effective use of digital technologies. Our explanations and instructions are clear. We use skilled questioning and engagement to promote curiosity, independence and confidence and to regularly enable higher-order thinking skills in all learners. We observe learners closely to inform appropriate and well-timed interventions and future learning. We use feedback effectively to inform and support progress in learning.

How closely aligned to key messages from education literature and research do you think this illustration is? For me, there is something of a disconnect.

This is a problem. One reason is because many schools in Scotland are using what is written in this guidance as their sole means to evaluate

---

76. Education Scotland (2015) *How Good Is Our School?* (Fourth edition). Livingston: Education Scotland.

and improve teaching quality. I recently heard a headteacher say to a colleague, 'If it's not in *How Good Is Our School?*, I'm not interested'.

Creating a Lesson Evaluation Toolkit

No two schools are the same, even if they operate within the same local authority or school cluster. Although there are common principles regarding what makes great teaching, it would be surprising if any two schools had – or needed to have – identical *Lesson Evaluation Toolkits*. Rather, schools should develop their own to fit their context. Doing so helps to create the sense of ownership which is so important to encourage staff to use it.

Start with why

In *Start with Why: How Great Leaders Inspire Everyone to Take Action*[77], Simon Sinek stresses the importance of leaders setting out a convincing case for change before expecting staff to follow them. If you are trying to convince members of your school community that a *Lesson Evaluation Toolkit* can be of value, then you need to be clear about why this is the case.

In explaining this to staff, your reasons might include that:

- There isn't a shared understanding of what great teaching is, or what the features of high-quality lessons are, across our school – a *Lesson Evaluation Toolkit* will help us to address that

- The feedback that teachers are getting from lesson observations is inconsistent, both in terms of what it is saying and how it is being delivered – a *Lesson Evaluation Toolkit* will help us improve the quality of feedback given to teachers

- We are unclear where our strengths and weaknesses exist as a school in terms of particular teaching practices – a *Lesson Evaluation Toolkit* will help us to get a better picture of these and plan strategically for continuous improvement

- Our in-school professional learning programme is unfocused – a *Lesson Evaluation Toolkit* will help us to focus on particular aspects of pedagogy

---

77. Sinek, S. (2011) *Start with Why*

For your *Lesson Evaluation Toolkit* to have impact – and there is no point in having one if it doesn't – teachers and school leaders need to believe in its potential to make a difference. Before they can believe in it, they need to understand what it is for. For this reason, prior to the development of a *Lesson Evaluation Toolkit* for your school, make sure that you take time to explain to staff why it is needed.

In the process of explaining why a *Lesson Evaluation Toolkit* is needed, you might find value in turning to the questions I asked you at the start of Chapter 1. For example, you might ask staff:

1. What makes great teaching?
2. How good is your teaching?
3. How do you know?
4. How would you rate the quality of your teaching out of 10?
5. How confident are you that your teaching is as good as you think it is?
6. Do you want to make your teaching better?
7. Do you know how to make your teaching better?

Discussion based on the first question will probably reveal that there isn't a shared understanding of what makes great teaching across your school. A case can then be made for why this needs to be addressed. Development and use of a *Lesson Evaluation Toolkit* can support this.

Discussion based on questions 2 to 7 will probably reveal that most staff are committed to improving their teaching practice (regardless of how good it is already), but that many are unsure how they can go about doing that. Development and use of a *Lesson Evaluation Toolkit* can support this too.

The 'how'

Once a case has been made for the value of a *Lesson Evaluation Toolkit* in your school, the next step is to create your own version. In planning such a process, I suggest that you ensure you have a **Teaching and Learning Improvement Group**. Strategic working groups of this kind are examples of 'Professional Capital'[78] in action, bringing together the

---

78. Hargreaves, A. and Fullan, M. (2012) *Professional Capital*

synergy of human, social and decisional capital which Andy Hargreaves and Michael Fullan have argued is so important to the development of great teaching in schools.

The Teaching and Learning Improvement Group should have staff representation from across your school, and all teachers should be invited to join. It should play a key strategic role in your school's continuous improvement agenda, and therefore should be empowered to make strategic decisions, such as arrangements for creating a *Lesson Evaluation Toolkit*.

Just as there is no definitive version of a *Lesson Evaluation Toolkit*, there is no definitive process by which a school should go about creating one. What follows is an example of an approach which *could* be taken. Such an approach has proven to be effective in schools I have worked in or supported to go through this process.

Step 1: Allocate time for a whole-staff meeting, the purpose of which is to develop a school *Lesson Evaluation Toolkit*. As a minimum, this should be one hour, but ideally more time will be available.

Step 2: Select a small amount of reading you would like all staff to engage with in advance of the meeting and share this with staff at least one week in advance. Encourage staff to read this in preparation for the meeting, making clear that they will get more out of the time available if they do so. Suitable examples could be:

- *Principles of Instruction*[79] by Barak Rosenshine
- Selected slides (I would suggest those on pages 12 and 22–25) from *What Makes Great Teaching?*[80] (presentation) by Robert Coe
- Selected effect size information from John Hattie's *Visible Learning* website[81]
- *10 Reasons Lessons Can Be Less Effective Than They Could Be*[82] (blog post) by Tom Sherrington

---

79. Rosenshine, B. (2012) *Principle of Instruction*

80. https://www.ibo.org/globalassets/events/aem/conferences/2015/robert-coe.pdf

81. https://visible-learning.org/hattie-ranking-influences-effect-sizes-learning-achievement/

82. https://teacherhead.com/2018/12/01/10-reasons-lessons-can-be-less-effective-than-they-could-be/

Step 3: At the meeting, start by making the purpose clear, which is for staff to identify what, for them, are the key features of great teaching in high-quality lessons. Staff returns will be used to help create a school *Lesson Evaluation Toolkit*. There would be value in asking for a show of hands to indicate the proportion of staff who managed to engage with the pre-meeting reading.

Ask staff to get into groups of two or three. Explain that each group will have access to a selection of teaching- and learning-focused literature, and that over the course of the time available, they should aim to extract from this what, for them, are the 'typical features of high-quality teaching in lessons'. This will likely involve reading, highlighting, discussing, note-taking and drafting. There may be value in setting a target number of features to identify – for example, a top 10. By the end of the meeting, each group should have what is, for them, a definitive list of the typical features of high-quality teaching in lessons.

Each group should have access to photocopies of the advance reading, plus additional reading for this meeting. This should be brief, otherwise it won't be possible for staff to engage with it meaningfully. You don't want staff to be spending too much time reading in this meeting. Far more important is that they are able to discuss – which will include arguing and agreeing – what they believe to be the key features of high-quality teaching in lessons. Reference to literature is important so that discussions are based on more than what teachers think they know already.

Step 4: Give staff the opportunity to continue their discussions and drafting after the meeting has finished. Some will want to do this and others won't, but it is important that you give everyone the chance. I would suggest that a fortnight would be an appropriate amount of time to allocate for this. All returns should be forwarded to the chair of the Teaching and Learning Improvement Group by a specified date.

Step 5: The next meeting of the Teaching and Learning Improvement Group should be used to analyse and discuss staff returns. The aim should be to produce a draft version of your school *Lesson Evaluation Toolkit*, informed by the returns. This will include determining an appropriate layout.

<u>Step 6</u>: Share the draft version of your *Lesson Evaluation Toolkit* with all staff, ask them to try it out, and invite feedback. Use the next meeting to review this feedback and adapt the draft version accordingly. You should now have a finalised version.

<u>Step 7</u>: Share the final version with all staff.

The *Lesson Evaluation Toolkit* which has been created will not be the version your school has forever – over time, it should evolve, in line with staff understanding of what makes great teaching. The features of your *Lesson Evaluation Toolkit* represent a synergy of the messages coming from the research that staff have been engaging with and the beliefs about great teaching which they already have. As staff continue to learn through reading, observation and discussion, your *Lesson Evaluation Toolkit* should evolve.

That said, I would caution against your *Lesson Evaluation Toolkit* changing too often – staff need to get used to it and feel comfortable with it. If it keeps changing, that won't be the case. People don't generally like change, and will typically react against it, at least initially. Therefore, I would recommend that your *Lesson Evaluation Toolkit* be updated and changed no more than once every two to three years. Any changes made to it should go through similar collegiate and collaborative processes as those used in the development of the original version.

Teachers or departments creating their own Lesson Evaluation Toolkits

While the focus of our discussion about creating a *Lesson Evaluation Toolkit* has been on schools creating one for whole-school use, there is nothing to stop departments and individual teachers creating their own *Lesson Evaluation Toolkits* through a similar process. While the development and use of a school *Lesson Evaluation Toolkit* is the best way to go about developing a shared understanding of what makes great teaching across a school, if, for any reason, a school is holding back from developing a whole-school version, I would encourage departments or individuals to take a lead and develop their own.

Using your Lesson Evaluation Toolkit

Creating a *Lesson Evaluation Toolkit* should be relatively straightforward – getting every teacher to use it in a way which supports the development of great teaching in every classroom presents more of a challenge. How easy this is will depend largely on the strength of the professional learning culture in your school.

The good news is that, even if the professional learning culture in your school is relatively weak, the process of developing a *Lesson Evaluation Toolkit* which staff 'own' will have played a key part in starting to strengthen it. As it is used over the weeks, months and years which follow its development, the professional learning culture of your school will continue to develop and strengthen.

Four interconnected areas

A *Lesson Evaluation Toolkit* has a variety of uses. These include four interconnected areas of school activity: **professional learning, self-evaluation, improvement planning** and **quality assurance**.

Figure 8.2: The four areas of school activity which your Lesson Evaluation Toolkit can support.

To be clear about what we mean by these terms:

- **Professional learning** is concerned with the development of pedagogical knowledge and skills
- **Self-evaluation** is concerned with asking questions about how well things are going: 'how good is this?', 'how do we know?'
- **Improvement planning** is concerned with taking action to improve areas you have identified as priorities as a result of your self-evaluation
- **Quality assurance** is concerned with ensuring that minimum standards are being met and that the things you think are going well are actually going well

These four align to a common goal: the pursuit of great teaching in every classroom in your school. Depending on where a teacher, department or school is in their development at any particular time, a greater focus may be required on one over others.

Principles for effective use

Earlier in this chapter, we explored key principles in relation to the *creation* of your school *Lesson Evaluation Toolkit*. In the chapters which follow, we will go on to discuss key principles in relation to its use.

How a *Lesson Evaluation Toolkit* is used will determine how it is perceived by staff. Used in the right way, it will be perceived as integral to the professional learning culture. Used in the wrong way, it will be perceived as nothing more than another top-down management tool which does little or nothing to support teaching and learning. A *Lesson Evaluation Toolkit*, in itself, changes very little – it is *how it is used* that determines its impact.

Figure 8.3 summarises effective and ineffective practice in terms of how a *Lesson Evaluation Toolkit* might be used in a school.

Ineffective practice	Effective practice
Used as a tick-list to ensure that teachers are teaching in a particular way.	Used to support lesson planning, self-evaluation, feedback, discussion, coaching and mentoring, the focus of professional learning programmes and improvement planning.
Used only by school leaders; for example, when they observe a lesson being taught.	Used by all teachers and school leaders.
Used infrequently, so that, for example, a teacher only looks at it or talks about it once or twice in a school year.	Used frequently. The *Lesson Evaluation Toolkit* is constantly being referred to and used.

Figure 8.3: Ineffective and effective use of a Lesson Evaluation Toolkit.

Evaluative language

To support the effective use of your *Lesson Evaluation Toolkit*, it can be useful to establish a common evaluative language across your school. In doing so, I suggest that you stick to the 'Einstein Principle': as simple as possible, but not simpler[83]. While not essential, establishing a common evaluative language can be very useful – for example, in supporting communication of key messages.

There are a variety of forms that evaluative language can take. For example, you could use a scale, such as 0–10. A three-point 'traffic light' system (green/amber/red) is the one I usually turn to. It is simple, clear and easily understood.

The precise definitions of 'green', 'amber' and 'red' can be determined by individual schools. As an example, these might be:

- **Green** – very good
- **Amber** – good
- **Red** – an area to improve

While there is always the risk that use of such language reduces complex messages to simplistic terms, sometimes there are benefits in doing so. One of the most important is that it encourages people to *think*. Nailing your colours to the mast and committing to a particular term (such as 'green' or '6') gets you to think critically. Thinking

---

83. Discussed in: https://www.nature.com/articles/d41586-018-05004-4

critically is key to improving your practice, both as a teacher and as a school leader.

In Chapters 10, 11 and 12, we will explore how a *Lesson Evaluation Toolkit* can be used to support the continuous improvement of teaching and learning in classrooms, departments and schools. Before we do, in our next chapter we will return to our discussion from Chapter 5 about what makes great teaching.

Chapter 9
Great teaching - Part 2

In Chapter 2, we discussed great teaching as a blend of **Specific Teaching** and **Non-specific Teaching** approaches, with the balance in favour of Specific Teaching.

In Chapter 4, we identified four components of Specific Teaching, these being high-quality:

1. **Pedagogical subject knowledge**
2. **Teacher–student relationships**
3. **Direct-interactive instruction**
4. **Formative assessment**

While great teaching will always involve a degree of Non-specific Teaching as well, in the interests of teaching students the knowledge they need to develop skills and to attain, we recognised that a focus on Specific Teaching is key.

In Chapter 5, we discussed how great teaching manifests itself through the pedagogy of lessons, arguing that lessons are the delivery units of great teaching. In general terms, we said that Specific Teaching should account for 80–90% of lesson time.

Towards the start of that chapter, we broke the Specific Teaching approach down into the specific pedagogy of high-quality lessons, arguing that high-quality lessons are those which typically include:

1. Activities that require students to **recall knowledge** from previous lessons, which may or may not be relevant to this lesson, but which needs to be learned as part of the course

2. Clear communication and use of **learning intentions and success criteria**

3. Activities that allow the teacher to **find out what students know or can do already** (in relation to what is being taught in this lesson)

4. Clear **teacher explanations and demonstrations** which hold student attention

5. Activities that allow students to **put into practice** what they are being taught

6. Appropriate levels of **support and challenge**

7. Use of **questions** to make students think and to check for understanding

8. Activities that get students to **discuss and learn with other students**

9. Clear **feedback** to individual students and to the class about their learning

10. Activities that **evaluate the impact of lessons**

11. Strong **teacher–student relationships**

12. **High expectations and standards** for student behaviour and quality of work

In Chapter 5, we explored the first three of these. In this chapter, we shall explore the next five.

> 4. Clear **teacher explanations and demonstrations** which hold student attention

As a school leader who observes a lot of lessons, including those which are a part of our school's recruitment process, it is often quite striking to me just how many teachers are reluctant to actually 'teach'. What I mean by this is how many are reluctant to lead the teaching using Specific Teaching approaches instead of letting students lead through Non-specific Teaching. Often, there seems to be an obsession with getting students to find out things for themselves or learn from one another, even when students don't know very much about a topic in the first place.

Recently, I observed lessons being taught by candidates applying for a history teacher position. Each candidate was asked to teach a lesson to a class of twenty 14-year-olds on the topic of the Wars of Scottish Independence. In most of the lessons I observed, after the learning intention and success criteria had been shared the lesson went something like this:

- Students were assigned to different groups.
- Each group was given a different information sheet, which the teacher had written themselves.
- Students were given a few minutes to read through this, discuss what they had learned with other students in their group, and one person was to write a summary of the main points.
- After five minutes, one member of the group was sent to join a different group, to ask them about what they had learned from their reading and discussion, and take notes from this.
- The process continued until someone from each group had been around all the others, after which they returned to their original group.
- The student who had collected all the information from the other groups reported back to their original group, and students took notes based on what they were being told.

Take a moment to think about whether or not you think great teaching (and by that, I mean teaching which leads to great *learning*) was taking place in such a lesson.

If you believe that Non-specific Teaching is better for teaching knowledge than Specific Teaching, then perhaps you'd say yes. Certainly, the candidates who were teaching these lessons believed that they had taught strong lessons, because they told me that in their interviews afterwards. They believed that students leading their learning, learning from one another with minimal teacher talk, had helped to make these lessons very good ones. Very few appeared to have engaged with educational research which, as we have discussed, tells us that direct-interactive instruction and formative assessment are key to teaching students knowledge. The example lesson involved little of either. For that reason, because of what the candidates were trying to teach, I didn't believe that lessons taught in this way had been as successful as the candidates believed they had. For me, the main activity served as little more than a version of Chinese Whispers. I was not convinced that many students had learned very much at all.

Had the learning intention been for students to be able to find out things from other people and then report back to a group, then I could be a little more convinced that the pedagogy was effective at achieving this – some students *did* manage to do that, although the accuracy of what was being reported back was never really explored; students could have been telling each other almost anything.

Contrast the lesson described with one taught by a different candidate. After sharing the learning intention and success criteria, this is how this candidate's lesson went:

- Students were assigned to different groups.
- Each group started at a station which had an A3 piece of paper with a drawing and name of a person on it – for example, Edward I or Robert the Bruce. Each group was given two minutes to discuss what they knew about these characters and write it down using the coloured pen they had been given (different groups had different coloured pens).
- After two minutes, each group moved to a different station, at which they were given a further two minutes to read what previous groups had written, discuss this, and amend or add to it as they saw appropriate.
- The teacher moved between groups as they were working, listening to student conversations and watching what they were writing.
- After each group had been to each station, the teacher called a halt to the activity and asked students to sit down. They opened a PowerPoint presentation which linked to, and built on, the previous activity. They used what they had seen and heard from this activity

to make teaching points, including addressing misunderstandings and gaps in knowledge. For example, a picture of Edward I appeared and the teacher asked, 'Who is this?' A sea of hands went up. A student was chosen who said, 'Edward I.' The teacher asked the class, 'Is she right?' and everyone said, confidently: 'Yes.' 'Good, that's correct,' said the teacher. 'As I saw and heard, most of you know that Edward I was the King of England. Who can tell me *when* he was the King?' And so it went on. The teacher used their voice to make key teaching points, raising and lowering it for effect, varying the pace, using moments of silence and repeating important points. What they were saying to the class was supported by visuals in their PowerPoint presentation – text, pictures and diagrams. Key words were in bold or different colours. The teacher homed in on some of these and said things like: 'Someone please tell us what this word means.' They adjusted their teaching according to right or wrong answers from students and moved things on as and when there was evidence that students understood what had been said. Occasionally, they would ask students to write a key word or sentence in their jotter as a note to which they might need to refer at a future point.

This is *Specific Teaching*. It is the sort of teaching which research tells us is most appropriate for teaching students knowledge. It is also the sort of teaching which gives you a buzz when watching it. Direct-interactive instruction and formative assessment were integral to the candidate's approach. They knew their subject well and they had strong relationships with the students they were teaching, even though this was their first lesson teaching this class. It wasn't their last: they got the job.

At some point in the recent past, some teachers seem to have got it into their heads that they shouldn't be presenting content to students, that Specific Teaching represents 'old-fashioned' teaching and that great teaching involves something else. But it doesn't: great teaching needs to include teachers presenting content directly and interactively to students and checking for understanding. It is true that if they do this in a way which fails to hold student attention then students will switch off, get bored and probably start to behave poorly. However, such behaviours come about as a result of *poor* presentation and interaction.

Holding student attention

Great teachers command the room. They hold students' attention with the way they use their voice, their movement around the room, the visuals they use, the stories they tell, with their passion and their enthusiasm, and with their expert knowledge of the subject they are teaching. They interact with students, making eye contact and asking lots of questions. They repeat key points and they ask students to repeat these back to them. Periodically, they tell students to 'make a note of that, because it's important.' Their explanations are clear and precise.

I have watched great teachers teach lessons of over an hour in such a way that not one student got bored, switched off or started to behave in an inappropriate way. Speaking to students after such lessons, they tell me that they 'loved it' and that it was 'a great lesson'. I ask them why and their answers are usually the same: 'It was really interesting' and 'I learned a lot.' Teaching which leads to students being interested and learning a lot is clearly great teaching.

The fact is, when I ask similar questions to students who have been taught in the way I described towards the start of this section, they usually tell me things like: 'I enjoyed the lesson' or 'It was fun.' Enjoying lessons and having fun are, of course, good things, but more important is that students are *learning*. Great teaching isn't about students enjoying lessons at the expense of learning: in great teaching, it's about both.

Death by PowerPoint

From time to time, a phrase I hear teachers and school leaders use is 'death by PowerPoint'. The inference is that if PowerPoint is used in every lesson, it will kill student learning, because it will cause students to switch off and get bored. If I accept this, then I must admit that I am probably guilty of killing a lot of learning, because when I am teaching, I use PowerPoint all the time. (Feel free to pause in your reading to gasp.) I hope you can accept that it isn't PowerPoint which kills learning – it is *poor use* of PowerPoint. Used well, PowerPoint will transform a lesson. If I'm being honest, the only resources I would ever insist on having for a lesson would be Show-me boards, my own board, Post-it notes and PowerPoint. Give me those resources and I know I can teach a great lesson.

Poor use of PowerPoint is when there is a lot of text, usually appearing all at once, with very few visuals. The teacher reads out what is written on the slides and gets students to do a lot of copying. The reason they are getting students to do a lot of copying is that they want them to have a set of high-quality notes. This might have been a good rationale in the 1990s, but we have moved on a lot since then. High-quality notes can be typed up by the teacher and made available to students as Knowledge Organisers, either on paper or online. Students don't need to be wasting time in class making copious notes: relatively little learning happens during the note-taking process. Instead, **lesson time should be predominantly used for activities which require a teacher** (such as direct-interactive instruction and formative assessment) **or which require other students** (such as think–pair–share, discussion and peer assessment).

I once got into a difficult exchange with my head of department when they questioned the results my students had achieved in a class test (which were very good) against the detail of notes in their jotters. 'I don't believe that these students could have achieved these marks from the notes in their jotters,' she said. I explained, as calmly as I was able under the circumstances, that I cared far less about the knowledge that was recorded in their jotters than I did about the knowledge in their heads. While I believe that it is important for students to set out work and notes neatly in their jotters, because I believe that standards of presentation matter, the quality of work and notes that students produce in their jotters tells you very little about how much they are learning.

The importance of clarity

Often when we explain things to students, they appear to understand what we are saying, but in actual fact, they don't. Sometimes, this is because they don't understand what key words are. Thinking back to my own school experience, I can remember sitting through an English lesson, thoroughly confused by the fact that we were being asked to write a discursive essay on the topic of 'Youth in Asia'. I was struggling to see how you could argue against there being young people in Asia when, clearly, there are millions of them. Of course, our teacher wasn't asking us to do that. Rather, they were asking us to write an essay to discuss the topic of 'Euthanasia'. Had the teacher written this word on the board when using it, I would have realised that what they were talking about was very different from what I initially thought. *Seeing* words is often as important as hearing them. In Specific Teaching, this is important for teachers to keep in mind.

Different words have different meanings in different contexts. Often, students will become confused because they have difficulty in understanding the meaning of a word in a particular context. When I am teaching students about the difference between physical and chemical properties, or about the difference in properties between metals and non-metals, the word which tends to get in the way of student understanding is 'properties'. Some students can't get past the meaning of this word in the context of 'belongings' (this is my 'property') or 'buildings' (again, this is my 'property'). I hadn't always recognised how much of a block this can be to some students. Recognising it now, I always take time to explore the meaning of key words in their specific contexts.

The importance of examples

In helping students to understand what words or concepts mean, examples are essential. In the context of the 'properties' scenario, if students are really to understand what physical and chemical properties are, it isn't enough just to give them a definition – they need examples as well.

Examples and non-examples

You might think that the more examples you give students, the better. However, this isn't quite right. Certainly, having more than one example is important. However, if all of the examples or too similar, student understanding will be limited by this[84]. Having a broad range of examples is as important as having many. For that reason, showing students non-examples is also important.

As a trainee teacher, I was once told that you should never give students examples of things that aren't right, because you will confuse them. That is some of the worst pedagogical advice I have ever been given. It took me a few years to recognise this.

---

84. Needham, T. (2019) in *The ResearchED Guide to Explicit and Direct Instruction*

Consider the following list of facts which could form a teaching sequence about mammals:

- 'Mammals are animals which have fur or hair, have mammary glands and give birth to live young (they don't lay eggs).'
- 'All three things need to apply – if only one or two apply, the animal is not a mammal.'
- 'An **example** of a mammal is a dog – dogs have fur, have mammary glands and give birth to live young.'
- 'Another **example** of a mammal is a tiger – tigers have fur, have mammary glands and give birth to live young.'
- 'A snake is **not an example** of a mammal – snakes *don't* have fur or hair, *don't* have mammary glands and *don't* give birth to live young (they lay eggs).'
- 'A spider is **not an example** of a mammal – spiders do have hair (sometimes it is hard to see), but they *don't* have mammary glands and they *don't* give birth to live young (they lay eggs).'
- 'A human is an **example** of a mammal – humans have hair, have mammary glands and give birth to live young.'
- 'A dolphin is an **example** of a mammal – dolphins have hair (it is very fine and hard to see), have mammary glands and give birth to live young.' (You chose this example to avoid a misconception that all mammals live on the land.)
- 'A bat is an **example** of a mammal – bats have fur, have mammary glands and give birth to live young.' (You chose this example to avoid a misconception that mammals can't fly.)
- 'A shark is **not an example** of a mammal – sharks *don't* have fur or hair, *don't* have mammary glands, but do give birth to live young.'
- 'A parrot is **not an example** of a mammal – parrots *don't* have fur or hair (they have feathers), *don't* have mammary glands and *don't* give birth to live young (they lay eggs).'

In this sequence, the examples and non-examples have been *carefully chosen* and *carefully sequenced*. Examples and non-examples which the teacher believed would prove challenging to students (such as the dolphin and the bat) were deliberately introduced after more straightforward ones. Deliberately again, the sequence fluctuated between examples and non-examples, taking students from one to the other and back again. Use of appropriate visuals (such as photographs in a PowerPoint presentation) would support students to develop an understanding of what is being said.

One important point about this illustration is that I am not suggesting that a teacher should simply reel off a list of facts like this and expect students to learn from that. That would not be great teaching. Rather, the process would be interactive, with the teacher asking questions to explore student thinking and to check for understanding at appropriate points (such as, 'Do you think that a mouse is a mammal? Why?'). We will discuss questioning in more detail in a later section. In the interests of illustrating how examples and non-examples might be sequenced, I have omitted teacher–student interactions.

Exceptions

As a final point before we move on, I would like to highlight a distinction between non-examples and exceptions. To make this point, consider the following as a possible addition to the teaching sequence we have just discussed:

- 'A duck-billed platypus is an **example** of a mammal – they have fur and they have mammary glands. However, they *do not* give birth to live young – they lay eggs. This makes them different from other mammals – they are an exception.'

Highlighting exceptions is important. However, so as not to confuse students, they should appear late in teaching sequences. This is an important distinction from non-examples, which can be introduced earlier.

Textbooks

Just as there are a significant number of teachers and school leaders who hold negative views about teacher-led presentations, including use of PowerPoint, there are a significant number who view use of textbooks in a similarly negative way. As with their views on teacher-led presentations, this is misguided.

Textbooks have an important role to play in teaching and learning. Lucy Crehan reports that use of high-quality textbooks is a key feature of schools in the world's highest performing countries[85]. Daisy Christodoulou highlights an important role for textbooks as progression frameworks[86], making clear to students and the teacher the content that needs to be taught. In addition, many textbooks are rich in practice questions, the use of which should be encouraged.

However, not all teachers use textbooks well. Some teachers rely too heavily on them, devoting too much lesson time to their use. If we accept that lesson time should focus on activities which require a teacher or other students, reading and note-taking from a textbook isn't the best use of time.

Sometimes, when a student asks their teacher a question, they get told to 'look it up' in a textbook. Why do teachers do this? I suspect it is because some teachers think it is important to teach students how to find things out for themselves. However, would it not have been far quicker just to have told them? Would there not be a greater chance of the student getting the right answer from the teacher than from the textbook? I have watched teachers who default to telling students to look things up for themselves. All that typically happens is that students get frustrated and time gets wasted. Textbooks shouldn't replace teachers, particularly when there is one on hand in lessons.

5. Activities that allow students to **put into practice** what they are being taught

In the previous section, I argued that, for the most part, lesson time should focus on learning activities which require a teacher or other students. On the face of it, you could argue that 'practice' is an activity that students can do in their own time, without the need for a teacher. This is partly true. However, research suggests that *independent practice* of this kind is most effective when it comes as the third stage in a three-part model, the first two parts being *guided practice* and *supported practice*[87].

---

85. Crehan, L. (2016) *CleverLands*
86. Christodoulou, D. (2016) *Making Good Progress?*
87. Rosenshine, B. (2012) *Principles of Instruction*

Figure 9.1: The three stages of practice. It can be useful to think about this as 'I do', 'we do', 'you do'[88].

Guided, supported and independent practice

In **guided practice**, the teacher carefully takes students through the steps of how to do something. They model how to do it by showing students and talking it through. The use of visuals to support verbal explanations is important to learning. The teacher breaks processes down into 'chunks' and pauses after each chunk to check understanding and repeat key points. They highlight to students the things that are particularly difficult or that students often get wrong. They work their example through to its conclusion and then they go through another example. The process is direct and it is interactive.

Once the teacher has gone through this modelling, students should be given the opportunity to have a go themselves through **supported practice**. The teacher is on hand to support them with this, moving around the room and watching carefully for what students are doing. They use visual cues to give praise and encouragement. This doesn't need to be lengthy or over the top; a simple 'That's good' or 'Well done' is enough. They don't interrupt students who are practising well, because they recognise that this risks disrupting their flow. They have established the conditions in which it is okay for students to work with and help each other, if they need to. This is important, because there is only one teacher and lots of students, and they don't want a student to be sitting stuck for too long. When they do stop to work with a student who is struggling, they talk to them in a quiet voice so as not to disrupt the work of the rest of the class. If, while going around students, the teacher discovers that there is a common area of difficulty or that a common mistake is being made, they stop the class and go back over this, offering extra pointers and strategies to address it.

---

88. Ashman, G. (2019) in *The ResearchED Guide to Explicit and Direct Instruction*

The teacher recognises that there is only so much time available in lessons for students to practise, because there is new content to be taught. Therefore, the teacher sets homework tasks that allow students to engage with **independent practice**. In such homework exercises, students complete tasks which relate to recent learning but also to less recent learning – the teacher has included some tasks that require students to recall knowledge that was taught some time ago, recognising the benefit to learning of doing so.

Spaced vs mass practice
This last point relates to research which tells us that '**spaced practice**' is better for student learning than '**mass practice**'[89]. An example of mass practice is when students practise lots of questions in one go but don't revisit these again. In spaced practice, they would practise questions when something is taught, but then revisit similar questions the next day, the next week, the next month and the next term. This links to the idea of retrieval practice, which we discussed in Chapter 5.

6. Appropriate levels of **support and challenge**

Of everything that teachers are expected to do, the concept of 'differentiation' is perhaps the most contentious. What does differentiation actually mean, and what should teachers be expected to do to 'differentiate' lessons? For example, does differentiation mean that teachers should plan and provide different learning activities for different students or groups of students, depending on their prior learning or ability? Should there be different levels of worksheet available, for example, categorised as 'bronze', 'silver' and 'gold', according to their degree of difficulty?

Support

In *CleverLands*[90], Lucy Crehan reports that differentiation is a common feature among schools in the world's highest performing educational countries. However, this is not differentiation by setting students different tasks. Rather, it is differentiation in terms of the *support* that is available. For example, this could include:

---

89. Hattie, J. (2009) *Visible Learning*
90. Crehan, L. (2016) *CleverLands*

- Whether or not they use their Knowledge Organiser to help them answer questions or complete a short piece of writing

- Whether or not a student makes use of a 'hints and tips' sheet or 'writing frame'

- Whether a student works individually or with a partner

- The amount of one-to-one time that a teacher spends with individual students or small groups

The opportunity for differentiated support doesn't start and end with the lesson. Support can also be offered to students by inviting them to out-of-lesson sessions or through resources that they are directed to, which they can access at home – for example, via the school website.

When thinking about differentiated support, people often forget to consider the opportunity feedback presents for this. As students are practising and the teacher is circulating the room, there is great scope for students to be given personalised feedback about their work. This doesn't need to take long – a single comment can suffice – and it doesn't need to be written down. However, it is important and, potentially, powerful.

Case study: Differentiate support (not content)

Recently, I heard a teacher say they thought that students in a class should be given differentiated Knowledge Organisers. In effect, they were saying that different students in the class should be given a different curriculum, because they would be learning different content. We got into a discussion about this, during which I explained that I fundamentally disagreed. The teacher's argument was that those students who found the content challenging needed to be taught less challenging content, which a different Knowledge Organiser would reflect. My argument was that it wasn't the fact that some students found the content easier and some found it more difficult that was the issue: the issue was the amount of *support* that students were receiving. Those who find the content easier need less support; those who find it more challenging need more. This is a principle of equity: equity isn't about giving everyone the same thing, it is about giving them what they need at any particular time.

Challenge

As well as differentiating the support available to students, it is also possible to differentiate the *challenge*.

As an example, imagine that you are teaching a maths class and students are learning to calculate the area of a triangle. As part of the teaching and learning, students are asked to practise solving different problems. These have been carefully sequenced in terms of difficulty, so that the easiest are first and the most difficult are last. Rather than every student being told that they must answer all of the questions, the teacher gives the students choice in relation to which questions they attempt. For example, they might say: 'If you are finding these straightforward, just attempt the even-numbered problems.' However, in doing so, you need to be mindful of the learning gulf that can be created in a class by letting some students move too far ahead of others. Students will work through problems and tasks at different paces, and often the pace that they work at will be related to how easy or difficult they find the work (although not always). Recognising this and allowing it to happen is important. However, just as important is the consideration of how far ahead you let the most able get. To let them get too far ahead risks not giving others the opportunity to catch up. With this in mind, Lucy Crehan quotes Bart Simpson: 'Let me get this straight. We're behind the rest of our class and we're going to catch up to them by going slower than they are?'[91]

One way to address this is through peer teaching; that is, getting students who have mastered something to work with and help teach students who haven't. Use of this approach can be powerful in helping to consolidate learning and tease out misunderstandings that might not otherwise have been picked up on.

Great teaching involves the teacher asking students lots of questions. When asking students questions, there is scope to differentiate. For example, knowing the students in their classes well, teachers can use their professional intuition to decide which questions to ask which students, depending on how challenging the question they are asking is.

---

91. Crehan, L. (2016) *CleverLands*

I once observed a lesson with a colleague and, as part of our post-lesson discussion, they made the point that the level of challenge was right because no one got stuck, asked for teacher help, or needed to refer to any of the support frameworks the teacher had provided. Would you agree with their conclusion? I have to say, I had a different conclusion, which was that the work being set was too easy. By its very nature, learning is difficult. It takes effort, perseverance and resilience. If students aren't displaying any of these attributes, then the teacher should question whether the work is challenging enough.

Choice

The concept of *choice* can be useful in supporting effective and efficient differentiation. In offering students choice, there are three important caveats to keep in mind:

1. The choice should be within the planned activity, rather than you planning lots of different activities for students to do

2. In presenting choices to students, you should encourage them to push themselves so that the support they are accessing is minimised and the challenge they are giving themselves is maximised

3. Any differences within activities should be kept as small as possible. This is important in terms of 'keeping students together' in their learning – you don't want to create conditions whereby some race ahead while others are left behind without having the opportunity to catch up – and in terms of keeping teacher workload manageable

Shirley Clarke has helpfully framed this idea in the concept of a 'chilli pepper challenge'[92]. In a chilli pepper challenge, differing levels of support and challenge are framed as 'mild', 'medium', 'spicy' and 'hot'. Students are encouraged to start at the level they feel is most appropriate to them (supported by teacher guidance as to which level to choose), and then move on to 'hotter' levels. Importantly, students are given the choice. The teacher is not using this to put students into ability groups. Yes, there will be students working in the class who are accessing differing levels of support and challenge, but the students have had

---

92. Clarke, S. (2014) *Outstanding Formative Assessment*

ownership about which level they want to be working at. Doing so has avoided the stigmatisation which can come from a teacher dictating who has to work in each group.

There is a difference between planning for differing support, challenge and choice within activities and planning completely different activities. In terms of the preparation time that a teacher reasonably has available to them, the first is reasonable, the second less so.

In summary, differentiation is incredibly important. However, it should be done smartly. It is best thought of as being about **differentiated support and challenge** which is given to individuals. **Choices** within activities fit this brief. Effective differentiation isn't about planning different learning and different activities for different students: it is about offering differing levels of support and challenge in relation to whole-class learning, and choices within the activities being set.

7. Use of **questions** to make students think and to check for understanding

Asking questions is one of the most important things a teacher can do to help students learn and to check their learning. If you ask a student a question, it requires them to *think*. To give you an answer, they need to *recall* information. Their answer *gives you feedback* about what they know and understand, and what they don't. You can then use this to *give feedback to them*, or to *make teaching points* to others that you might not have considered otherwise. Asking questions is a powerful formative teaching practice.

All that said, it requires skill to ask questions in a way that makes all students think and moves learning forward. In general, there are three key aspects to consider:

1. What questions you are asking
2. How you are asking questions
3. How frequently you are asking questions

We will explore each in turn.

What questions you are asking

Which of these questions is the best?

1. Which King was killed at the Battle of Bosworth?
2. What do you know about the Battle of Bosworth?
3. True or false: Henry V was killed at the Battle of Bosworth.
4. Which King was killed at the Battle of Bosworth?

   a. Richard II

   b. Richard III

   c. Henry V

   d. Henry VI

Would you categorise any of these as 'good' questions or 'bad' questions? Why? Thinking about this leads to a different question: what makes a good question? Perhaps the answer is 'any question which makes a student think'. But all questions make students think. So, what makes a good question? The key principle to keep in mind is the 'Goldilocks principle': ask questions which are appropriately challenging – not too easy and not too difficult.

The questions you ask should be ones which students have a reasonable chance of answering. For example, you might ask about something that has previously been taught, that students might have learned outwith class, or that is a logical extension of something you are currently teaching. It would seem reasonable to ask 10-year-old students, as part of a modern studies lesson, 'Who is the president of the United States of America?' and expect that many students will know the answer. If there is little or no chance that any student will be able to answer a question, there is little or no point in asking it. Students switch off or go off task pretty quickly if the questions they are being asked are too easy or too difficult. Arguably, the latter is worse. At least with questions that are too easy, students are able to experience success (albeit success which is rather superficial). With questions that are too difficult and which students have no chance of answering, they quickly default to a feeling of 'what's the point?'

The wrong kind of thinking

A caveat on the importance of thinking is that *not all thinking leads to useful learning*. For example, I once saw a chapter in a maths textbook for 13-year-olds which asked questions like:

- What do you think is a safe amount of money to carry in your wallet or purse?
- What is the most amount of money you have ever carried in your wallet or purse?

In a geography textbook, for the same age group, I have seen questions such as:

- Where is the hottest place you have ever been?
- Would you rather live in a hot or a cold country? Why?

While questions of this kind can be useful at stimulating student interest, they do very little to advance learning, because students aren't being taught anything new. They may be getting students to think, but they aren't getting students to *think hard*. Questions of this kind just aren't challenging enough to get them to think hard. They keep students busy, but being busy is a poor proxy for learning[93]. Used sparingly, questions like this can have a place, but teachers need to take care with regard to how much space they are given.

Open and closed questions

Let's return to the questions that were asked at the start of this section and apply the 'Goldilocks principle'. If students hadn't been taught anything about the Battle of Bosworth, questions 1, 3 and 4 wouldn't be particularly good questions to ask at the start of a lesson, because students wouldn't have a reasonable chance of being able to answer them – the questions are too difficult; they are 'closed questions' relating to knowledge students are unlikely to have. Question 2 would be a good question to ask near the start of a lesson, because there is far more of a chance that students will be able to come up with an answer, as this is an open question. Even if the answer is 'nothing', that is useful for the teacher to know, because it establishes a baseline. Questions 1, 3 and 4

---

93. https://www.ibo.org/globalassets/events/aem/conferences/2015/robert-coe.pdf

would be better questions to ask towards the end of the lesson in which students had been taught that Richard III was killed at the Battle of Bosworth, or at the start of the next lesson, or in a lesson some days, weeks or months after this content had been taught, as part of Daily, Weekly or Monthly Review.

Whether 'open questions' are better than 'closed questions', or vice versa, depends on what has already been taught and on what you are trying to achieve by asking the question. If you want to get an idea of how much students know about something, then open questions usually offer the best way to do that; if you want to know if precise facts and concepts have been learned, then closed questions offer the best way to do that. A misconception that some teachers and school leaders hold is that open questions are better than closed. They might be, but they might not. It depends on what you are trying to find out.

Higher-order questions

Another misconception that some teachers and school leaders have about questioning relates to Bloom's Taxonomy. They say things like 'higher-order questions are better questions to ask students than lower-order questions'. What I say to them is: why do you believe that? Whenever I do, they tend to get stuck. Often, they will say something like, 'Because someone told us that they were.' Is this a good reason? Clearly not.

The misconception that some teachers and school leaders have about the importance of higher-order questions links to the discussion that we had in Chapter 2, where we discussed the fact that **higher-order questions are not necessarily better questions to ask than lower order questions**. Any question which is appropriately challenging and makes students think is a good question to ask. Lower-order questions have an important role to play in Specific Teaching too.

How you are asking questions

For the purposes of this discussion, we are thinking about a teacher asking verbal questions, rather than students being set written questions to answer. With that in mind, there are two ways in which you can ask students questions. You can:

1. Ask a particular student a question and wait for their response

2. Ask the class or a small group a question and wait for a response

We touched on the themes of asking questions in Chapter 2 when we asked: 'What is the capital city of Australia?' There would be benefit in you going back and rereading that section. The approach discussed in that section can be summarised as: **pose, pause, pounce, bounce**[94]. In other words:

- Ask your question
- Allow *thinking time* for everyone
- Ask someone for an answer
- Ask someone else something about the answer that was given

Below are a selection of useful phrases which help set up the 'pause' and 'bounce' sections of questioning:

Pause	Bounce
• 'Everyone think about that for a moment.' • 'Take 10 seconds to think about that.' • 'Think about that – everyone.' • 'Chat to a partner for 30 seconds.' • 'Take a minute to talk about that.'	• 'Are you sure?' • 'How sure are you? Give me a 0-10.' • '(Name), do you agree?' • 'Who agrees?' • 'Does anyone disagree?' • 'You're half right, but not fully. Have you any idea what wasn't quite right?' • 'Can anyone help with that?' • 'Who would like to comment or build on that answer?'

Figure 9.2: Examples of instructions that can be given and questions that can be asked to initiate 'pause' and 'bounce' during 'Pose, Pause, Pounce, Bounce' questioning.

Teachers are generally good at 'pose' and 'pounce'; they are generally less good at 'pause' and 'bounce'. Pausing and bouncing take up lesson time.

---

94. https://www.theguardian.com/teacher-network/2011/nov/17/lessons-good-to-outstanding-afl-questioning

A scenario in which you ask a question and take an answer from the first student who puts up their hand can take fewer than 10 seconds. Pausing and bouncing takes considerably more time. But this is not wasted time. In fact, it is quite the opposite: this is making the most of the time that you have with students to get them *all* to *think* and to *learn from each other.* Teachers need to make time for this.

'Random name generators', 'lollipop sticks' and 'no hands up'

From time to time, when I talk to teachers about questioning techniques or when I watch lessons, I hear about or see 'random name generators', 'lollipop sticks' and 'no hands up'. I must admit, I am not much of a fan of any of these. While I understand the logic which underpins their use, I think it is flawed.

The theory behind random name generators and lollipop sticks is that their use encourages all students to think, because no one knows who is going to get asked a question. Also, they help the teacher involve all students in answering questions, rather than just the ones who always put their hand up. While I agree that getting all students to think and to involve all students in questioning are the correct principles, the flaw is that use of random name generators and lollipop sticks removes the ability of the teacher to differentiate teaching through questioning. Teachers know students in their classes well, so they know which students are usually confident at answering questions and which students aren't. When they have a difficult question to ask, they know not to pick a student they recognise is unlikely to be able to answer it. When they have a more straightforward question and they are looking to build the confidence of a particular student and involve them in the questioning process, they need to be able to use their professional intuition to select which student to ask. Random name generators and lollipop sticks stop them from being able to do that.

Equally, I appreciate the theory which underpins 'no hands up'. The logic is that, if you allow students to put their hand up to answer questions, you will typically find that it is always the same students who put up their hands and so it is always the same students who end up answering your questions; those students who don't put up their hands don't get asked and don't get to answer. Worse, they will rely on the fact that they don't have to come up with an answer. But this logic works on the assumption that you have to ask students who have put up their hand: but you don't. It is perfectly possible for you to allow students to put up their hands but not choose one of these students to answer, instead saying something like, 'I'm going to choose someone who's not got their hand up this time, because I'd like to hear from some other people.' I actually think there is a lot of value in getting students to put up their hands, because by doing so, the teacher is given an indication about how many students think they know the answer. This, in turn, gives the teacher an indication of how easy or difficult students have found the question, or how well students think they know something. A show of hands can be a useful formative tool.

Shouting out

The one thing I am really not a fan of in questioning is shouting out. Shouting out smothers thinking. If you ask a question and allow students to shout out, you prevent every other student from having the opportunity to think about your question. You need to establish the rules for student behaviour when you are asking questions. My rules are usually:

- Don't shout out
- Put up your hand if you think you have an answer
- Listen to each other's answers
- Don't make fun of anyone for their answer

Show-me boards

As you may have picked up from earlier sections of this book, I believe that Show-me boards and great teaching go hand in hand. They are an invaluable formative assessment resource and every teacher should have a class set. They should be as integral to teaching and learning in classrooms as a jotter. I find it hard to understand why a teacher wouldn't be using them in a lesson.

Show-me boards can play a key role in the 'pause' and 'bounce' sections of questioning: you ask a question, everyone writes down an answer on their Show-me board (this is the 'pause'), you look at these (either while students are doing this or by asking them to hold them up once everyone is done), and then you use what you see on boards to make teaching points: for example, by holding up particular boards to show other students what someone has written or drawn (this is the 'bounce'). The question you ask could require a one-word answer ('What is the capital of Australia?'), a few words ('Write an example of a metaphor') or a picture ('Show me what you think electricity looks like'). Used in this way:

- They help get *everyone* to think
- They help you to see what *all* students are thinking
- They help you to give feedback to all students based on what other students were thinking – in other words, they help *everyone* learn from one another

---

Case study: Making thinking visible

I once taught a lesson for a science teacher who was off work ill. The head of department explained to me that, in the previous lesson, students had been carrying out an experiment to investigate the effect of changing voltage on the brightness of a bulb. The purpose of today's lesson was, in part, to teach students how to draw a graph of the results from this experiment.

I began the lesson by asking students what it was they had been doing in their last lesson. They told me that they had been carrying out an experiment. I then asked them: 'What was the purpose of this experiment?' I asked them to use their Show-me boards to write this down, then hold them up and show me. Student answers included:

- 'To find out how much voltage was in the bulb'
- 'To find out how much voltage you can get from a bulb when the brightness changes'
- 'To find out if increasing or decreasing the voltage impacts on the brightness of a bulb'

You don't need to be an expert in physics to appreciate that each of these answers is different. The third answer was a good answer, but the first two indicated that these students had gaps in their understanding of what the experiment was about. More than this, their answers suggested that they had deeper misunderstandings in

---

terms of the physics which underpinned the experiment (for example, believing that voltage was 'in the bulb' indicates a misunderstanding about what voltage is).

Had I asked the question about what the experiment was about to just one student, I probably wouldn't have found any of this out. The power of Show-me boards is their ability to give the teacher instant feedback about the learning of *all* students. The teacher can then use what they are seeing to give instant feedback to students.

One final point in relation to Show-me boards is that students, no matter what age, tend to really like using them. In that sense, they can motivate students to participate. This is particularly true of shy students, who might have been reluctant to answer a question out loud, but who are comfortable writing something on their Show-me board.

How frequently you are asking questions

In Specific Teaching, the frequency with which a teacher asks questions is very high. There are two reasons for this:

1. To make students think
2. To make thinking visible, as a formative assessment strategy

As a rule of thumb, I would suggest that there should be at least one question asked for every minute of teacher exposition. In saying this, I would caution that there is a fine line between asking lots of good questions and asking lots of questions just for the sake of it. Care should be taken not to drag things out more than necessary, which can have the opposite effect of that intended: killing the pace and student engagement.

We will explore the use of frequent questions by way of example.

Asking frequent questions

Imagine a chemistry lesson on the topic of chemical bonding for 15-year-old students. This lesson is going to be about ionic bonding, but the teacher taught a lesson on covalent bonding last week and wants to find out how much the students learned before moving on to ionic bonding. The first 10 minutes of the lesson go something like this.

Teacher: 'Last week we were learning about covalent bonding. I would like you to take two minutes and chat to a partner: **what do you know about covalent bonding?**'

Over the course of the next two minutes, the teacher wanders the room and listens in to conversations. If they hear something they think would make for a useful teaching point to the class, they say to the student, 'Please write that on your Show-me board when I ask you to.'

The teacher addresses the class again.

Teacher: 'Okay, that's two minutes up. Stop there. Now, **please write on your Show-me board one thing you know about covalent bonding.**' (I accept that, technically, this isn't a question, but the statement achieves the same outcome as asking a question.) 'I would like you to make sure that whatever you write is different from the person you chatted to. I would also like you to write a number at the top of your board which indicates how confident you are that what you have written is right – 10 means you are certain and 1 means you think there is a good chance that it's wrong. Hold your boards up so that I can see them, when you are ready.'

A minute or so passes.

Teacher: 'Okay, so I am seeing that some of you have written, "You get covalent bonding in elements." Without shouting out, **who thinks that's right?**'

Some hands go up.

Teacher: 'Okay, thank you. Well, let's be clear about this: that *is* right. We *do* get covalent bonding in elements. Well done. If you didn't know that, please make a note of that point. We *do* get covalent bonding in elements.'

The teacher pauses to allow students time to make a note of this.

Teacher: 'Now, a different question for you to think about: **do we get covalent bonding in *all* elements? Take 30 seconds and chat to a partner about that.**'

30 seconds pass.

Teacher: 'Okay, so the question was, "Do we get covalent bonding in all elements?" **Who wants to tell us something about that?**'

The teacher pauses, surveying the class for 10 seconds.

Teacher: 'Okay, so I'm seeing a few hands, but I was hoping a few more of you would have something to say about that.'

The teacher pauses. A few more hands go up. The teacher chooses one of these students.

Teacher: 'Audrey, **what do you think?**'

Audrey: 'Yes, I think we do get covalent bonding in all elements.'

Teacher: **'How sure are you?'**

Audrey: 'Pretty sure.'

Teacher: 'Okay, thanks. Derek – **is that right?**'

Derek: 'Um, yes.'

Teacher: **'How sure are you?'**

Derek: 'Not very.'

Teacher: 'Scott, **do you agree that there is covalent bonding in all elements?**'

Scott: 'No, I don't think that's right.'

Teacher: 'Okay, **why not?**'

Scott: 'Because I don't think you get covalent bonding in metal elements.'

Teacher: 'Okay. That's interesting. **Can you say any more about that?**'

Scott: 'I think there's a different kind of bonding in metals.'

Teacher: 'Okay, that's interesting, too. So Scott is saying we don't get covalent bonding in metal elements and that metal elements have a different kind of bonding in them. **Who agrees?**

Who disagrees? Why?'

The teacher pauses for five seconds and surveys the room.

Teacher: (To a student with their hand up) 'Kelly, **what do you think?'**

Kelly: 'I think that's right. Metal elements have metallic bonding, but not covalent bonding.'

Teacher: 'Spot on. Well done. So that's an important point: metal elements don't have covalent bonding – they have metallic bonding.'

The teacher pauses to emphasise the importance of the point they have just made.

Teacher: 'If you didn't know that, please make a note of it. I'll repeat: metal elements don't have covalent bonding – they have metallic bonding.'

The teacher pauses to allow students time to make a brief note of this.

Teacher: 'Okay, so if we're saying that we *do* get covalent bonding in elements but that *metal elements don't have covalent bonding* in them, I guess that means that non-metal elements are the ones with covalent bonding in them. **Is that right?** Take a moment to think about that yourself, please. The question is: **true or false – non-metal elements have covalent bonding in them.'**

The teacher pauses for 20 seconds and surveys the room.

Teacher: 'Okay, **so who would like to say something about that?'**

The teacher waits. Some hands go up.

Teacher: 'Okay, Jamie, **what do you think?'**

Jamie: 'I think that's right, but I don't think all non-metal elements have covalent bonding in them.'

Teacher: 'Oh, that's interesting. **Hands up if you agree**: not all non-metal elements have covalent bonding in them.'

Very few students put up their hand. Most look unsure.

Teacher: 'Okay, so most of you have kept your hands down, which I'm taking to mean that most of you think that Jamie is wrong. Fiona – you've got your hand up, though. **Do you want to tell us why?**'

Fiona: 'I think Jamie's right. Noble gas elements don't have covalent bonding in them.'

Teacher: **'Why not?'**

Fiona: 'Because noble gas elements don't have any bonding in them.'

Teacher: 'That's absolutely right, Fiona, and another important point. *Most* non-metal elements have covalent bonding in them, but some don't. The noble gas elements are an example of non-metal elements which don't.'

The teacher draws a diagram on the board to illustrate this point.

Teacher: 'Let's summarise the key points from what we have been discussing. Covalent bonding is found in elements, but not all elements have covalent bonding in them. For example, metal elements don't have covalent bonding. Most non-metal elements do, but an exception is the noble gas elements. **On your Show-me board, write the chemical symbol for two elements which don't have covalent bonding in them and, on the other side of your board, two that do. When you are ready, hold up the side which shows the two that don't.**'

This is Specific Teaching in action. Through frequent questioning, the teacher can *drill down* to explore student understanding in detail. Where they find mistakes, they can provide feedback to address these. In the example we have looked at, in a relatively short space of time the teacher has asked more than 20 questions. Through the way that they have been asked, all students are engaged in the process, thinking and learning from the teacher and from one another.

In order to teach in this way, teachers need to have a strong knowledge of the subject they are teaching. Beyond knowledge of the subject, they need to have knowledge of how students think about the subject, including the things that students typically find challenging or commonly misunderstand. They also need to have strong relationships with the students they are teaching, with students trusting that the teacher will use the answers that are given – right or wrong – in a constructive way to support the learning of everyone in the class. They know that they will never be mocked or humiliated for giving incorrect answers. Rather, they recognise that, so long as they are trying their best, their teacher actually values incorrect answers, because through these, they get high-quality feedback.

8. Activities that get students to **discuss and learn with other students**

Discussion doesn't necessarily mean whole-class discussion. Rather, discussion can happen in pairs or small groups. Often, discussion in pairs or small groups is more beneficial to student learning than whole-class discussion. The smaller the group size (with pairs being the smallest group size you can have), the more individual students realise that they are expected to take part in the discussion. In larger groups, students have more of an opportunity not to take part.

Discussion can be very powerful when used as part of whole-class questioning, when the teacher uses phrases such as '**chat to a partner**' or '**take a moment to discuss that**', which we have previously discussed. During such moments, the teacher can circulate and listen to what students are saying to one another. This is another strategy to make student thinking visible. It gives feedback to you about what students are thinking – for example, their prior knowledge on a topic or how well they have learned something. You can then use things you have heard during discussions to make whole-class teaching points. For example, you might say: 'As I was wandering around the room, I heard one or two groups say this... I wonder what other groups think about that?' In this way, discussion is supporting the 'bounce' idea we discussed as part of effective questioning techniques.

It is usually best if your time is spent listening in to conversations, rather than getting involved in them. While it can be useful to join in (for example, it can help get a conversation going or move it in a particular direction), if you get too drawn into any one discussion, you are missing a valuable formative assessment opportunity for yourself. Students can also be quick to notice when a teacher is involved in talking to other students and can use this as an opportunity to go off task.

A powerful approach to discussion is '**think–pair–share**'[95]. In this approach, students are asked to take a moment to think about a question themselves, then given the instruction to discuss their thinking with a partner, before they are invited to share their thinking more widely, perhaps with the class.

～ᒪᖇ～

In this chapter, we have continued our discussion on the typical pedagogy of high-quality lessons. We shall return to this in Chapter 13. Before we do, we are going to turn our attention to how a *Lesson Evaluation Toolkit* can be used to help transform teaching practice in classrooms and departments across a school.

---

95. Clarke, S. (2014) *Outstanding Formative Assessment*

PART 3.

Towards great teaching in every classroom in every school

Chapter 10
Lesson planning and self-evaluation

There is more to great teaching than what happens in a lesson. Great teaching requires careful planning in advance of lessons and evaluation following lessons. The plan–teach–evaluate cycle (illustrated in Figure 10.1) is key to great teaching.

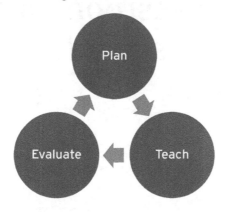

Figure 10.1: The plan–teach–evaluate cycle.

In this chapter, we will explore how your school *Lesson Evaluation Toolkit* can support high-quality lesson planning and evaluation.

Lesson planning

Regardless of experience or expertise, there are occasions when all teachers teach lessons which fall short of the standard they had expected or are satisfied with. When this happens, it is typically a result of poor lesson planning. Careful lesson planning is a prerequisite to great teaching.

Using your Lesson Evaluation Toolkit to support lesson planning

Used as a tool to support planning, a *Lesson Evaluation Toolkit* helps to achieve the development of a shared understanding of what makes great teaching across a school. By functioning as a pedagogical *aide mémoire*, it helps to keep pedagogy first and foremost in the minds of teachers when planning a lesson. The more it is used, the more familiar the included pedagogy becomes, and the less time needs to be spent referring to it. Teachers will start to remember what the key pedagogy to consider is and planning for this will become more automatic. Whether you are new to a school or have worked in a school for 30 years, a *Lesson Evaluation Toolkit* helps to remind you of the typical pedagogical features of high-quality lessons. Being reminded of these helps you plan for them.

There are a variety of ways that you might use your *Lesson Evaluation Toolkit* to support your lesson planning. For example, you might use it as a reference tool, keeping it to hand and referring to it during planning. You might not use it to help plan every lesson, but periodic reference to it will be useful to you.

Alternatively, the *Lesson Evaluation Toolkit* might become your planning tool of choice, which you use to help you plan every lesson. In the 'notes' section, you might record details which relate to a lesson. For example, you might record what the learning intention is, what the success criteria are or the key questions you will ask students. If used electronically, your planning notes might include hyperlinks to saved files or webpages.

Use of the *Lesson Evaluation Toolkit* in lesson planning is not about making all lessons look the same – it is about getting all teachers to think about the same pedagogy as part of their planning. As I said in Chapter 8, when we talk about the importance of achieving consistency across a school, the important thing is consistent *high quality*, not every teacher teaching in the same way. A *Lesson Evaluation Toolkit* is not saying: *you must do this.* Rather, it is saying: *remember, there could be value in doing this – think about it.*

Collaborative planning

A *Lesson Evaluation Toolkit* can also be used to support collaborative planning. For example, two maths teachers teaching the same topic might use the *Lesson Evaluation Toolkit* to support their joint planning of the lessons they will be teaching. Its power is that it keeps pedagogy (as opposed to content) first and foremost in the minds of those doing the planning.

For example, assuming that 'plenary' is included as an element of the *Lesson Evaluation Toolkit* of a school, plenaries will be discussed as part of the planning process. If one teacher has good ideas about lesson plenaries, the teacher they are planning with can learn from that. Without reference to the *Lesson Evaluation Toolkit* in planning, a lesson plenary may or may not get discussed. In this way, some of the benefits of teachers observing other teachers are achieved, without as much of a time investment.

Evaluation

As important to great teaching as careful lesson planning is teacher evaluation (which is often referred to as 'self-evaluation') of a lesson after it has been taught. In evaluating a lesson, key questions for a teacher to ask themselves are:

1. How good was this lesson?
2. How do I know?
3. Which elements of this lesson were strongest/weakest?
4. Why do I think that?
5. What might I do differently if I were to teach this lesson again?
6. How does all of this influence the next lesson?

The importance of regular self-evaluation

Great teachers self-evaluate teaching and learning from lessons as a matter of course. While it would be unrealistic to expect teachers to complete a structured self-evaluation of every lesson they teach, the periodic use of the school's *Lesson Evaluation Toolkit* to self-evaluate a lesson can be very powerful.

In terms of how you might go about doing this, an effective process is to sit down with the *Lesson Evaluation Toolkit* soon after a lesson has been taught and apply an evaluation system (such as green/amber/red or 0-10) against elements and/or illustrations as set out, adding notes as you deem appropriate.

Figure 10.2 shows an example.

Lesson Evaluation Toolkit: typical features of high-quality lessons		
Elements	Illustrations	Notes
Structural features		
Daily Review (including Weekly & Monthly Review)	• Low-stakes assessment, promoting recall from everyone. • Includes material required for the lesson, recent and less recent material.	*GREEN* The true or false quiz was low-stakes recall. It was effective in identifying gaps in student knowledge. Covered material needed for the lesson.
Learning intentions	• Set out precise learning goals ('Know...' 'Understand...' 'Be able to...'). • Clearly communicated (verbally and visually, if possible) in student friendly language. • Revisited during lesson and in plenary.	*AMBER* Discussed quite late into the lesson because I had to spend more time than I'd planned recapping content (following poor student performance in Daily Review). I included these in my PowerPoint presentation. Should have referred back to them later.

Success criteria	• Clear communication of what you are looking for/ what success looks like, e.g.:
	  • 'I can...' statements
	  • Key features
	  • Exemplars
	• Used to support feedback and student self-evaluation.
		RED
		Explained but not referred back to. I'm not sure all students understood them.
		Will need to bring the focus back to these in the next lesson to help students self-evaluate their work.

Figure 10.2. An extract from a teacher's self-evaluation of a lesson, completed using the school Lesson Evaluation Toolkit, which encourages critical reflection.

Use of an evaluation system is important. It encourages you to think about the pedagogy you are evaluating and ask yourself critical questions about this. For example:

- 'Was this element "green", "amber" or "red"?' or 'How would I evaluate this element out of 10?'
- 'Why do I think that?'
- 'What could I have done to move this from an "amber" to a "green", or closer to 10?'

Without such a system, it is possible to go through the *Lesson Evaluation Toolkit* and think to yourself: 'I *did* that' or 'I *didn't* do that.' In other words, the *Lesson Evaluation Toolkit* would become a tick-list, rather than an evaluative framework. The power of the *Lesson Evaluation Toolkit* comes from when it is used to ask *evaluative questions*, rather than ticking things off as having happened or not. Used in this way, it can function as a diagnostic tool which you can use to identify elements of teaching practice which are typically strong (and which you might then share with others) and tease out elements of teaching practice which are typically less strong (and which you will focus on improving).

Such a process is not about self-reporting teaching quality. In themselves, green/amber/red and 0–10 self-evaluations mean little. Rather, it is about supporting **structured critical reflection** and **continuous improvement**, with a clear focus on pedagogy. The more you use the *Lesson Evaluation Toolkit* in this way, and the more you encourage others to watch you teach and use the *Lesson Evaluation Toolkit* to discuss elements of teaching practice with you, the more reliable your self-evaluation will become and the better you will know yourself as a teacher.

One size doesn't fit all
It is important to recognise that while many teachers will see value in using a *Lesson Evaluation Toolkit* in this way, there will be some who will not. For that reason, it is worth reminding ourselves that one of the reasons that we refer to this framework as a 'toolkit' is because it can be used in a variety of ways. Not everyone needs to be using it in exactly the same way. What is more important is that everyone is using it in *some* way; a way which they perceive to be of benefit to them.

On that basis, while I believe that there is real merit in asking teachers to use the school's *Lesson Evaluation Toolkit* to complete a structured self-evaluation on a regular basis, school leaders should take care regarding how hard they push anyone who is reluctant to buy into such an approach, particularly in the early stages of using your *Lesson Evaluation Toolkit*. As Michael Fullan cautions, command and control strategies don't tend to be particularly effective in schools[96]. Instead, the development of *culture* is key.

As the professional learning culture of your school develops, the likelihood is that more and more teachers will buy into the approaches you are advocating, particularly if this culture is grounded in collaboration. Be careful not to view consistency as 'everyone doing exactly the same thing'. It is important that there is room for a degree of professional autonomy.

Collaborative evaluation

Teacher engagement in a structured self-evaluation of a lesson becomes most beneficial to their professional learning when it is the first step in a more collaborative process; for example, through discussion of a lesson with colleagues. There are a variety of ways in which such discussion might come about, which we shall explore.

Discussing lessons with colleagues

Imagine that a head of department or year has created an expectation that, once a month, all teachers use the school's *Lesson Evaluation Toolkit* to self-evaluate at least one lesson. Teachers are expected to bring a completed copy of their self-evaluation to the weekly department meeting, to share and discuss with others. The first element of the *Lesson Evaluation Toolkit* is 'Daily Review', and the head of department starts the discussion by saying: 'Let's talk about our self-evaluations of Daily Review in lessons this week.' A discussion based on teachers' self-evaluation follows, including why teachers evaluated this element in the way that they had (green/amber/red or 0–10). The process supports critical thinking, discussion and professional learning.

---

96. Fullan, M. (2008) *What's Worth Fighting for in Headship?*

Because a climate of **trust** and mutual **respect** has been developed in this team, teachers feel comfortable to share and engage in discussion of this kind, regardless of whether their self-evaluation is highlighting strengths or weaknesses. They don't believe that a self-evaluation of 'red' or '3/10' means: 'I am failing as a teacher.' Rather, they feel comfortable about being honest in their self-evaluation and in their discussions.

It may be the case that, normally, a teacher self-evaluates a particular element of teaching practice positively. However, for the lesson they have self-evaluated, this element of the lesson wasn't as good as it normally is. The most and the least experienced teachers in the department might both have self-evaluated Daily Review as 'red' for this lesson. Equally, the most expert and the least expert teachers might have done the same. Alternatively, it may be the case that a particular teacher recognises that Daily Review is rarely a strong element of their lessons, so their self-evaluation of this lesson is quite typical. This being the case, the teacher recognises that by engaging in discussions with colleagues, it is likely that others will be able to offer suggestions as to how Daily Review might be improved. Other teachers will chip in and say things like, 'Have you thought about doing this...?' or 'I recently watched a teacher do this and it was very effective.' Used to support such discussions, the *Lesson Evaluation Toolkit* is supporting collaborative professional learning.

One-to-one discussions

As an alternative example, imagine that a head of department or year asks teachers to complete a self-evaluation of a lesson they have recently taught, but rather than asking them to bring this along to the next department meeting to discuss as part of a group, they asked them to bring it along to a one-to-one meeting. Like the departmental meeting, the purpose is to support critical thinking, discussion and professional learning. However, being one-to-one, the approach can be more personalised.

The head of department or year didn't observe the lesson, so you might think: 'How can there be any sort of meaningful discussion if they weren't in the lesson to see what was going on?' The answer relates to how the head of department or year leads the discussion, with coaching and mentoring approaches being key.

Coaching and mentoring

Coaching

Coaching is about asking questions which make people think, listening carefully to what they say and then asking further questions. In this way, the person being coached can be led towards their own conclusions – the coach helps tease out the answers. The role of the coach is to act as a facilitator for critical reflection.

A coaching approach to discussions about lessons might include questions and phrases such as:

- 'Talk me through your self-evaluation.'
- 'Were there any elements of this lesson that you self-evaluated as "green"?'
- 'Why did you evaluate that element as "green"?'
- 'Were there any elements that you self-evaluated as "red"?'
- 'Why did you evaluate that element as "red"?'
- 'What do you think would have moved this element from "red" towards "amber" or "green"?'
- 'How typical is your self-evaluation of 6/10 for "feedback"?'
- 'How confident do you feel about your understanding of how to give students effective feedback in a lesson?'
- 'Is there a way in which you could share that with others? I think there would be real benefits in doing so.'

People who are coaching should do a lot of listening and watching – listening to what is being said, listening to how it is being said, and watching for body language cues. Depending on what is being heard and observed, this may lead to further questions, such as:

- 'I'm picking up, from the way you are talking about this, that perhaps you aren't as confident about this element of practice compared with others – is that fair?'
- 'Why do you think that is?'
- 'Do you think there would have been any value in using Exit Tickets?'

- 'Have you ever watched a teacher use Exit Tickets?'
- 'How do you think you could go about improving this element of your practice?'
- 'Is there anyone who could help you with that?'

A teacher's self-evaluation is not being used to *draw conclusions* about teaching quality – it is being used to *ask questions*. In this way, it can be used to support self-evaluation and professional learning, in the spirit of continuous improvement. The process can help a school leader to get to know teachers better, including in relation to their self-identified strengths and areas for improvement, their confidence, their ability to reflect and think critically, and their understanding of what makes great teaching.

Regular coaching conversations are important. Whether or not these happen, and their quality, provides a good indication as to the strength of the professional learning culture in a department or school. Without them, teachers will be left to self-evaluate on their own, which will limit the effectiveness of the process. Some teachers won't self-evaluate lessons at all. Therefore, protecting time for teacher self-evaluation and discussion of this self-evaluation is important. School leaders should build this time into departmental and whole-school calendars (which I call 'Teaching and Learning Calendars', and which we shall discuss in Chapter 14).

GROW
Some people find it useful to use mental models to help them coach. One such model is GROW:

- **G**oal – what do you want to achieve?
- **R**eality – describe the current situation
- **O**ptions – what options do you have?
- **W**ill – what action will you take?

In terms of providing a structure to support coaching conversations, such models have a lot going for them. However, I do not believe they are essential to high-quality coaching. What is essential is that the coach listens, watches, asks good questions and does more listening.

I have been on the receiving end of coaching conversations in which it was quite clear to me that the coach was thinking more about what comes next in the GROW model than they were about the answers I was giving to their questions. If using a model to support their coaching, coaches should be mindful not to let the model get in the way of the coaching.

Mentoring

Coaching conversations don't work for everyone and they don't work in all contexts. Sometimes, **mentoring** is a more effective approach.

Mentoring is different from coaching in that it is more directive, with the person doing the mentoring offering suggestions and advice, rather than asking questions to help the other person come up with their own solutions. For example:

- 'I faced a similar problem. What I did was…'
- 'Have you thought about doing this…?'
- 'I think that's a very good idea. I like it because…'
- 'I'm not so sure about that. I'm unsure because…'
- 'I really don't think that's a good idea. I'm saying that because…'
- 'That was a very good piece of work. What I thought was so good was…'
- 'Okay, so I'm going to be honest with you here: I don't think you handled that as well as you could have.'
- 'While I thought that went quite well, I think it could have been improved. Rather than (this), I would have liked to have seen more of (this).'
- 'Moving forward, I would like you to do (this).'
- 'I would like you to consider changing how you do (that). Instead, I would like to see something more like (this).'

The mentoring approach is more instructional than coaching. It involves more feedback and it gives a clearer direction and steer. It drills down into specific details more than coaching does and is generally more black and white in its approach: *this* is what I would like you to think about; *this* is an example of an effective way to do this; *this* is what success would look like; I really don't want to see *this*.

Mentors need to be knowledgeable in the area that they are mentoring. As with teaching, while experience can be useful, it is *expertise* which is more important. People don't generally take advice and instructional messages on board if they don't understand or trust what they are being told. If they don't understand what has been said, or if they don't trust it, then they are unlikely to act upon the suggestions and advice. They certainly won't put it into practice in the way that the mentor had hoped that they would. The more expert a mentor is on the topic being discussed, the better equipped they will be to communicate clear messages and the more confidence the person being mentored will have in them.

Coaching versus mentoring

Figure 10.3 presents a summary of the differences between a coaching and a mentoring approach:

Coaching	Mentoring
• Asking questions	• Offering advice
• Listening	• Directive
• Leading people towards their own conclusions	• Suggesting or advising people on what they should do

Figure 10.3: A comparison of the differences between coaching and mentoring approaches to conversations. In reality, conversations with staff usually involve a combination of coaching and mentoring approaches, but it is always worth keeping the distinction between the two in mind. As a general rule, people with more expertise (note: not experience, which is different) tend to benefit more from coaching rather than mentoring; the opposite is true for people with less expertise.

No single approach tends to be effective on its own. Coaching conversations in the absence of any mentoring input can become frustrating and fruitless for the person being coached, especially if the conversation fails to make clear what needs to be done as a result of the conversation. Mentoring conversations in the absence of any coaching input can become frustrating for the person being mentored if they aren't given any space to think for themselves but are instead just told what to do (or not do). The balance of approach taken should be informed not only by the expertise of the person being coached or mentored, but also by how they respond to the approach being taken.

Case study: Coaching and mentoring middle leaders

As a deputy headteacher, I do a lot of coaching and mentoring. I believe that this is a key aspect of my job. I line manage nine middle leaders (eight of whom are heads of department while the other has a whole-school remit) and I meet with each of them once a fortnight for 40 minutes for a one-to-one meeting. The purpose of our meetings is to catch up and discuss departmental and whole-school issues, with a teaching and learning focus.

Our standing agenda typically covers:

1. Calendar – we look at what's coming up in the departmental and whole-school calendar over the next fortnight
2. Staff matters
3. Student matters
4. Improvement Plan (we will discuss this in Chapter 12)
5. Teaching & Learning Calendar (we will discuss this in Chapter 14)

I recognise that my day-to-day and week-to-week contact with individual teachers is limited – there are simply too many teachers in the school for me to work with meaningfully on an individual basis every day or week. This is one of the reasons why the school employs heads of department, who play a crucial middle leadership role. It is the head of department – not me – who makes contact with individual teachers in their department on a daily basis. Accordingly, it is the head of department who is in the stronger position to influence teaching and learning in classrooms. As deputy headteacher, an important part of my role is to coach and mentor middle leaders to develop their leadership, helping to ensure that their influence is making the positive impact it needs to.

Recently, as part of a one-to-one meeting, a head of department raised an issue with me that was bothering them. They had been asked by the local authority to lead a piece of work which they didn't really understand how to go about leading. What should they do?

In our meeting, we talked this through. I did some coaching, asking questions such as: 'What do you think are your options?'; 'Of these, which is the most preferable to you?' I also did some mentoring, saying things such as: 'I found myself in a similar situation once. What I ended up doing was (this). However, that didn't really work out because of (this). So, I'd caution you against doing (that).'

By meeting with this person on a fortnightly basis, I knew them well. I remembered that they had told me a few months ago about a book they had read, which I had also read. I felt that there was a solution to their problem in that book, which I mentioned. This became a light-bulb moment – they agreed: what they had read in that book did present a solution. I hadn't told this middle leader specifically what they needed to do, but I had acted as a coach and as a mentor, asking questions to explore the problem and discuss the options, offering suggestions and advice, and helping to signpost a potential way forward.

<hr>

In this chapter, we have discussed how use of a school *Lesson Evaluation Toolkit* can support high-quality lesson planning and evaluation. As part of our discussion, we touched on the idea that self-evaluation becomes most beneficial to professional learning when it is the first step in a more collaborative process, such as through discussion of a lesson with colleagues. These discussions are richest when they are with a colleague who has observed the lesson which the teacher is self-evaluating. It is to the topic of lesson observations that we will turn our attention next.

Chapter 11
Lesson observations

Lesson observations have the potential to offer invaluable professional learning to both teachers and school leaders. Through the process of watching a teacher teach, teachers and school leaders alike can develop and refine their understanding of what makes great teaching. Depending on its quality, the feedback that teachers receive from professionals who have observed them teaching can help to transform their teaching practice.

Why is it, then, that the very mention of the phrase 'lesson observation' provokes such a defensive and negative reaction from some teachers? Why is it that something which has the potential to help teachers develop and improve their teaching is viewed with such suspicion and hostility? Why is it that so many teachers see it as a threat? Why is it that when I talk to other school leaders about the importance of regular lesson observations in their school, some of them say things like, 'We can't do that – the trade unions won't allow it' or 'We're only allowed to observe teachers teach for 20 minutes at a time, and no more than 3 times a year'? These are questions we are going to explore in this chapter.

Just leave me to get on with it!

Recently, in my school, I heard a teacher with around 20 years' experience and whom we had only recently appointed say to a colleague, 'I just want them to leave me to get on with it.' The 'them' to whom they were referring were members of the school leadership team, and the specifics of what they were referring to were lesson observations. Why were they so reluctant to have someone observe a lesson?

I sat down with this teacher and we had a chat about it. What I discovered was that their experience of lesson observations in the past had been very negative. In their previous experience, school leaders had come into classrooms and formed judgements about the overall quality of teachers' teaching. If teaching was deemed to be poor, a teacher would be given negative feedback, and told that they needed to improve and that the school leader would be back to check that they had. Also, a rating was assigned to lessons; for example, 'outstanding' or 'unsatisfactory'. No wonder this teacher was wary of lesson observations. If I felt that someone coming in to observe my teaching was going to use that lesson to arrive at a judgement about my skills as a teacher, that I might receive negative feedback, or that my lesson might be assigned a negative rating, there is not a chance I would welcome this. Who in their right mind would feel comfortable about that?

Mindset

Not all teachers' experiences of lesson observations are so negative. Nevertheless, most teachers do feel at least a little nervous at the prospect of having a lesson observed by another professional. I know that I do. There is no getting away from it: when another professional is watching us teach, there is at least a small part of us which feels we are being judged. Often, our behaviour changes as a result. This relates to a scientific phenomenon called 'The Hawthorne effect'[97], which states that the awareness of being observed alters the way that people behave. For some reason, we seem to believe that this one observed lesson is going to define us as a teacher and we think that the opinion of the professional who is observing matters an awful lot more than it does. As I have said, I still find myself slipping into this mindset.

Importantly, I recognise that this is the wrong mindset. A far better, healthier mindset would be for me to see it as a positive thing that another professional is observing me teach, because they can learn something from me by doing so. I believe that there are elements of my teaching which are very good and I am keen to help improve someone else's teaching by letting them watch me teach. At the same time, I

97. https://www.sciencedirect.com/topics/computer-science/hawthorne-effect

recognise that there are elements of my teaching practice which are less strong. I also recognise that the elements which are less strong might actually be those I thought were good. Having another professional watch me teach creates an opportunity for feedback and discussion. The feedback I get from them will be based on their professional *opinion*. It is nothing more than that. When I receive it, I will think about it. I will give it serious thought and consideration. I might find myself agreeing with it or I might not, but I will certainly consider it. Either way, the opportunity to get better is not something I should fear, but welcome.

What I also recognise is that not all professional opinions have equal worth. The feedback which is likely to be most valuable to me is feedback from someone who I am confident has a good understanding of what makes great teaching. If I don't believe they have this, while I certainly won't be dismissing their opinion, I will take into account their professional knowledge and understanding when I consider it. If I find myself disagreeing with it, I might decide to invite a different professional to observe a lesson and to seek an alternative opinion.

I recognise that the nervousness and feelings of judgement that I have in relation to lesson observations, in part, come about as a result of the fact that professionals don't tend to observe me teach very often. As a result, when someone does come to observe me teach, the stakes feel higher. If I had professionals in to watch me teach more often, the stakes would feel lower, I would probably feel more comfortable about it and I would have more opportunities to learn from feedback. Other professionals would learn more from me as well. Carried out with the right ethos, lesson observations offer powerful professional learning. Anyone who doesn't embrace the opportunity to improve their teaching is, dare I say, suffering from the very teaching delusion we are trying to address.

Professional learning

A focus on professional learning is the key to successful lesson observations, both in terms of how they are perceived by teachers and in terms of their impact on teaching practice. Conducted in the spirit of professional learning, lesson observations should come to be welcomed by teachers. Teachers should want their lessons to be observed regularly. They should feel disappointed and frustrated if they haven't received feedback from a lesson observation. How are teachers supposed to improve the quality of teaching in their classrooms if they don't receive feedback?

Using golf as an analogy, the world's top 100 golfers all have swing coaches. The swing is the fundamental aspect of the golfing game – scores are made as a result of a golfer's swing at a ball. It doesn't matter how experienced the professional golfer is; it doesn't matter how good their game currently is – they could be the world number one and have won their last six tournaments; they will still be working with a swing coach (someone who knows what they are talking about and who provides them with high-quality feedback) week by week.

Use of the coach isn't their only means of evaluating their performance – their scores help with that, just as student test scores can help a teacher with their self-evaluation of their teaching. But a professional golfer can have a bad score, having played well, and a good score, having not played well. The score in itself isn't enough to evaluate the quality of their swing. Feedback from their coach is key.

It is imperative that school leaders and teachers carry out lesson observations with an understanding that, first and foremost, they are about professional learning. Conducted in this way, lessons observed can be used to:

1. Provide **feedback** to teachers
2. Support teacher **self-evaluation**
3. Support the **sharing of practice** among teachers
4. Support **improvement planning** at teacher, department and whole-school levels

Without lesson observations, and without lesson observations carried out in the spirit of professional learning, a school cannot claim to have developed a professional learning culture. Without a professional learning culture, there cannot be a culture of improvement. Schools that don't make use of lesson observations, or in which lesson observations are used exclusively for the purposes of quality assurance, are not *learning schools*: they are static schools. Schools do need to measure, but they also need to move. Moving is more important than measuring. Accordingly, professional learning is more important than quality assurance.

All of this said, while research suggests that lesson observations offer a potentially powerful means by which to improve teaching quality in a school[98], it also suggests that, used poorly, they won't have much impact. Indeed, they may have a negative impact on mindsets and climate which, as we discussed in Chapter 7, influence the strength of a school's professional learning culture. In the next section, we will explore why this might be.

Why lesson observations often fail to make a difference

Lesson observations often fail to impact on teaching practice for four reasons:

1. The feedback given to teachers is poor
2. There is no feedback given to teachers
3. The person giving the feedback isn't confident about delivering it
4. Nothing is done with the feedback given

We will explore each of these in turn.

The feedback given to teachers is poor

It is assumed that school leaders who observe lessons will have a clear idea about what makes a typical high-quality lesson. But do they? And if they do, would two school leaders working in the same school share the same views?

As we discussed in Chapter 1, the answer to both of these questions is a resounding no. What follows is a selection of comments I have heard school leaders, including headteachers, make in relation to lesson observations:

- 'I don't know what good teaching looks like.'
- 'I never know what I am looking for in lessons.'
- 'I don't observe lessons because I already know that teaching in my school is very good.'

---

98. Coe, R. *et al.* (2014) *What Makes Great Teaching?*

- 'I don't observe the good teachers – they should just be left to get on with it.'
- 'It's not my job to tell teachers how they should be teaching.'
- 'I don't have time to do lesson observations.'
- 'I don't believe that doing lesson observations makes any difference to teaching and learning.'

As a result, many school leaders simply don't 'do' lesson observations.

Fortunately, there are many who do. However, without being clear about what makes great teaching and what they are looking for in lessons, school leaders can't be clear in the feedback they are giving to teachers. School leaders who aren't clear about what makes great teaching are those who aren't doing much reading, aren't in classrooms very often and aren't taking the opportunity to engage in professional discussion with teachers. As a result, they have weak frameworks from which to draw upon when observing lessons, because their understanding of what makes great teaching is limited. What they believe makes great teaching typically relates to how they themselves would teach. I have had conversations with teachers whose teaching has been observed by such school leaders, who have reported that the feedback they received was 'a load of rubbish', that they 'didn't agree with any of it' and that 'it was just waffle'.

Thankfully, there are many school leaders who are clear about what great teaching looks like and, as a result, have a clear idea about the pedagogy they are looking for in lessons. Even if they aren't teaching themselves, the best school leaders are present in classrooms a lot, working constructively and supportively with teachers. They keep their professional knowledge up to date through regular reading and discussion. In this way, although they might not be teaching themselves, they do have a very good understanding of what they are talking about and, as a result, the feedback they give to teachers is perceptive, constructive and useful.

Your school's *Lesson Evaluation Toolkit* can support school leaders to give consistent, high-quality feedback to teachers, regardless of who is observing the lesson and the subject being taught. Whether it is a lesson in PE, maths, geography or science, observed by the headteacher, deputy headteacher, head of department, principal teacher or a school leader from another school, use of your *Lesson Evaluation Toolkit* will focus feedback on specific features of pedagogy. No longer will you have feedback which says, 'Be more creative in delivery, e.g. use games' (which is an example of what we saw given in Chapter 1), unless your *Lesson Evaluation Toolkit* highlights this as a key pedagogical feature of lessons (which I hope it won't).

Before we move on, it would be worth repeating a crucial point from Chapter 8: **your *Lesson Evaluation Toolkit* should not be used as a tick-list in the lesson observation process.** Instead, it should function as an *aide-mémoire*, reminding the teacher and the observer of the typical pedagogical features of a high-quality lesson. In doing so, it will support post-lesson discussion and feedback.

There is no feedback given to teachers

Why would any school leader observe a lesson and not give feedback? I will suggest two reasons, neither of which is good.

One might be that they don't feel they have time. At the very least, this is discourteous. The second might be that they don't think that giving feedback is important. If this is the case, they are failing to appreciate the crucial role of lesson observations in professional learning. I actually believe that giving feedback to teachers about teaching practice is one of the most important things that school leaders can do with their time. School leaders need to make time to give feedback to teachers and to treat this as a priority. What else is more deserving of a school leader's time than a conversation with teachers about pedagogy? If school leaders aren't going to do this, then who is? And if it is decided that someone else could do it (perhaps other teachers via Peer Observation Programmes), then how are school leaders going to ensure that this feedback is high quality?

In schools with strong professional learning cultures, time is protected for school leader lesson observations and for having feedback conversations soon after. School leaders see it as a priority to provide teachers with high-quality feedback. While they understand the important role that lesson observations play in the school's quality assurance procedures, they also understand that, first and foremost, lesson observations are about supporting professional learning.

The person giving the feedback isn't confident about delivering it
Surely all school leaders are confident in delivering feedback on observed lessons to teachers? Surely they have all had training on how to do this? Surely you can't become a school leader unless you are qualified in giving feedback? None of these is necessarily true.

Giving effective feedback isn't easy. In fact, I would argue that it can be one of the most difficult jobs a school leader has to do. As has already been discussed, a prerequisite to giving effective feedback is being clear about what you are giving feedback on, which a *Lesson Evaluation Toolkit* supports. But assuming that you are clear about this, how do you go about giving feedback?

Knowing your staff well
A key principle relates to knowing your staff well. The manner in which you deliver feedback to a particular teacher may be very different from the manner in which you deliver it to another. This will depend on various factors, such as their personality, experience and the quality of your relationship with them.

Some teachers will appreciate being invited to a school leader's office to receive feedback, perhaps because they value time out of their classroom and they feel that doing so formalises the process, which they like; others will feel intimidated by this and would much prefer to receive feedback in the more familiar environment of their own classroom. Some teachers will respond very well to praise; some will feel embarrassed by it. Some teachers will respond well to constructive criticism and will welcome it; others will become upset by it, even if the school leader believes that it is light touch. Some teachers will want to spend 30 minutes discussing feedback together; others will take more from the process if it is limited to 10 minutes. Some teachers will respond well to coaching approaches (in which you ask good questions, listen and guide the teacher to their own conclusions), while others will prefer, or may need, more of a mentoring style (in which you offer suggestions and advice, which is more directive than coaching).

Clumsy feedback
There is no single 'right way' to give feedback, but there are lots of wrong ways to do it. The more lessons a school leader observes, the more

confident they should become in delivering feedback. They will have a greater wealth of experience from which to draw upon and, assuming that they are giving feedback after each lesson they observe, they will have had more practice at delivering it.

However, even the most experienced school leader can slip up when giving feedback. One clumsy word, or taking the wrong tone, can lead to feedback which was intended to be supportive being received negatively. This can lead to upset and resentment. Knowing your staff well can go a long way to mitigate this, as can being prepared. Taking time to plan the things you want to say in advance of the meeting, including how you intend to put your points across, is generally time well spent. As with effective teaching, giving effective feedback relies on careful planning. Your school *Lesson Evaluation Toolkit* can help you to be clear about the specifics of what you would like to say.

Reading body language and visual cues from the person you are giving the feedback to is also important. Depending on what you are seeing and hearing, you may need to adapt your approach.

Be focused

As is the case when giving feedback to students, it is generally best to start with some positives. Most people don't mind how many positives you highlight to them, but most do have a limit to the number of negatives they are willing or able to receive. Therefore, if there are areas you would like to highlight as focal points for improvement – and there should be, otherwise you are not operating with a mindset of continuous improvement – you should be clear about what these are in advance of the meeting, and stick to these. Resist the temptation to bring up every area which could be improved – in theory, every area could be improved. Instead, stick to the one or two which you believe are the most important.

'Talk me through your self-evaluation'

A *Lesson Evaluation Toolkit* can help school leaders to prepare their feedback in advance, but it also has the power to help facilitate discussion about the lesson, which is often the most useful part of any feedback meeting. Contrast the meeting in which the school leader says: 'Well I thought you did "this" and "this" very well, but I would like you to focus on developing "this"' with the one in which the school leader first invites the teacher to talk through their self-evaluation of the lesson, which the teacher has completed using the *Lesson Evaluation Toolkit*, before the feedback meeting takes place.

If the teacher has completed their self-evaluation and sent a copy of this to the observer in advance of the meeting, then the observer can get an indication of what the teacher thought about their lesson before going into a meeting to discuss feedback. This can influence the way feedback is given. If the teacher has used an evaluative system such as green/amber/red and has self-evaluated with lots of 'green' and 'amber' – and the school leader has evaluated the lesson in a similar way – then this will lead to a particular sort of conversation. However, if the teacher has self-evaluated with lots of 'green' and 'amber' – but the school leader has evaluated the lesson with a lot of 'red' – then this will lead to a different sort of conversation.

Regardless of whether the school leader receives a completed self-evaluation from the teacher or not in advance of the feedback meeting, an important phase of this meeting is the beginning, when the school leader should ask the teacher to talk through their self-evaluation. Often, a teacher will then ask, 'How would you like me to do that?', to which the best answer usually is: 'It's up to you.' The teacher could go through the lesson sequentially according to the different elements of the *Lesson Evaluation Toolkit*, or they could go through it chronologically, discussing the different phases of the lesson as it was taught. Alternatively, they could go through the pedagogy which they self-evaluated as 'green', 'amber' or 'red'.

The discussion during the meeting should be guided by the *Lesson Evaluation Toolkit*. If this highlights 'guided practice' and 'independent practice' as typical features of high-quality lessons, you can imagine a conversation going along these lines:

Teacher: 'I thought that the opportunities for practice were good in this lesson. Students engaged well with these.'

Observer: 'That's good. Was the focus more on guided practice or independent practice?'

Teacher: 'It was independent practice in this lesson. But actually, I think there might have been some benefit in spending more time on guided practice, with a few more examples, because I was picking up on a few students making the same mistake as I walked around the room.'

Without a *Lesson Evaluation Toolkit* which sets out 'practice' as a key element of lessons, practice may or may not be discussed in the feedback meeting. **Use of the *Lesson Evaluation Toolkit* ensures that it is discussed.**

Nothing is done with any feedback which is given

Regardless of the quality of feedback a teacher receives from an observed lesson, its impact on teaching practice will be limited or non-existent if the teacher doesn't do anything with this. They could have accepted it, valued it, and agreed with it, but the logical next step is for something to happen with it. This requires both planning and practice. In the next chapter, we will return to this when we discuss teacher Professional Learning Plans.

The lesson observation process

Having explored a variety of reasons why lesson observations can fail to make an impact on teaching practice, we will now go on to explore good practice in terms of the lesson observation process.

Setting up a lesson observation

In setting up a lesson observation, school leaders must conduct themselves in a way which shows professional respect to the teacher whose lesson they plan to observe. As previously discussed, for a variety of reasons teachers will often feel anxious about being observed teaching. Some may not wish to be observed teaching at all. However, as also discussed, regular lesson observations which are followed up with high-quality feedback discussions are an integral feature of a school's professional learning culture. *All* teachers and school leaders need to be involved with these. It is not okay for any teacher in a school to 'opt out' of lesson observations, or to be 'just left to get on with it'. The lesson observation process is too important.

It is good practice for a school leader to give the teacher whose lesson they will be observing advance notice that they would like to observe it, and to check this will be okay. In my experience, the vast majority of teachers will say yes. If a teacher does express unhappiness about a lesson being observed, arrange to sit down with them and have a chat about it. Explain why you would like to observe the lesson, give them choice over which lesson you will observe, and generally go about putting them at ease. A key message for you to get across is that the observation will be about supporting professional learning and continuous improvement, not about finding fault.

Case study: Resistance to lesson observations

In one school I started work in as a deputy headteacher, lesson observations hadn't been happening for some time and there was a culture of 'us' and 'them' – the 'us' being teachers and the 'them' being senior school leaders. There was real suspicion when, within my first few weeks of starting, word got around that I was starting to set up lesson observations. However, in partnership with my senior leadership team colleagues, during my first three months in the school we managed to observe over 40 lessons, taking a department-by-department approach, and taking time to meet with every teacher to discuss teaching and learning soon after the lesson. Feedback from teachers was that they valued the process and did not find it threatening. Most said it was refreshing that school leaders were taking time to watch what was going on in classrooms and spend time talking with teachers about teaching and learning.

In my fourth month in the school, I planned to observe lessons in the science department. I got in touch with the head of department about this, who expressed in no uncertain terms that 'we' (i.e. members of the senior leadership team) had 'no right' to be doing this. I asked him for a meeting to discuss the matter, to which he agreed. Over a coffee, I asked him why he was unhappy about the prospect of lessons being observed in his department. He began by quoting sections from trade union guidelines, saying things like, 'School leaders are not allowed to observe any teacher more than once a year.' This told me a lot about this teacher's perceptions regarding the purpose of lesson observations. In his mind, lesson observations were about quality assurance and judgement. He was anticipating that the process would be a negative experience. There was an element of insecurity and one of wanting to protect his team. He wasn't going to let senior leaders come in and spy on the work of his teachers, or to tell them that they weren't doing their job well enough.

By the end of our meeting, his mindset had changed. By taking time to listen carefully to his concerns and not dismissing them, I was able to discuss these with him. Being clear in my own mind that the purpose of lesson observations is to support teachers through feedback and professional discussion, I was able to get him to understand this point. I talked him through how we would go about setting up the observations, that teachers would have a choice about which lesson someone would observe, and what would happen after the observation – teachers would complete a structured self-evaluation using the *Lesson Evaluation Toolkit* and there would be a meeting to discuss this soon after the lesson. Following this conversation, he said that he was happy for the observations to go ahead, which they did, and teacher feedback about the process was very positive. Regular lesson observations are now standard practice in this department.

Agreeing a focus

At the same time as agreeing a date for a lesson observation to take place, there can be value in agreeing a focus for the observation. My view is that lesson observations present an opportunity for lessons to be evaluated against each of the elements of a school's *Lesson Evaluation Toolkit*. That said, there can be value in a teacher identifying, in advance, specific pedagogy which they would like the school leader to focus on in particular, or in the school leader identifying this specific pedagogy.

There is usually value in the teacher sharing a lesson plan with the school leader in advance. While not essential, it can be useful to compare what was planned with what was delivered. This can help identify and subsequently explore the adaptability of the teacher in light of the requirements of the class, and the reasons why some things may have been omitted.

During the observation

Different people have different opinions as to how an observer should conduct themselves during a lesson observation. My own view is that the observer should be as unobtrusive as possible and that their presence should not affect the teaching and learning of the lesson. If you hadn't been there, the teaching and learning would have been the same. Once, when I was observing a lesson with another colleague from a different school, I witnessed my co-observer conducting themselves in a way I found wholly inappropriate. They rummaged around in trays, scrutinised jotters and asked students leading questions, all of which gave the impression that they were looking to find fault. They had the wrong mindset.

Ideally, the observer will arrive at the classroom before the lesson starts and ask the teacher if they have a preference for where they would like them to sit. If they can't get to the lesson before it starts, my recommendation is that the observer enters the room quickly and quietly, drawing minimal attention to themselves. A smile to the teacher and class, or perhaps a quiet 'Hello' is appropriate, courteous and a nice touch.

The observer should bring a copy of the school *Lesson Evaluation Toolkit* with them, some blank paper (in case they end up writing more than they can fit in the 'notes' section of the *Lesson Evaluation Toolkit*) and something to write with. In a lesson where there is unlikely to be a desk to lean on (perhaps a PE lesson), it is generally a good idea to bring a hardback notebook, but clipboards should be avoided – they bring with them too many connotations of the old-fashioned tick-sheet approaches which we are trying to move away from.

If I am observing a lesson, I typically position myself behind students at the back of the room, so that they are not looking at me. Instead, they are focusing on the teacher, their peers or their own work. I try to listen and watch as much as I can, but I always write notes. I don't trust my memory about what I've been seeing and hearing – if I don't write it down, there will be important things that I forget.

As a general rule, I don't write down anything that I wouldn't be happy for the teacher to read if they wanted. I think this is important, because it helps create a climate of trust. Generally, though, nobody ever asks to see what I have written down. Instead, the feedback meeting is used to discuss this.

Professional learning for observers

Lesson observations should be hard work for the observer, because the *Lesson Evaluation Toolkit* should be making them really think. Really, **the person observing the lesson should be working as hard – if not harder – than the teacher**. As we have already discussed, learning happens when people have to think hard, and lesson observations offer opportunities for excellent professional learning, as much for the observer as for the teacher teaching the lesson.

During the observation, the observer should be referring to the *Lesson Evaluation Toolkit* constantly and thinking critically against it. In their head, they are asking themselves questions like:

- Am I seeing this?
- If I am seeing this, *how good* is this?
- Why do I think that?
- Could this be better?
- How could this be better?
- Could this have been done any differently and, if it could, would this have made it any better (or would it just have been different)?
- How does this compare to how I have seen other teachers do this?
- Is there another teacher in the school who I think could help the observed teacher develop this?
- Is this practice which is worth sharing with others?
- If I'm not seeing this, should I be, or might it not be relevant to this lesson?

With every lesson a school leader observes, through critical reflection against the *Lesson Evaluation Toolkit* they should have developed and refined their understanding of what makes great teaching. The more lessons they observe, the more developed and refined this understanding will become.

Once the lesson is finished, I thank the teacher for letting me watch their lesson and I ask them to complete a self-evaluation using the school *Lesson Evaluation Toolkit*. I ask them when would be a good time to meet to discuss the lesson, and to email a completed copy of their self-evaluation to me in advance.

Soon after the lesson, I devote around 15 minutes to reading through my notes, which I use to help me complete a green/amber/red evaluation of the *Lesson Evaluation Toolkit* elements. I do this by writing 'G', 'A' or 'R' next to each element, or I use highlighter pens. I recognise that these simply reflect my *impressions* – they are not absolute measures of quality. But they do give me a simple and very useful visual summary of my evaluation of the quality of pedagogy. In doing this, **I am not making an overarching judgement about the quality of this teacher's teaching**. Rather, I am *evaluating the pedagogy of this particular lesson* – as a snapshot of practice – on which I hope to base the supportive feedback I will offer.

The feedback meeting

In the meeting to discuss the lesson, I will ask the teacher to talk me through their completed self-evaluation. As we discuss this, I will usually refer to the notes I wrote during the lesson. However, I am very unlikely to share my completed *Lesson Evaluation Toolkit* (with my green/amber/red evaluations) with the teacher at any stage, including in the feedback meeting, unless they ask me to. The *Lesson Evaluation Toolkit* helped me to reflect on the pedagogy of the lesson and structure my thoughts. However, there is little value in getting hung up about whether I evaluated a particular element as 'green', 'amber' or 'red' – a discussion of this is not the purpose of this meeting. Rather, the purpose of the meeting is to discuss *pedagogy*.

If I felt the lesson was a poor one (perhaps I have evaluated all or most of the *Lesson Evaluation Toolkit* elements as 'red'), I am unlikely to bring this to the teacher's attention. What would be achieved by doing that? Rather, in having prepared for this meeting – ideally, with a copy of the teacher's completed self-evaluation to hand – I will have planned what, *specifically*, I would like to discuss. If they ask me directly which elements I evaluated as green/amber/red, I will, of course, tell them. However, teachers almost never ask me to do that and there is little point in doing so. The green/amber/reds, in themselves, mean very little. It is the thinking which underpins them that is most important.

If I felt the lesson was a very strong one (perhaps I have evaluated all or most of the elements as 'green'), I will still offer some suggestions as to what I think could be improved further. If I don't, this gives the impression that the teacher has reached an end point, that their teaching is so good that it can't be improved. But of course it can – it always can – and it should. Offering suggestions about *what* and *how* to improve further are important. Often, it's not necessary that I make suggestions, because through their self-evaluation and the discussion we have using a coaching approach, the teacher reaches their own conclusions, which, generally, I will agree with.

Written feedback

Just as there can be value in giving students written feedback, so too can there be value in giving written feedback to teachers. While written feedback is not essential, many teachers value receiving it. If you don't do this as a matter of routine, it is generally good practice to ask the teacher if they would like feedback in writing.

An advantage of writing feedback is that it keeps a record, which can be referred to in the future by the teacher and the school leader. Because they will be carrying out a lot a lesson observations, it can be helpful for school leaders to have written feedback to refer to the next time they go in to observe a lesson that this teacher is teaching. Keeping a written record also helps remove ambiguity over what was said.

If the person observing a lesson was the headteacher or a deputy headteacher, producing a written record of feedback means that it can be easily shared with the teacher's head of department or year, who should be kept in the loop.

Use of a Lesson Evaluation Toolkit to support written feedback

Use of your school *Lesson Evaluation Toolkit* can help to create a degree of consistency in the feedback given to teachers following an observed lesson. Figure 11.1 provides an illustrative feedback *pro forma*.

Elements of teaching practice which I thought were strongest:	Elements of teaching practice which I suggest you focus on improving (in the spirit of continuous improvement):
Relationships	Plenary
Teacher-student relationships were excellent. This meant that the ethos in the room was perfect for learning. You clearly know each student very well.	Consider how the final minutes of lessons can be used to:
Learning intentions and success criteria	• Summarise key teaching/ learning points
The learning intention and success criteria were clearly communicated and frequently referred back to. The What/How/Why? prompt on the whiteboard really helped you to make the success criteria clear. Your modelling on the whiteboard was exemplary.	• Evaluate the success of the lesson in terms of what students have learned. Use of 'Exit Tickets' would really support this.
Making students think and checking for understanding	
You used questioning very effectively to engage students and check their understanding, including very effective use of Show-me boards. You made good use of 'chat to a partner' moments, which helped to engage everyone in learning during questioning. Use of a 'deliberate mistakes' exercise was also an effective way to critically engage students.	
Challenge and support	
The self- and peer-assessment activity was well designed. I particularly liked the idea of getting students to use different coloured pens depending on what stage of the activity they were completing. You had a nice phrase here: 'This is about looking at your work as an editor would.'	

Suggested professional learning activities to support continuous improvement: Could include: 1. Reading 2. Observing others 3. Others observing you 4. Discussions with colleagues 5. Practising specific things Try to <u>be specific</u>, e.g. **What** should you read? **Who** should you observe?	I would like you to work with (teacher A) to develop effective plenaries. This should include you asking them to observe you teach and offer you feedback. I would like you to observe some other teachers in the school, with a specific focus on lesson plenaries. Teachers with strong practice in this area include: • Teacher B • Teacher C • Teacher D
Follow-up When will we follow up on this?	I would like to observe a lesson again in roughly one month's time. Please set a date and invite me back.

Figure 11.1: An example of a completed observation feedback pro forma. The comments being made in the top two boxes link to specific elements of the school's Lesson Evaluation Toolkit.

In this example, the teacher is given feedback relating to lesson *strengths* and *suggested improvement areas*. Crucially, the feedback has been written so that it links clearly to specific elements of the school's *Lesson Evaluation Toolkit*.

The *pro forma* also includes a section which suggests specific professional learning activities which could support the teacher to improve. Finally, it includes a section relating to follow-up.

Follow-up

As we have already discussed, there is little point in giving feedback to a teacher if they don't act on it. In all likelihood, acting on feedback will require them to do something in a different way, which will require practice. In my experience, too often teachers are left to get on with this on their own, with no follow-up feedback. Often, a year or more can pass before another professional observes them teach again. Revisting a sporting analogy, no professional sportsperson would work in this way. Instead, in the interests of becoming the very best that they can, they demand *continuous feedback*. If we are serious about a continuous improvement agenda in schools, teachers require high-quality, *continuous* feedback as well.

Summary of the effective lesson observation process

Figure 11.2 summarises the key messages from our discussion of the effective lesson observation process.

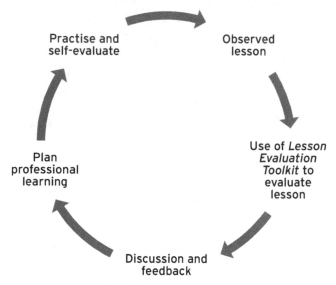

Figure 11.2: The effective lesson observation process.

Joint lesson observations

In our discussion up to this point, we have assumed that lessons are being observed by one person. In 'joint lesson observations', more than one person observes the same lesson. This has two advantages over just one person observing:

1. It 'upskills' the professionals who are observing
2. It leads to improved feedback to teachers

By observing lessons together and discussing pedagogy afterwards, teachers and school leaders can learn from each other, developing their understanding of what makes great teaching. This is excellent professional learning. As a result, they are better equipped to give higher-quality feedback to teachers whose lessons they observe. Rather than the feedback being based on the impressions of one professional, it is based on two. By doing so, schools can move away from the scenario in which, if one person observes, you get particular feedback, but if a different person observes, you get different feedback. Instead, the feedback teachers receive from lesson observations is much more consistent and accurate. As a result, it will be much more valued.

Whenever I observe a lesson in school, as far as possible I do this jointly, with a middle or senior leader. Every time I do, through our discussions afterwards I end up thinking about the pedagogy of the lesson differently from how I would have had I just observed the lesson myself. I believe the same to be true of the other observer. In this way, we develop our understanding of what makes great teaching.

Because some teachers can be reluctant to have even one person observe a lesson, it is important that you have a conversation with teachers to explain why you would like two people to observe. If a teacher indicates that they aren't comfortable with this, I would encourage you to respect their wishes. The chances are that, as they hear about this working successfully in other teachers' classrooms, they will buy into such an approach.

Following a jointly observed lesson, the observers should meet to discuss it. They should use their completed *Lesson Evaluation Toolkits* to guide their discussion, comparing green/amber/red evaluations and notes. They should ask each other questions such as, 'Why did you evaluate that as "green"?' and then have a discussion about this. In doing so, each can learn from the other.

It is not necessary for both observers to give feedback. So long as there has been a meeting between the two to discuss the lesson, either one should be able to discuss the agreed feedback with the teacher.

Peer Observation Programmes

Teachers should take advantage of every opportunity to observe and learn from other teachers. Because the perfect teacher does not exist, every teacher has something to learn and improve in their teaching. An essential part of this learning is watching other teachers teach.

How often should teachers be doing this? This is a question for school leaders and teachers to answer themselves. Once a week? Once a month? Once a term? Once a year? There are some schools in which it is expected and has become the norm that teachers will use at least one of the non-teaching periods they have in any week to observe another teacher. This requires a significant investment, but it is time well spent. The professional learning culture in such schools is a strong one.

Professional learning from peer observation
It is one thing to get teachers to observe other teachers; it is quite another to maximise the learning which comes from this. To achieve this, you first need to understand that there are two types of learning which come from lesson observations:

1. The learning of the teacher *teaching the lesson* – from discussion and feedback afterwards
2. The learning of the teacher *observing the lesson* – from what they are seeing in the lesson

Establishing and co-ordinating a Peer Observation Programme
Let's assume you have created a culture in which teachers *want* to be observed by other teachers. They don't feel threatened by this and actually welcome it. How can a whole-school Peer Observation Programme be established and co-ordinated? How do you get the ball rolling?

Start with why
In Chapter 8, we emphasised the importance of starting with *why*. If you are to get people on board with any new initiative, they have to understand why you are asking them to do so. If they don't understand why, they are far less likely to do it, or they view it as just another 'thing we have to do'.

So why are you asking teachers to observe each other teaching? There are a number of reasons, which include:

- Because our school is committed to *the continuous improvement of teaching and learning*. No matter how good the quality of teaching is in our school already, we are determined to make it even better.

- Because peer observation offers *excellent professional learning.* Many teachers report that they learn more from observing 50 minutes of another teacher's lesson than they do from attending full-day courses. Peer observations help teachers to observe theory in practice. They will help you to broaden your horizons and think about pedagogy in ways that you might never have considered yourself. Peer observation is all about teachers learning with and from other teachers. It is about the principle 'we are better learning together' than we are learning on our own.

Use a calendar

Because schools are incredibly busy places, with the best will in the world, professional learning initiatives such as Peer Observation Programmes sometimes get nudged to one side and don't end up happening. One strategy to help avoid this is to include 'Peer Observation Weeks' or 'Peer Observation Fortnights' in the whole-school calendar. Doing so helps to establish the importance of peer observation and an expectation that it will take place, as a minimum, at identified points. As teachers get more and more used to watching other teachers teach and having other teachers in their lessons to watch them teach, there is a strong chance they will start to initiate their own peer observations more often.

Use your Teaching and Learning Improvement Group

As we discussed in Chapter 8, your school Teaching and Learning Improvement Group should play a key strategic role in planning, co-ordinating and evaluating your in-school professional learning programme. Key questions for this group to consider might include:

1. How many Peer Observation Weeks or Fortnights should there be in the year?

2. When should Peer Observation Weeks or Fortnights take place?

3. How will teachers pair up during these? Should they do this themselves or should pairing up be co-ordinated?

4. Should teachers work in pairs or threes (that is, should two teachers observe lessons together rather than one)?

5. How can learning from peer observation be shared more widely (that is, beyond the observers)?

Professional learning – not quality assurance

As you set up your school Peer Observation Programme, it is important that you make clear what peer observation is about – professional learning – and what it is not about, which is quality assurance. Peer observation is about *learning from each other*, not *checking up on each other*. Peer observation is not about getting teachers to go into other teachers' lessons and evaluate quality. Sadly, I know of schools who have misunderstood this. The result has been to fuel resentment and disengagement. No learning comes from peer observation carried out in this way.

In considering the type of discussion that teachers have following a peer observed lesson, I present two examples:

Example 1:

Teacher 1: 'I really enjoyed watching your lesson. Thank you for having me in.'

Teacher 2: 'Thank you. I hope you thought it was okay.'

Teacher 1: 'Absolutely. I thought it was a great lesson.'

Teacher 2: 'Was there anything that you think I could improve?'

Teacher 1: 'No. I thought it was great.'

Teacher 2: 'Did you learn anything from watching it?'

Teacher 1: 'Oh yes, lots. Thanks again.'

Example 2:

Teacher 1: 'I really enjoyed watching your lesson. Thank you for having me in.'

Teacher 2: 'Thank you. Could we discuss what you thought were the strongest elements of the lesson and any elements that you thought could be improved?'

Teacher 1: 'Absolutely. Well, we'd agreed that I was going to focus on the "Making students think & checking for understanding" element of our *Lesson Evaluation Toolkit*.'

Both teachers are now referring to the *Lesson Evaluation Toolkit*.

Teacher 1: 'I thought you used "thinking time" really well. Whenever I ask questions in my lessons, I'm too quick to choose a student to answer and I'm not giving everyone else a chance to think about it. I really liked how you did that and I'm going to try and do that more myself. I'd heard people talk about thinking time before, but until I saw you using it, I hadn't really appreciated how it works in lessons.'

Teacher 2: 'Thank you. That's really useful feedback. Thinking time is something I've been working hard to get better at. Do you have any feedback about anything you think could improve my questioning technique further?'

Teacher 1: 'I think that you could probably try to ask more questions than you do. Over the lesson as a whole, you asked four or five, and you were really engaging students in thinking when you were doing that. I think there might be scope for you to do more of that.'

Teacher 2: 'That's really helpful. I am conscious of that but sometimes I'm just in such a hurry to get through everything that I stop asking questions, so to get feedback like that is really useful. I'll start to practise doing that. Would you mind coming back to observe in a few weeks' time as a follow-up?'

Teacher 1: 'I'd be delighted to.'

In a *learning school*, the aim is to move teachers away from the type of discussion exemplified in Example 1 and towards that in Example 2. Use of the school's *Lesson Evaluation Toolkit* helps to do that.

Sharing practice

Peer observations offer a powerful way to 'open the black box' of the classroom[99]. If teachers share practice they have observed with other teachers, this serves the twin purposes of supporting other teachers to learn and giving the teacher whose lesson they observed a metaphorical pat on the back.

---

99. Cole, P. (2012) *Aligning Professional Learning, Performance Management and Effective Teaching*

It should be the job of the school's Teaching and Learning Improvement Group to plan, co-ordinate and evaluate methods to share practice across the school. We will use a case study to consider how this could be done.

Case study: Sharing practice

An idea which came out of the Teaching and Learning Improvement Group in my school was to set up two '**sharing practice noticeboards**' in the staffroom. The staffroom was chosen because this is an area staff go to every day, often several times a day.

Noticeboard 1 is called our 'Post-its board'. On this, there are 13 A3 sheets of paper, each representing one of the 13 elements of our school *Lesson Evaluation Toolkit*. Each has a heading (such as 'Daily Review', 'Learning intentions', 'Making students think & checking for understanding') and a large blank area. Following a peer observed lesson, teachers are asked to make a record on a Post-it note of practice they feel is worth sharing with other teachers and to stick this onto the relevant sheet on the board. Doing so supports teachers to see where there is practice taking place which could support their professional learning. For example, if a teacher has identified 'learning intentions' as an area to focus on improving, they can look at this board and read about practice which has been identified by other teachers as worth sharing. This might prompt them to have a conversation with the teacher whose practice has been highlighted, or to observe that teacher teaching.

Noticeboard 2 is for staff to share photos and examples of work. For example, if someone has observed a lesson in which Daily Review was very strong and in which there was a PowerPoint slide relating to Daily Review, they might take a photo of this, print it out and stick it on the board. Alternatively, they might ask the teacher to email the presentation to them and print the slide directly off that. Either way, the good practice that was taking place in this lesson is being made visible to other staff.

There is always a danger that initiatives of this kind get off to a good start and then stall. In the case of the noticeboards described, these might be created and populated, but then sit dormant, with nothing new being added to them. As a result, staff will stop looking at them. While initially they acted as powerful resources to support professional learning, through lack of maintenance they become little more than wallpaper. A key duty of the Teaching and Learning Improvement Group is to ensure this does not happen.

Another sharing practice strategy has been to create a **Teaching and Learning Website** using an online platform such as WordPress. A member of the Teaching and Learning Improvement Group has been assigned responsibility for updating and maintaining this site. The posts they add to it relate to practice from both within and outwith the school. They add a new post once a week and draw staff attention to this via email and at our weekly staff meeting. It is important that staff attention is drawn to the website on a regular basis, otherwise they can forget about it. Doing so by email and via staff meetings is a useful 'belt and braces' approach.

Whenever they add a post, they 'categorise' it. A category is really a label which helps to identify the post. Because there are hundreds of posts, categories help staff find what they are looking for. The categories that we assign to posts are named after the elements of our *Lesson Evaluation Toolkit* (such as 'Plenaries' and 'Feedback'). Because there are 13 elements, there are 13 categories. If a member of staff wants to develop their practice in relation to a particular element, they can go to our Teaching & Learning Website and 'filter' by a particular category. At a click, they can access all of the posts which relate to this element.

Having a single member of staff as the 'gatekeeper' for this website is important. Without this, there is a danger that staff won't make use of the website because:

1. They get swamped by too many posts being added in too short a space of time (the result of which is that they don't read any of them)

2. The quality of posts falls short of minimum standards (the result of which is that they don't read any of them)

Sharing practice noticeboards and a **Teaching and Learning Website** are two examples of how teaching practice might be shared across a school. Systems of this kind empower teachers to lead their own professional learning and to learn from colleagues.

The purpose of this chapter was to emphasise the key role that lesson observations can and should play in the professional learning culture of schools. One of the roles of lesson observations is to give teachers feedback to help them improve. It is to the theme of improvement and, specifically, improvement planning that we will turn in our next chapter.

Chapter 12
Improvement planning

In schools with strong professional learning cultures, planning for improvement is never-ending. The mindset is: no matter how good standards are already, they can always be better. That said, without due care, improvement planning has the potential to swamp a school and smother it. If you try to improve too many things at any one time, the likelihood is that you won't improve anything, certainly not to any significant extent. **Proportionate, streamlined improvement planning** is the order of the day.

Streamlining

To streamline improvement planning, school leaders need to have a clear idea of what it is their school is trying to achieve. That is, they need to know their **vision** and their **objectives**. Vision is about the big picture; objectives relate to more specific goals.

The number of objectives which a school can realistically focus on achieving is directly linked to how many members of staff a school has working in it. Regardless of the size of your school, school leaders need to keep in mind that the more objectives you have, the less focused your improvement agenda will become. Breadth is the enemy of depth. A small number of carefully aligned objectives usually makes for the most effective improvement planning.

Objective-strategy-tactics

In *Leadership Matters*[100], Andy Buck highlights what, to me, is a very useful model by which to think about improvement planning: **objective–strategy tactics**. He uses the example of the Labour party in the 1990s to illustrate what is meant by each component: the *objective* was to get elected; the *strategy* was to focus on the concept of 'New Labour'; the *tactics* were varied and numerous (such as referring to 'New Labour' whenever possible in interviews), but they were always aligned with the strategy.

As I have already argued, a core objective of all schools should be to continuously improve the quality of teaching across the school. Using the objective–strategy–tactics model, the components of an Improvement Plan could look as follows:

Objective	Strategy	Tactics
Continuously improve teaching quality	1. Develop a shared understanding of what makes great teaching 2. Develop a strong professional learning culture	• Establish a Teaching and Learning Improvement Group • Create a school *Lesson Evaluation Toolkit* • Establish a Professional Reading Group • Introduce a Peer Observation Programme • Improve the quality of our senior leader lesson observation programme • Set up a teacher-led workshop programme • Improve the systems we have to gather student feedback about teaching quality • Introduce a middle leadership development programme

Figure 12.1: An example of how an 'objective–strategy–tactics' model could support teaching and learning improvement in a school.

---

100. Buck, A. (2016) *Leadership Matters*

Capacity for improvement

The number of objectives that a school can focus on achieving is also linked to the capacity of its staff. By this, I mean the ability of staff to focus on and deliver improvement. Staff capacity to do this is affected by factors which include:

- The *time* they have available to them to focus on improvement-related activities
- The *resources* they have available to support them with these activities
- Their professional *knowledge*
- Their professional *skills and attributes*

By way of example, imagine that a school objective is to continuously improve the quality of teaching across the school. Imagine that the school has a member of staff who is enthusiastic and positive and has excellent interpersonal skills – they have strong attributes. However, their knowledge of what makes great teaching is quite weak. How strong a contribution do you think this member of staff will be able to make to the school's objective? There is little doubt that they will work hard and try their best. However, they are not going to be as successful as they could be at making an impact unless action is taken to help them develop their knowledge of what makes great teaching. Doing so would increase their capacity to help deliver improvement.

Imagine a different scenario: a member of staff has a very strong knowledge about what makes great teaching but they have poor interpersonal skills. How strong a contribution do you think this member of staff will be able to make to the school's objective? The chances are that many staff won't get on board because this person doesn't understand how to motivate and influence people. They are not going to be as successful as they could be at impacting on improvements to teaching quality across the school unless action is taken to help develop their interpersonal skills. Doing so would increase their capacity to help deliver improvement.

Where are we now?

Improvement planning is about 'going somewhere'. However, before you can determine where you want to go, how you are going to get there and likely timescales for getting there, you need to establish *where you currently are*. 'Where are we now?' is a question staff should keep returning to. This is a question about **self-evaluation**. Accordingly, schools need to know about areas that are relatively strong and those that are weak. In terms of the core business of a school, this relates to teaching practice.

As we have previously discussed, there is little or no point in assigning 'ratings' to lessons based on their perceived quality. However, I would argue quite strongly that there can be a lot of value in evaluating the quality of specific pedagogy in lessons (such as use of learning intentions, success criteria, questioning) as a means to support professional learning and improvement planning. Knowing which teachers' practice is typically strong or less strong in relation to specific pedagogy is important if school leaders are to be able to target professional learning, guide and facilitate teachers to learn from each other, and support teachers to develop and improve their practice. Without this knowledge, schools will fail to achieve consistent, high-quality teaching and learning across the school.

Teaching evaluation systems

In *What Makes Great Teaching?*[101], Robert Coe *et al.* explore what sort of teaching evaluation systems can be useful and less useful at supporting improvements to teaching quality. The paper identifies the following as potentially useful features of any school evaluation system:

- Classroom observations by peers, headteachers or external evaluators (i.e. **lesson observations**)
- Student ratings (i.e. **student evaluations**)

Below are direct quotations of what this paper says about each.

---

101. Coe, R. *et al.* (2014) *What Makes Great Teaching?*

Classroom observations

Successful teacher observations are primarily used as a formative process – framed as a development tool creating reflective and self-directed teacher learners as opposed to a high-stakes evaluation or appraisal. However, while observation is effective when undertaken as a collaborative and collegial exercise among peers, the literature also emphasises the need for challenge in the process – involving, to some extent, principals or external experts.

Levels of reliability that are acceptable for low-stakes purposes can be achieved by the use of high-quality observation protocols. These include using observers who have been specifically trained – with ongoing quality assurance, and pooling the results of observations by multiple observers of multiple lessons.

Student ratings

Collecting student ratings should be a cheap and easy source of good feedback about teaching behaviours from a range of observers who can draw on experience of many lessons. There is evidence of the validity of these measures from use both in schools and, more widely, in higher education.

The paper stresses that any teaching evaluation system should be built on the principles of **continuous formative assessment**, as opposed to infrequent, 'high-stakes' assessment. Assigning ratings to lessons is high-stakes; evaluating the quality of particular elements of pedagogy is low-stakes.

It also stresses the importance of viewing the evidence coming from these sources as being *suggestive*, rather than definitive. It is evidence which is based on perceptions, impressions and opinions. A single lesson observation might *suggest* that a teacher's use of questioning to make all students think is high quality (or not), but it should never be used to assert this definitively. It should be used as a starting point from which to explore this area further – for example, via further observations or using information from other sources.

Triangulation

The reliability of evidence coming from one source is strengthened when it is compared with and confirmed by evidence from another. For example, supporting the information which comes from lesson observations, student evaluations could be used to find out more about the quality of a particular element of teaching practice. Comparing evidence from one source with evidence from another is often referred to as 'triangulation'[102]:

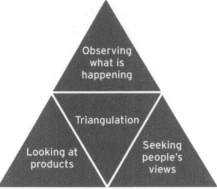

Figure 12.2: The components of a triangulated approach to evaluation: observing what is happening, seeking people's views and looking at products.

Figure 12.3 offers examples of the sorts of evidence which would fit into each category.

Observing what is happening	Seeking people's views	Looking at products
Lesson observations	Evaluations and surveys	Course or lesson planning
	Focus groups	Resources used in lessons
	Informal conversations	Examples of student work
		Attainment data

Figure 12.3: Examples of how teachers and school leaders can collect evidence to support triangulated evaluation of teaching and learning.

---

102. For example: https://sites.educ.ualberta.ca/staff/olenka.bilash/Best%20of%20Bilash/Triangulation.html

Data

When people think about data, they generally think about it relating to student attainment, such as test and examination results. However, as we have previously discussed, this is but one piece of the self-evaluation puzzle. Other sorts of data are just as important. In this section, we shall explore examples of the sorts of data which could be gathered.

The importance of data

If you are asking yourself, 'How good is the teaching in my classroom, department or school?', gathering relevant data should support your self-evaluation of this. In the absence of data, teachers and school leaders might think that they know something, but in reality, this isn't how it is. Data can help to produce a clearer picture of what's going on.

Analysing the data you collect will help you to identify areas of relative strength and weakness, which in turn can inform your improvement planning focus. Assuming you have taken steps to improve something that you identified as an area of relative weakness, by gathering data again at a future point and comparing it with your previous data the data gathering process can support you to evidence impact.

While gathering data can be of great benefit to a school, the time spent gathering it and the volume of data being gathered must be proportionate. It is all too easy for schools to drown themselves in data by attempting to measure everything that moves (and doesn't). Data is important, but it is what is done on the back of messages learned from data that is most important. Often, the most important thing to happen is a conversation. Because time is precious, more needs to be spent acting on data than gathering it. Data on its own changes nothing.

One of the reasons that data can be powerful is because it is visual and therefore can be used to communicate messages in a clear and direct way. However, a caveat on this is that data can also be unreliable and misleading. Accordingly, it is important to take care in how data is collected, recorded and used. Isolated pieces of data should not be used to draw conclusions. Instead, they should be used as a starting point from which to ask questions.

In the sections that follow, we will consider two examples of data which can be gathered to support self-evaluation of teaching and consider how use of a *Lesson Evaluation Toolkit* can support data collection and analysis.

Data from lesson observations

Schools should consider whether or not they believe there is value in making use of lesson observation programmes and their *Lesson Evaluation Toolkit* to support data gathering. From experience in a number of schools (primary and secondary), I believe there are real benefits in doing so. Data of this kind can help schools to get to know themselves better and sharpen the focus of improvement planning and professional learning. I ask you to consider a suggested approach and to make up your own mind about whether or not it might have benefit in your department or school. Carried out in the right way, I believe that it can.

Figure 12.4 presents an example of data which can be collected through a lesson observation programme in a school:

Figure 12.4 (opposite): An example of how a green/amber/red evaluation system can be used to gather data in relation to the perceived quality of specific pedagogy in lessons. In this example, eight lessons have been observed across five different teachers (identified as A–E). Each lesson has been observed by two people (identified as M–Q). The data suggests that, of the lessons observed, 'Daily Review', 'Presentation of content' and 'Relationships' are relatively strong; 'Plenary' is the weakest area.

Teacher	Team	Class	Date	Daily Review	Learning intentions	Success criteria	Presentation of content	Practice	Plenary	Challenge and support	Feedback	Relationships	Observers
A	Team	Class	Date										
B	Team	Class	Date										
C	Team	Class	Date										
A	Team	Class	Date	G	R	R	A	A	R	A	A	G	M & N
B	Team	Class	Date	A	R	A	A	A	R	R	A	G	M & O
C	Team	Class	Date	R	G	A	G	G	R	A	A	A	M & P
A	Team	Class	Date	G	R	R	R	R	R	R	G	A	Q & N
B	Team	Class	Date	G	R	A	G	G	G	A	G	G	Q & O
C	Team	Class	Date	G	R	G	G	G	A	A	A	G	Q & P
D	Team	Class	Date	G	G	A	A	A	R	A	A	G	P & N
E	Team	Class	Date	A	G	A	G	A	R	A	R	G	P & O

Elements from school Lesson Evaluation Toolkit

The example shows how a green/amber/red evaluation system can be used to gather data in relation to particular pedagogy of lessons. In this example:

- Selected elements from this school's *Lesson Evaluation Toolkit* are set out along the top of the chart (such as 'Daily Review' and 'Learning intentions')
- Details of the lessons observed are set out to the left of the chart – five teachers (identified as teachers A–E) have been observed teaching, with Teacher A, Teacher B and Teacher C each having been observed teaching twice
- A green/amber/red evaluation system has been used to evaluate the different pedagogical elements of lessons
- Each lesson has been observed by two observers, who have discussed and agreed the green/amber/red evaluations against each element (observers have been assigned letters, M–Q)

Note: **the overall quality of lessons is not being evaluated**. Instead, it is *specific pedagogical elements* of lessons that are being thought about, as identified in the school's *Lesson Evaluation Toolkit*. Mapping green/amber/red evaluations against specific pedagogical elements produces a visual guide relating to perceived strengths and weaknesses, in terms of specific pedagogy. The perception is that of the person (or people) observing a lesson. **The fact that the evaluation is nothing more than a *perception* must always be emphasised**. The usefulness of such data is dependent on the pedagogical knowledge and understanding of whoever was observing the lesson. In other words, such data is only of use if whoever was observing a lesson understands what makes great teaching.

By recording green/amber/red evaluations with regard to specific pedagogy (rather than to lessons as a whole), over time a picture starts to develop across a department or school, and areas of relative strength and weakness in relation to pedagogy can be identified. Teachers and school leaders can then use this data to inform the focus of improvement plans and in-school professional learning programmes.

For example, if the data gathered is suggesting that lesson plenaries are relatively weak, then 'improve lesson plenaries' should become a focus of a school or department Improvement Plan. A high-quality, in-school professional learning programme focusing on lesson plenaries can be put together, which the school's Teaching and Learning Improvement Group could plan.

Over time – perhaps 6 or 12 months later – if improvement planning and professional learning processes have been successful, schools and departments should see changes in the data, turning 'reds' into 'ambers' and 'ambers' into 'greens'. In other words, the data collected should help to evidence impact.

Should you choose to, lesson observation data can be analysed in a different way. By using spreadsheet software, formulae can be created which convert 'greens', 'ambers' and 'reds' into numbers: green = 3, amber = 2, red = 1. Figure 12.5 presents an example of such an approach.

Figure 12.5 (on following page): An example of how data collected from lesson observations can be collated and analysed, helping to inform improvement priority areas. In this example, 50 lessons have been observed. Each element from the school's Lesson Evaluation Toolkit has been evaluated as 'green', 'amber' or 'red' for each lesson. The 'averages' have been calculated by multiplying the total 'green' by 3, the total 'amber' by 2 and the total 'red' by 1, adding these together, and then dividing by the number of lessons observed (50). Comparing data year on year can help to evidence impact and improvement.

Number of lessons observed	Evaluation	Total number of green/amber/red evaluations for each element of the school *Lesson Evaluation Toolkit*									
		Daily Review	Learning intentions	Success criteria	Presentation of content	Practice	Plenary	Challenge and support	Feedback	Relationships	Average
50	Green (value = 3)	34	29	10	25	19	6	10	12	38	
	Amber (value = 2)	9	6	26	13	19	6	12	25	11	
	Red (value = 1)	7	15	14	12	12	38	28	13	1	
	Average	2.5	2.3	1.9	2.3	2.1	1.4	1.6	2.0	2.7	2.1

Taking such an approach can help provide clearer messages about areas of relative strength and weakness across a department or school. In the example above, 'Relationships' and 'Daily Review' appear to be relatively strong; 'Plenary' and 'Challenge and support' are relatively weak. This data suggests that the school (or perhaps this particular department in the school) should focus on improving lesson plenaries and challenge and support. It also suggests that they have practice worth sharing with others in terms of Relationships and Daily Review.

A school or department can, of course, evaluate the quality of teaching without the need for such data. However, what this data can do is support and add weight to such evaluation. Schools are accountable to different bodies (such as school boards, local authorities, parent councils and inspectors) and are expected to report on standards and evidence. Lesson observation data can help with this. In my own school, data of this kind has played a key role in persuading the local authority and inspectors that our school knows itself well. Schools with whom I have worked to develop similar approaches have all reported similar benefits. While practices in schools should not be driven by a need to please local authorities and inspectors, it would be naïve to pretend that they are not accountable to such bodies.

Data from student views
When triangulating data, gathering the views of students is an important part of the process. There are a number of ways that student views can be collected, but they generally fall into two categories: **evaluations** and **focus groups**.

Most students don't receive training about what makes great teaching. Instead, their views on the quality of teaching are based on their day-to-day experiences. Students aren't experts in teaching. If teachers are to receive useful feedback about their teaching based on student views, I would argue that it is important to steer students towards specific elements of practice. This is where the *Lesson Evaluation Toolkit* comes in.

Student evaluations can be developed using the elements of the school *Lesson Evaluation Toolkit* to steer what they are being asked about. These can be completed by individual teachers, departments or at whole-school level. The different elements of the *Lesson Evaluation Toolkit* can be turned into 'student friendly' statements. Figure 12.6 presents an example.

Element of *Lesson Evaluation Toolkit*	Statement students are asked to evaluate	Evaluation (e.g. green/ amber/red or 0-10)	Comments
Learning intentions	Learning intentions are shared in lessons and help me to understand what we are learning		
Feedback	My teacher gives me regular feedback, which I find useful		
Support	I feel that my teacher gives me enough support		

Figure 12.6: An example of how elements from a school's Lesson Evaluation Toolkit can be used to collect data relating to student views about specific teaching practices. This can be triangulated with related data, such as from lesson observations.

How students evaluate specific elements of teaching practice will depend on three factors:

1. Whether or not these happen
2. How often these happen
3. Their perceived quality

Statements which students are asked to evaluate should align as closely as possible to the specific elements of your school *Lesson Evaluation Toolkit*. This will support triangulation against other data, for example, from lesson observations. As a general rule, I advise that it is better to use statements rather than questions, because questions often lead to yes/ no responses.

We are not using this process to ask students to 'check up' on their teachers – we are using this process as a supportive, formative evaluation tool for teachers. If we believe that we are in the business of supporting, challenging and inspiring students to learn, it is difficult to argue against the importance of seeking their views in relation to this.

Coming up with good statements for students to evaluate isn't easy. The wording will depend on the age and stage of the students being surveyed. Before students complete such evaluations, time should be spent talking them through the process, explaining why they are being asked to do this, and checking that they understand what each statement is saying. For example, if the statement reads 'Daily Review is used to support my learning', it is essential that students understand what Daily Review is.

The percentage of students who evaluate particular elements of lessons as green/amber/red (if that is the evaluation system you are using) can be analysed at individual teacher, department and whole-school levels. Depending on the size of your school, an electronic survey package could be used to help facilitate data collection. Repeating the process on a regular basis (perhaps every six months) will produce data which supports improvement planning and evidence of impact. Figure 12.7 presents an example of this.

Statement students are asked to evaluate	Percentage 'green' or 'amber'		
	November 2018	May 2019	November 2019
Learning intentions are shared in lessons and help me to understand what we are learning	71	84	90
My teacher gives me regular feedback, which I find useful	89	90	91
I feel that my teacher gives me enough support	84	90	89

Figure 12.7: An example of summarised student evaluation data collected over a one-year period.

As with data gathered from lesson observations, caution should be applied in relation to its validity. How students complete such evaluations can be influenced by factors such as whether they were having a good or a bad day and at what stage in the day they were asked to complete them. However, assuming there is a sufficient sample size, the collated data can serve as a useful starting point from which to ask further questions. Particular themes and individual responses can be followed up through focus groups and one-to-one conversations.

> ### Case study: Linking improvement planning and professional learning via an in-school workshop programme
>
> In my school, we use data we have gathered from lesson observations and student surveys to inform the focus of our in-school professional learning programme. An important feature of this is **staff-led workshops**.
>
> If our data is suggesting that 'questioning' is an aspect of pedagogy which is relatively weak across the school, we ask teachers whose practice we know is strong in this area to lead workshops for other staff. We encourage staff who are leading workshops to make use of the high-quality teaching practices we are aiming to see in lessons (such as use of learning intentions, success criteria, Show-me boards and Exit Tickets). In this way, good practice can be modelled. We vary which staff are leading the workshops and encourage staff to lead workshops together – perhaps a teacher who has experience of leading workshops supporting one who hasn't.

Where are we going?

Once a school or department has an understanding of where its teaching and learning strengths and areas for improvement lie (based on triangulated evidence, such as the data we have just discussed), it can start to plan for improvement. In doing so, it is important that the focus is on improving the 'right' things. Without a focus on the right things, teachers and school leaders will be working hard, but their efforts are likely to be in vain. Nobody wants to waste their time, so understanding what the right things are is important. This is the theme to which we will turn our attention next.

The 'right' and the 'wrong' things

Most schools and departments develop annual Improvement Plans. Unfortunately, these plans often focus on the 'wrong' things.

Let's take a random school as an example and consider their most recent Improvement Plan. It has two objectives:

1. 'Raise attainment'
2. 'Develop students' Core Skills'

Are these the 'right' or the 'wrong' things to be focusing on? We will explore both.

Objective 1: 'Raise attainment'
Attainment matters. It is right that schools focus on improving it.

While schools are about more than students attaining qualifications, there is no getting away from the fact that qualifications can transform lives. The more qualifications students attain (which may be academic or vocational), and the better their quality, the more options they will have available to them when they leave school. It doesn't matter how well-rounded an individual you are, if you don't have the necessary qualifications, you aren't going to get to become a dentist, physiotherapist or building surveyor. Schools recognise this, which is why a focus on raising attainment will always be important.

But what is the key to raising attainment? In its Improvement Plan, this school identifies two strategies: *'Develop an ethos of ambition and resilience'* and *'Develop students' study skills'*. This is where it starts to go wrong. We shall explore why.

The wrong strategy
In Chapter 5, I argued that the key factors influencing student learning (and attainment as a result of this learning) are:

1. **High-quality teaching**
2. **Hard work** on the part of the student

If a school's objective is to raise attainment, these are the areas on which its strategy should focus. Both are important. Arguably, teaching quality is most important. For me, it definitely is. However, this plan does not focus on that. Instead, it focuses on students – their ambition, resilience and study skills. While these are important, a lack of focus on *teaching quality* is a significant strategic weakness.

The Improvement Plan reads: 'The quality of teaching in our school is strong. What we need to do is develop an ethos of ambition and self-belief.' In effect, what it is saying is: 'The quality of teaching in our school is *good enough* – the reason that students aren't attaining as highly as they could is because they aren't setting their goals high enough and they lack confidence. We need to focus on these things directly.' There are two reasons why this is misguided.

Firstly, it misses the point that the way to address issues of ambition and self-belief is through a focus on developing *high-quality teaching*. With improved teaching will come improved learning. When students experience success in their learning, they develop ambition and self-belief. Ambition and self-belief are products of learning; they cannot be taught directly.

Secondly, by putting all of the improvement focus on students, it suggests that the attainment issue is a student issue, not a teaching issue. But it is both. With improved teaching quality will come improved attainment.

This is not an isolated example. I once heard a headteacher say to a teacher that there was no need for them to worry about improving their teaching or exam results because both were good enough (out of a class of 20 students, 18 had achieved A grades and two had achieved B grades). The teacher was not altogether pleased. 'But I want my teaching to keep getting better!' they protested. 'And that's exactly what I'm going to make sure happens.' This is the mindset of a great teacher. This is the mindset that all teachers and school leaders should have. **If a school wants to improve its attainment, a focus on teaching quality is key.**

Objective 2: 'Develop students' Core Skills'
We talked a lot about 'skills' in Chapter 2. While there is no debate about whether or not skills are important (they are), where there *is* debate is in relation to the very meaning of the word. When people talk about the importance of schools teaching students 'skills', what do they actually mean by that?

Without delving too deeply into this issue again, I present to you a random selection of skills:

- Being able to hit a backhand shot over the net in tennis
- Being able to crack open an egg without the yolk breaking and mixing with the egg white

- Being able to skim-read
- Being able to carry out multiplication calculations without a calculator
- Being able to carry out multiplication calculations with a calculator
- Being able to lay bricks
- Being able to evaluate the usefulness of a historical source
- Being able to address an audience without notes
- Being able to address an audience with notes
- Being able to make an audience laugh
- Being able to write a word equation for magnesium reacting with water
- Being able to recite the lyrics to your favourite song
- Being able to sing your favourite song at karaoke

Through these examples, the point I wish to make is that the word 'skills' is broad, vague and ambiguous. To simply talk about 'skills' is meaningless. Arguably, everything that you can do is a skill. The spectrum of skills which exist is infinite. Clearly, the school we are discussing isn't aiming to teach students *everything*, so what skills are they actually aiming to teach them?

Core Skills
The Improvement Plan's strategy pinpoints four 'Core Skills': 'leadership', 'teamwork', 'problem-solving' and 'a positive attitude' (whether or not 'a positive attitude' is a 'skill' or an 'attribute' is a debatable point, but we'll go with it). The tactics for developing these are:

- 'All learning intentions should include a Core Skills focus'
- 'Every slide in PowerPoint presentations should highlight which Core Skill students are developing'
- 'Lessons dedicated to the teaching of Core Skills will be introduced'

Identifying 'Core Skills' and focusing on them in this way is a good thing to do, isn't it?

Perhaps… to a point. Drawing attention to Core Skills reminds students and teachers of the importance the school attaches to the development of these skills. Putting them on posters in corridors and classrooms can help to keep them at the forefront of people's minds. The idea is that students will be more likely to refer to such skills when writing job applications and at an interview.

However, this works on the assumption that it is important for students to be able to talk about such skills in a generic way. For me, that is a little naïve. If a student is able to say 'I have developed leadership and teamwork skills' in an application for university or interview for a job, just how valuable is that? While universities and employers are generally interested in qualifications, experience and attributes (such as work ethic and character), I would argue that they are far less interested in generic skills of the kind we are discussing. Rather, they are interested in *specific* skills.

If a student is applying for a job as an office assistant, the application process will generally aim to find out about their skills relating to this job (such as in word processing). Their leadership skills probably won't come into it. If they did, more likely they would be asked to give an example of something they have led. The ability to say 'I have learned leadership skills' is really neither here nor there.

Problems with Core Skills
It could be argued that, even if you don't accept the value of drawing attention to Core Skills, there is no harm in doing so. However, there actually can be. If teachers are being told that 'All learning intentions should include a Core Skills focus' and 'Every slide in PowerPoint presentations should highlight which Core Skill students are developing', this is going to lead to problems.

As was argued in Chapter 2, in the interests of students learning and attaining as best they can, it is essential that teachers **focus on teaching knowledge (declarative and procedural) using Specific Teaching approaches**. Including 'leadership', 'teamwork', 'problem-solving' and 'a positive attitude' in learning intentions and PowerPoint slides confuses this. As was argued in Chapter 5, learning intentions should relate to the *specific* knowledge, understanding and skills to be learned in lessons. 'Leadership', 'teamwork', 'problem-solving' and 'a positive attitude' do not fit this brief. If learning intentions are written to include such skills, we end up with things like:

Learning intention

To use our teamwork skills to help us learn about how metals are extracted from ores.

If nothing else, this over-complicates the learning intention (a far better one would be 'Understand how metals are extracted from ores'). But worse, the inclusion of 'teamwork' in the learning intention will likely lead to the teacher choosing inappropriate pedagogy. Instead of planning the best pedagogy to teach students about how metals are extracted from ores (which would be using Specific Teaching approaches), the teacher will instead plan activities which allow students to use teamwork skills, perhaps through discovery learning or groupwork. An over-emphasis on Core Skills adversely affects teaching quality. As a result, student learning suffers.

Lessons dedicated to teaching Core Skills

The idea that Core Skills can be taught in lessons dedicated to this purpose is also problematic. 'Leadership' and 'teamwork' cannot be taught in isolation. Rather, they require a knowledge context. You cannot lead on an area you have little or no knowledge about. Rather, your ability to lead is dependent on what you know about what you are leading. Similarly, the extent of your contribution to any teamwork activity will be determined by how knowledgeable you are in the context.

You cannot teach students 'problem-solving' in a generic way: you can only solve the problems you have the underpinning knowledge to solve, using schema. For example, if you ask students the question, 'If a coat is put on a snowman, would the snowman melt faster or slower than it would without wearing the coat?', you are asking them to solve a problem. The only way that this problem can be solved is by having knowledge of the relevant facts and concepts which relate to this problem (such as melting and insulation). You cannot solve this problem without this declarative knowledge. When school leaders argue that students need to be taught how to solve problems, they are right, but what they are really saying is: students need to be taught a broad and deep body of knowledge, which they can recall and apply to problems, as and when it is required. The broader and deeper the knowledge they have been taught, the more they will understand, and the better they will be at solving problems, both in range and complexity. Their success in solving any problem will be reliant on the strength of the knowledge they have relevant to that problem.

'Positive attitudes' generally come about when students feel that they have a chance of succeeding at something (note: not that they *will* succeed, just that they have a realistic chance). A lack of knowledge about something or how to do something is top of the list of reasons why students give up and develop a negative attitude towards it. No amount of coaxing, encouraging or rewarding is going to give them that knowledge – the only thing that is going to do that is high-quality teaching. The only thing that is truly going to do that is teaching them relevant knowledge. If we want to develop resilience and confidence in students, then we need to link this to helping them experience success. A positive attitude, resilience and confidence are all products of success – you can't plan lessons to teach them.

PACE

Having explored examples of the 'wrong' things for schools to be focusing on in Improvement Plans, what are the 'right' things?

In Chapter 2, I argued for the importance of school leaders 'prioritising the priorities' and streamlining the work of schools and departments to a focus on a core business of *learning*. With schools being the incredibly busy places that they are, it is all too easy to lose sight of what is important and to get distracted by initiatives which have little or nothing to do with this core business.

To help maintain focus, I suggest that teachers and school leaders keep in mind a simple acronym, **PACE**:

- Pedagogy
- Attainment
- Curriculum
- Ethos

This might be better represented as $\mathbf{P^A C_E}$, or as the diagram shown in Figure 12.8:

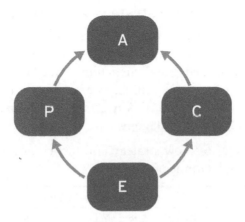

Figure 12.8: The acronym PACE provides a useful reminder of the key areas which schools, departments and teachers should focus on in improvement planning.

Attainment is not something which can be improved directly. Rather, it can be improved *indirectly* through a focus on **pedagogy, curriculum** and **ethos**. Attainment is a product of the interplay between pedagogy, curriculum and ethos. If a school or department wants to improve attainment, then pedagogy, curriculum and ethos are the key areas to focus on in order to achieve that.

Pedagogy, curriculum and ethos

As we have previously discussed, pedagogy and curriculum relate to the 'how' and 'what' of teaching and learning. In effect, pedagogy and curriculum *are* teaching and learning.

Ethos is not teaching and learning, but it does underpin it. It manifests itself through the attitudes and behaviours of everyone who works in and with a school. In the absence of a positive ethos, high-quality teaching and learning won't happen. However, a positive ethos in itself won't achieve high-quality teaching and learning: high-quality pedagogy and a high-quality curriculum are the keys to achieving that. Of these, pedagogy is the most important. In the PACE model, pedagogy comes first.

Improving attainment: strategy and tactics

Returning to the objective–strategy–tactics improvement model which we discussed at the start of this chapter, if 'raising attainment' is the objective, improving pedagogy, curriculum and ethos should be key components of any strategy. All three are important, but to repeat: pedagogy is the most important. **Any strategy to improve attainment should include a focus on pedagogy.**

Figure 12.9 summarises how strategy and tactics can be aligned to an objective of raising attainment.

Objective	Raise attainment		
Strategy Focus on...	**Teaching & learning**		**Ethos**
	Pedagogy	**Curriculum**	
Tactics Focus on...	Pedagogical subject knowledge Questioning techniques Use of Show-me boards Daily Review Use of Exit Tickets Homework which focuses on retrieval practice	The breadth and depth of subjects available to students ('academic' and 'vocational') The content taught in subjects	Teacher-student relationships Student behaviour Students' study habits Work ethic Pastoral support Parental engagement in student learning

Figure 12.9: In the interests of improving student learning and attainment, Improvement Plans should focus strategy on improving pedagogy, curriculum and ethos. The tactics which underpin each strategic area in this table are examples of the more specific areas that schools could focus on improving.

The word itself, 'PACE', is as important as the components of the acronym. School leaders and teachers need to pace themselves. Go too quickly and you will leave people behind or make mistakes; go too slowly and there will be little or no improvement to the experiences and outcomes of the students you are currently teaching.

Teacher improvement planning

To this point, we have been focusing on whole-school and departmental improvement planning. However, individual teacher improvement planning is just as important. Just as lessons are generally more successful if they are carefully planned, a teacher's professional learning will generally be more successful if it, too, has been carefully planned. What we mean by 'successful' in this context is that professional learning has a positive impact on teaching and learning. The key to achieving this impact is a high-quality **Professional Review and Development** programme, built on structured **self-evaluation** and clear **professional learning planning**.

Professional Review and Development

Most schools carry out annual staff review processes. In some schools, these take the form of an appraisal. In an appraisal, there is discussion and feedback in relation to how well someone is carrying out their job. Typically, this is documented by the person leading the appraisal, and the member of staff is given performance targets. The process can be thought of as 'Performance Review'.

In other schools, the staff review process has little in common with appraisals. Instead, the emphasis is on teacher reflection, self-evaluation and supportive discussion. There is a focus on coaching, and teachers are encouraged to take 'ownership' of their development as a teacher, maintaining a **Professional Learning Plan**. In this sense, the process can be thought of as 'Professional Review and Development'.

Which is better? For me, there is no question: Professional Review and Development will always trump Performance Review. Empowering teachers to take ownership of their professional learning is an integral feature of schools with strong professional learning cultures.

That said, we are all accountable as professionals for the quality of our work. This means that none of us can just do whatever we like whenever we like. This is not a bad thing. Empowerment and accountability can coexist. So long as it is proportionate, accountability can also be motivating and will often help us to do our jobs better than we would without it.

The focus of Professional Review and Development
In the Professional Review and Development process, who should decide what a teacher should focus on reviewing and improving? The teacher? Their head of department or year? The headteacher?

Once again, the answer lies with balance. The focus of Professional Review and Development should strike a balance between a teacher's identified development priorities and those of their department and school. The only caveat I would put on this is, regardless of who is identifying the priorities, there must always be a focus on improvement of teaching and learning. Training as a First Aider or as a hockey coach are both examples of worthwhile professional learning for teachers who are interested in developing in this way. They should be supported with this. However, this cannot be at the expense of a focus on teaching and learning improvement. **A focus on teaching and learning improvement must always be central to any Professional Review and Development process.**

If a school or departmental Improvement Plan has identified 'improving the use of Exit Tickets' as a priority, then discussion of this needs to happen in Professional Review and Development meetings and teachers need to include this in their Professional Learning Plans. If, through their self-evaluation, a teacher has identified a need to improve their skills in behaviour management, then this, too, should be discussed and included. School and departmental priorities should not trump individual teacher priorities, but neither should the opposite happen. A balance of both is important.

Structured self-evaluation

As preparation for their Professional Review and Development meeting, teachers should be given time to complete a **structured self-evaluation**. I suggest this has two parts:

- Part 1: A self-evaluation against the elements of the school's *Lesson Evaluation Toolkit*
- Part 2: A short report describing recent professional learning activity and its impact on teaching practice

Examples of each part are included below.

Part 1: Self-evaluation against Lesson Evaluation Toolkit elements

Use our green/amber/red system to self-evaluate your teaching practice against the elements of our *Lesson Evaluation Toolkit*. Use the following evidence sources to triangulate and support your self-evaluation:

1. Your self-evaluation of lessons
2. Feedback from lesson observations
3. Feedback from student evaluations or focus groups

Lesson Evaluation Toolkit: typical features of high-quality lessons		
Elements	Illustrations	Notes
Structural features		
Daily Review (including Weekly & Monthly Review)	• Low-stakes assessment, promoting recall from everyone. • Includes material required for the lesson, recent and less recent material.	*AMBER* I am beginning to build this into every lesson. It is 'amber' because I am still finding different ways to do this. I am using retrieval practice more regularly, including end of week 'Weekly Review'.
Learning intentions	• Set out precise learning goals ('Know...' 'Understand...' 'Be able to...'). • Clearly communicated (verbally and visually, if possible) in student friendly language. • Revisited during lesson and in plenary.	*GREEN* This is now an embedded feature of my practice.

Success criteria	• Clear communication of what you are looking for/what success looks like, e.g.:
	  • 'I can...' statements
	  • Key features
	  • Exemplars
	• Used to support feedback and student self-evaluation.
		GREEN
		I use success criteria in every lesson. Modelling is a regular feature in lessons – for example, co-constructing paragraphs in writing and then evaluating them with a class.

Lesson Evaluation Toolkit: typical features of high-quality lessons		
Elements	Illustrations	Notes
Structural features		
Presentation of content	• Clear presentation, including explanations and visuals which stimulate interest. • Checking what students know or can do already. • Interactive – includes frequent checks for understanding. • Repeating and summarising key points.	*AMBER* Start making a habit of checking that the class understands instructions by having them repeat them prior to embarking on the task.
Practice	• Guided, supported, then independent. • Co-operative learning opportunities. • Over-learning – lots of opportunities to master content. • Teacher circulating class.	*AMBER* More opportunities for co-operative learning could be provided.
Plenary	• Revisits the learning intention and success criteria. • Reinforces the main learning points of the lesson. • Gathers further evidence about what has been learned, was difficult, or not learned (e.g. via Exit Tickets). • Summarises next steps.	*RED* Still needs improvement.

Lesson Evaluation Toolkit: typical features of high-quality lessons		
Elements	Illustrations	Notes
Key principles		

Challenge & support	• Availability and use of support resources, e.g.:
	  • Knowledge Organisers
	  • Checklists and scaffolds
	  • Peer teaching
	• Choices within activities, with differing levels of challenge.
	• Balance of familiar and less familiar content.
		AMBER
		Regular use of the 'chilli pepper challenge' to provide support and challenge.
		I am considering how to increase challenge in junior classes.

Making students think & checking for understanding	• Strategies to make everyone think and their learning visible, e.g.:
	  • **Questioning**: pose, pause, pounce, bounce
	  • **Discussion** (e.g. chat to a partner, think–pair–share)
	  • **Active assessment methodologies** (e.g. true/false, multiple-choice)
	  • **Show-me boards**
		GREEN
		I am increasingly embedding formative assessment opportunities into lessons. I frequently use Show-me boards when questioning.
		I give careful thought to questioning. I regularly use think-pair-share. I will continue to work on this area.

Feedback	• Clear and precise. • Recognises positives and points to next steps – 'what' and 'how'. • Links to success criteria (e.g. 'I can' statements, key features or exemplars). • Individual and whole-class messages. • Time available for students to take on board feedback and improve (maybe via homework).	*RED* Aware of the importance of the time required to do this but it is often difficult to balance it with the pace of the lesson. It is something that I need to improve.

Lesson Evaluation Toolkit: typical features of high-quality lessons		
Elements	Illustrations	Notes
Learning environment		
Relationships	• Knowing students well. • Positive and professional interactions. • Recognition of positives, particularly effort.	*GREEN* I feel these are strong with all classes.
High expectations	• High expectations of effort, behaviour and quality of work. • Target/goal setting (e.g. personal bests). • Encouragement.	*GREEN* Look at ways to challenge targeted students through goal setting.
Management	• Calm, ordered, under control. • Effective use of time, space and resources. • Appropriate pace.	*GREEN* This is a strength.
Behaviour	• Students are on task, engaged, interested, motivated. • Poor student behaviours are dealt with promptly and in as low-level a way as possible.	*RED* An area to focus improvement on, particularly in my third/fourth year classes, to avoid taking time from the lesson to the detriment of the lesson and other students' learning.

Part 2: Professional Learning Report

Please write a *brief report* (in the region of 200–400 words) giving:

1. An overview of the **teaching- and learning-focused professional learning activities** you have engaged in over the past 12 months (these might include: reading, workshops, peer observations, observation feedback you have received, student feedback, sharing practice, discussion)

2. An evaluation of the **impact** of this professional learning on your practice (i.e. the elements of your teaching which have improved as a result)

I have been using this new version of the school *Lesson Evaluation Toolkit* to self-evaluate my lessons and have found it very helpful, especially as a planning tool.

This academic year, I have read *Practice Perfect* by Doug Lemov. This book has made me think about the importance of drill, practice and mastery of material and has validated my approach of getting students to learn lists of irregular verbs, prepositions and articles. Students also commented favourably on this in evaluations and at parents' evening. I have also started to use 'Quizlet' in lessons to help with the learning of vocabulary. I am currently reading *The Learning Rainforest* by Tom Sherrington, which examines the importance of core knowledge within the curriculum. I have read Andy Buck's chapter on 'Strategy, Vision and Values' from his book *Leadership Matters* and participated in a thought-provoking discussion on this at a meeting of our Middle Leadership Development Programme.

I engaged in peer observation with Teacher A in December; I received positive feedback on the pace and challenge within the lesson, the good mix of activities and the positive relationships I had with the students. I received good advice from Teacher A regarding success criteria. He suggested that I show these on the screen and link them directly to the questions I ask in Exit Tickets. I liked the idea of an 'entrance task' which I saw in his lesson; this was effective in settling the students down quickly. Since this observation, and also as a result of the reading I have done, I have worked hard on producing lesson starters which review and consolidate prior learning.

I was also observed by my line manager, who suggested that I ask pupils to have two pens – one to complete the initial task and another to correct this work so they can see clearly what they need to work on. This is a simple but effective technique. He commented that through improved use of Show-me boards, student learning had become much more visual, which was helping to guide the focus of my teaching.

In Part 1, use of the school's *Lesson Evaluation Toolkit* is key to focusing the minds of teachers and school leaders (who will be leading Professional Review and Development meetings) on specific pedagogy. Teachers are asked to draw on evaluative information from a variety of sources to support critical reflection on their teaching practice. In Part 2, teachers are asked to reflect on the impact of professional learning on their teaching practice.

Professional Learning Planning

Having completed their two-part self-evaluation, teachers are in a far stronger position to create a **Professional Learning Plan** to support their professional learning. This plan should set out:

1. The elements of pedagogy the teacher will focus on improving (linked to the school *Lesson Evaluation Toolkit*)

2. Details of professional learning activities which will support them to improve these

3. A review-by date

An example is included opposite.

Professional Learning Plan	
Name:	**Date:**
WHAT Which elements of our *Lesson Evaluation Toolkit* are you going to focus on improving?	Plenaries
HOW What **types of professional learning activity** will help support this? 1. **Read** (books, research, blogs, Twitter) 2. **Observe** (other teachers or professionals) 3. **Practise and self-evaluate** (using our *Lesson Evaluation Toolkit*) 4. **Get feedback** (from peers, school leaders, students) 5. **Participate** (in discussions, workshops, working groups) 6. **Share** (your learning, good practice) Try to **be specific** (What do you plan to read? Who do you plan to observe? When do you plan to do this?)	• Professional Reading: continue *The Learning Rainforest* • Observation: Teacher C, to see her use Exit Passes (in May) • Observation: Teacher D, to see a lesson plenary (in June) • Monthly self-evaluation of lessons using *Lesson Evaluation Toolkit* • Feedback: from Teacher E and Teacher F as part of Peer Observation Fortnight (in May); deputy headteacher observation (in September) • Discussions at departmental meetings and as part of the Professional Reading Group
REVIEW When will progress with this plan be reviewed? Who will you review progress with? As a general rule, reviews should take place **once a term (about every 10 weeks).**	Review in September, November, January and March. I will ask my line manager to review my progress with me during one-to-one meetings.

Figure 12.10. An example of a teacher Professional Learning Plan. This should link closely to the school Lesson Evaluation Toolkit and Professional Learning Model. It should be reviewed and updated roughly once every 10 weeks.

It is best for teachers to be asked to create their Professional Learning Plan in advance of their Professional Review and Development meeting (rather than after it). The meeting can then be used to discuss both the teachers' two-part self-evaluation and their Professional Learning Plan. Through the discussion during the meeting, the plan may be amended.

It is important that both teachers and their line manager have a copy of the finalised Professional Learning Plan. Over a 10-week period, teachers should take steps to act on their plan. In other words, they should lead their professional learning, guided by their plan. After 10 weeks, teachers should have a follow-up meeting with their line manager, during which progress in relation to their plan should be discussed. Following this, their plan should be updated. In these follow-up meetings, there shouldn't be a need for teachers to complete a two-part self-evaluation again. Rather, this is best carried out annually.

Having spent time in this chapter exploring the theme of improvement planning and how a *Lesson Evaluation Toolkit* can be used to support this, in Chapter 14 we will turn our attention to the topic of leadership. Before we do, in our next chapter we will return to our discussion from Chapters 5 and 9 about what makes great teaching.

Chapter 13
Great teaching - Part 3

In Chapter 2, we discussed great teaching as a blend of **Specific Teaching** and **Non-specific Teaching** approaches, with the balance in favour of Specific Teaching.

In Chapter 4, we identified four components of Specific Teaching, these being high-quality:

1. **Pedagogical subject knowledge**
2. **Teacher–student relationships**
3. **Direct-interactive instruction**
4. **Formative assessment**

While great teaching will always involve a degree of Non-specific Teaching as well, in the interests of teaching students the knowledge they need to develop skills and to attain, we recognised that a focus on Specific Teaching is key.

In Chapter 5, we discussed how great teaching manifests itself through the pedagogy of lessons, arguing that lessons are the delivery units of great teaching. In general terms, we said that Specific Teaching should account for 80–90% of lesson time.

Towards the start of that chapter, we broke the Specific Teaching approach down into the specific pedagogy of high-quality lessons, arguing that high-quality lessons are those which typically include:

1. Activities that require students to **recall knowledge** from previous lessons, which may or may not be relevant to this lesson, but which needs to be learned as part of the course

2. Clear communication and use of **learning intentions and success criteria**

3. Activities that allow the teacher to **find out what students know or can do already** (in relation to what is being taught in this lesson)

4. Clear **teacher explanations and demonstrations** which hold student attention

5. Activities that allow students to **put into practice** what they are being taught

6. Appropriate levels of **support and challenge**

7. Use of **questions** to make students think and to check for understanding

8. Activities that get students to **discuss and learn with other students**

9. Clear **feedback** to individual students and to the class about their learning

10. Activities that **evaluate the impact of lessons**

11. Strong **teacher–student relationships**

12. **High expectations and standards** for student behaviour and quality of work

In Chapter 5, we explored the first three of these. In Chapter 9, we explored the next five. In this chapter, we shall explore the final four.

9. Clear **feedback** to individual students and to the class about their learning

Feedback is fundamental to learning. It has three purposes:

1. To help students understand how they are doing
2. To highlight ways they could improve
3. To motivate and encourage

It achieves these three by identifying clear **strengths**, **areas for improvement** and **next steps**.

Giving feedback

Feedback can be given to students in a variety of ways. These include:

- Giving a piece of work a score or a grade
- Using a coding system on a piece of work, such as green/amber/red
- Writing comments on a piece of work
- Having a conversation with individuals or groups
- Pointing things out during Specific Teaching

Which of these do you think is the best way to give students feedback?

While there is a place for all of them, I would argue that the last two are generally the best. They involve the teacher *talking* to students. Not only can this give students the clearest feedback, it is usually the smartest use of time. Feedback doesn't need to be lengthy – it needs to valuable.

A misconception that teachers often have about feedback is that it is only given in response to assessed tasks, rather than being an integral feature of lessons. While feedback in response to assessed tasks is important, more important is *immediate* and *continuous* feedback as part of direct-interactive teaching and formative assessment during lessons.

Students are asked a question; based on their answer, they are given feedback. Students are asked to write something on their Show-me board; based on what they write, they are given feedback. Students are asked to discuss something; based on what they are saying, they are given feedback. Students are practising questions; after a quick check from the teacher, they are given feedback.

The value that feedback has to students will depend on its quality. But what makes high-quality feedback?

High-quality feedback

If students are to understand how they are doing and how to improve, they need to be clear about what they are learning and what success looks like. Accordingly, learning intentions and success criteria are integral to feedback. Of these, it is **success criteria** which are most important.

Ensuring feedback is linked to success criteria helps to ensure that it is more than just a set of qualitative statements. While it is important for students to be clear about quality, feedback should always be about more than that. In high-quality feedback, the word 'because' keeps coming up:

- 'This is good *because...*'
- 'This isn't quite right *because...*'
- 'I really like this *because...*'

The 'because' should link to success criteria.

Regardless of whether feedback is coming from the teacher or from a peer, it should always link to success criteria. The clearer that teachers and students are about success criteria, the clearer their feedback will be.

High-quality feedback is **specific** feedback:

- '*This* is what was good; *this* is what wasn't.'
- 'To improve, you need to do *this*.'
- '*This* could make that better.'
- 'You've nearly got that. There's just one mistake, and it's with *this*.'
- 'That is good. What you should focus on next is *this*.'

There is no ambiguity and there are no grey areas. Everything is specific: success criteria, strengths, areas for improvement and next steps.

The ability of teachers to be specific and clear in their feedback is dependent on their pedagogical subject knowledge. The better a teacher knows and understands their subject, including areas in which students typically struggle, where common mistakes tend to be made, what common misconceptions are and how students generally think about particular concepts, the better equipped they are to give high-quality feedback.

Coaching approaches

Sometimes there can be value in using **coaching approaches** to give feedback. Rather than jumping to tell students, '*This* was good'; '*This* wasn't so good'; 'Improve *this*', the teacher points things out and asks questions in a way designed to help them generate their own feedback.

For example, if a teacher looks at a Show-me board on which a student was asked to write three examples of metaphors, the teacher might say, 'Two of those are right but one is wrong. Which one do you think is wrong? Why?' So long as a student isn't left in the dark for too long (which will frustrate them and switch them off), coaching approaches can be a useful means to get students to think and come up with their own feedback.

Check for understanding

Once feedback has been given, teachers need to **check it has been understood**. One way to do this is by giving students an opportunity to act on it. This might be immediate ('Right, go and take 10 minutes to have a go at that') or require more time ('I'd like you to have another go at that by Wednesday and bring it back for me to have a look at with you.')

Another way would be for the teacher to ask a student to explain back what has just been explained to them ('Okay, so you're telling me that you understand this. That's good. I'd like you to explain back to me what I have just said.') Doing so is putting the student in the position of teacher and works on the principle that to be able to explain something to someone, you have to understand it.

Motivating and encouraging students

A key purpose of feedback is to motivate and encourage. All feedback is motivating and encouraging, isn't it? No. In fact, feedback has the potential to be the opposite. When that happens, it is usually because it:

- Is unclear
- Is overly negative
- Is *always* negative
- Is given in a way which comes across as unsupportive

Clearly, no teacher aims to demotivate and discourage students. To avoid doing so, teachers need to make feedback as specific and positive as they can. Where they need to highlight areas for improvement, they should do so in a supportive way. Typically, this will mean starting with positives and then highlighting negatives.

Students need to believe that their teachers are doing their very best to support them. The more they believe this, the more willing they will be to receive and act upon negative feedback. Feedback and support go hand in hand.

10. Activities that **evaluate the impact of lessons**

Every lesson should have purpose. As a result of every lesson they attend, students should learn something new or something better. No lesson should be wasted.

A key role for teachers is to evaluate the difference that lessons make to student learning. As we have previously discussed, John Hattie says that teachers should see themselves as 'evaluators of impact'[103]. In order to do this, student learning needs to be made visible. Teachers need to find out what students know or can do already, what they are learning during lessons, and what they have learned by the end of lessons. Used well, lesson plenaries have a key role in supporting this.

Lesson plenaries

A lesson plenary has two purposes:

1. Summing up what *should* have been learned in a lesson
2. Formative evaluation of what *has actually* been learned in a lesson

---

103. Hattie, J. (2012) *Visible Learning for Teachers*

Summing up what should have been learned

In great teaching, 'signposting' is important. The teacher makes it clear to students: *this* is where we are going; *this* is what I am looking for; *this* is what an excellent piece of work looks like; *this* is a common mistake to make; *this* is what we are going to do next. This is Specific Teaching.

Revisiting learning intentions and success criteria towards the end of a lesson helps to ensure that there isn't a mismatch between what you thought the purpose of the lesson was and what students did. With so much being said and done in lessons, it is easy for students to lose sight of what they are supposed to be learning. Revisiting the learning intentions and success criteria helps to stop that from happening. It helps to ensure that students leaving a lesson are clear about what they were supposed to have learned.

Formative evaluation of what has actually been learned

If learning intentions and success criteria are revisited in a lesson plenary, students will leave clearer about what they *should* have been learning. But *did* they learn it? A lesson plenary can also be used to find out if they have.

Imagine you are teaching a lesson about tropical storms. This has a learning intention and success criterion as follows:

<u>Learning intention</u>

We are learning about tropical storms, specifically:

– To understand the causes of tropical storms

<u>Success criterion</u>

You can *state* the six conditions which must be met for tropical storms to happen

In a lesson plenary, you could:

- Ask students to indicate, with a show of hands, who thinks they have achieved the success criterion.
- Ask students to indicate, on a 0–10 scale, how confident they feel about having achieved the success criterion.
- Ask students to close their jotters and list each of the six conditions on a Show-me board, holding this up for you to see.

- Give out Post-it notes ('Exit Tickets'), on which you ask students to write the six conditions, giving these to you as they leave the room. After the lesson, you read through these to get a feel for what students have learned or not learned, including common mistakes or difficulties, which you will give whole-class feedback on at the start of the next lesson.

- Give out Post-it notes ('Exit Tickets'), on which you ask students to write two things (on different sides):

  1. The six conditions which must be met for a tropical storm to happen

  2. Anything they found difficult, didn't understand or have questions about from this lesson.

- Project a list of six possible conditions, some of which are correct and some of which are not. You ask students to identify which are true and which are false, either through a show of hands, on a Show-me board, or on a Post-it note ('Exit Ticket'), which you collect.

What are your thoughts on these possible lesson plenary activities? Are there any that you think are better than others? Why?

Each of them asks students to *think* about their learning. So, in that respect, you could argue that each of them has value. However, the first two ask students to self-evaluate without producing any *evidence* of their learning. While this might have *some* formative value to the teacher (for example, they may have asked students to do this at the start of the lesson and compared responses with the end), it is not reliable evidence of learning. To be reliable, *specific evidence* of learning needs to be produced. Students need to *prove it*. The last four of the activities above get students to do that. Accordingly, they are better lesson plenary activities than the first two.

Case study: Evaluating learning

I once observed a home economics lesson in which the learning intention was 'To be able to decorate a sponge cake'. Students had made the sponge during the previous lesson and in this lesson were to decorate it with icing, which they would be piping. A number of success criteria were projected up, which the teacher read out to the class. These included:

- Use the correct equipment
- Work safely and hygienically
- Wash and tidy up your dishes properly

Students decorated their cakes. Towards the end of the lesson, the teacher said, 'I'd like everyone to evaluate how they did today. Please hold up your traffic light cards.' All of the students did. Of 15 students, there were 10 'greens' and 5 'ambers'. The teacher said, 'That's great. Thank you. You've all worked really hard today and done some great work. Well done.' The lesson was over.

What are your thoughts about this? What do you think of the success criteria? What do you think about the way that students were asked to evaluate their learning towards the end of the lesson?

I sat down with this teacher the day after the lesson had been taught. I'd asked her to self-evaluate the lesson, but she hadn't used any sort of framework (such as a *Lesson Evaluation Toolkit*) to base this on. Rather, she had reflected on what she thought went well and less well. On the whole, she said that she thought this lesson had been a success. Students had been productive, they had done what they were told, they had all behaved and they had all finished in time. Her instructions had been clear and she had gone around helping. Students had all evaluated how they did as 'green' or 'amber' – there were no 'reds'. It had been a successful lesson.

I told her that I agreed with a lot of what she had said. However, with some tact, I went on to raise a point about 'being busy' versus 'learning'. I said that if the purpose of the lesson had been for students to be busy, on task and well behaved, and for all to produce a final product in the time available, then yes, the lesson had been a success. However, if the purpose was about *learning* – learning something new or learning to do something better – then I didn't think we could say it had been as successful. Students had all created a decorated sponge – of varying quality – but there was no evidence that any student had actually learned anything.

We discussed how the lesson could have been better focused on learning. One suggestion was that the learning intention be changed from 'To be able to decorate a sponge cake' to 'To be able to decorate a sponge cake, with a focus on the quality of the piping of the icing'. The success criterion would then relate to how the final product compared to either clear statements of standards (such as 'The iced peaks are all of similar size and spread out evenly around the perimeter of the cake') or photographs of exemplars of differing standards. Students could then be asked how they thought theirs compared against standards or exemplars, identifying strengths, areas for improvement and next steps. A template for such an evaluation might look something like this:

Evaluation out of 10 (based on the success criterion)	
Strengths - the things that were best about it	
Improvements - the things that could have been better	
Learning - what I should do differently or focus on improving next time	

Such an activity could be completed towards the end of the lesson, as part of a plenary, or as homework. Such a *pro forma* could be used for self-evaluation, peer evaluation or teacher evaluation.

The subtle shift in the focus from 'doing' to 'learning' moved the learning intention from being task orientated to learning orientated. It also moved the success criterion from being about process to being about product. Success criteria relating to product, or outcomes, tend to be more useful than those that relate to process. Evaluation of a product or outcome can lead to feedback about the process. For example, feedback to a student from this lesson might be that they need to take care to use the right equipment, because they had used a metal spoon instead of a wooden spoon when stirring the icing and this had a detrimental effect on the final product.

11. Strong **teacher–student relationships**

In *The Magic-Weaving Business*[104], Sir John Jones argues that, while students will forget most of what you teach them, they will always remember how you made them feel. Positive professional relationships are at the heart of great teaching.

What you do and what you say matters

Such relationships start with the teacher knowing the names of every student in their class. They then develop with every interaction: the smile and 'hello' as a student enters the room, the recognition of their effort, improvement, or a particularly good answer to a question, and taking time to take an interest in individual students and their work.

The behaviour of teachers sets the tone for lessons. If teachers are positive, passionate, organised and professional, students will generally respond very well. If they are negative, moaning, nagging or sarcastic, students are not going to respond well. In fact, they are probably going to disengage from the learning process. Who would want to be stuck in an environment with the person in charge acting like that? This is an important point for teachers to keep in mind: in a single moment, through their words or body language, teachers have the power to make a student feel like a million dollars. They can also do the opposite.

---

104. Jones, J. (2009) *The Magic-Weaving Business*

Case study: How we make students feel

To this day, I remember going with great excitement to my first history lesson in secondary school. Early on in the lesson, the teacher asked the class to think about different sources of historical evidence. Students were asked to put up their hand if they wanted to share an answer. Enthusiastically, I put up mine. The teacher started to ask for answers, which included 'television' and 'films'. The student who answered before me said, 'Newspapers'; when I got asked, I said, 'Magazines'. I expected to get some form of positive affirmation from the teacher. Instead, I got: 'There is no difference between a newspaper and a magazine' in a blunt, curt tone. It wasn't so much what he said, it was the way he said it. The class laughed. I didn't put my hand up again for the rest of the year. And I have never forgotten that.

In a different example, I can recall a teacher whose students, year on year, achieved excellent exam results. I achieved excellent results with this teacher. Her teaching was high quality. However, everyone was terrified of her. Discipline in her classroom was excellent and everyone did exactly as they were told, but the majority of students in the class were too scared to ask questions when they were unsure of something, and became rabbits in the headlights whenever they were asked to answer. When I think back to lessons with this teacher, I can hear their voice saying, 'Don't be so stupid!', in response to an incorrect answer. How a teacher interacts with students matters, because it can influence whether or not students want to go on to study a subject. As soon I was able, I chose not to continue studying the subject taught by this teacher, not because I didn't like the subject – I did – but because I was scared of the teacher.

'I am not there to be liked'

I have heard some teachers say things like, 'I am not there to be liked.' Perhaps this is true – a teacher is there to teach. But teaching becomes an altogether more rewarding and satisfying process for both the teacher and the students if everyone enjoys what they are doing and gets along well.

I have also heard teachers say things like, 'I am not there to be their friend.' This is true. The relationship between a teacher and the students they teach is a professional one. As experienced teachers will know, a common mistake that novice teachers make is 'being too friendly' with students. Establishing positive relationships is important, but becoming overly familiar with students will, ultimately, lead to problems.

Authority

Sometimes I hear people discuss the teacher–student relationship as being one of equals. This always concerns me, because it isn't. The teacher is an adult and a trained professional. The student is a child, teenager or young adult and not a trained professional. The teacher is in a position of authority and is being paid to be in that position, with all of the accountability that goes with it. None of this applies to the student. While students can, of course, be involved in making and shaping the rules of the teacher's classroom, it is the teacher's classroom, and, ultimately, what the teacher says must go. The teacher is responsible for the safety, wellbeing and learning of all of the students they are teaching; ensuring that rules, standards and expectations are made clear and are met is essential to ensuring great teaching.

Accepting this is not the same as accepting that the teacher is always right. Teachers are people, and people make mistakes. As and when they do, teachers should own up to these and apologise where necessary, just as a student should be expected to.

A spring in their step

I once interviewed a candidate for a principal teacher position. During the interview we were talking about what makes a high-quality lesson. As part of their answer, the candidate said: 'I want students to be walking out of the room with a spring in their step.' I thought this was an excellent part of their answer and it has stuck with me. Through the quality of their teaching and the relationship that they have with their students, great teachers have students leaving their classroom with a spring in their step.

12. **High expectations and standards** for student behaviour and quality of work

I am a great believer in the principle: people will only jump as high as you set the bar. I also believe that people will behave as you allow them to. If you set low expectations, you will get low outcomes; set them higher and outcomes will be higher.

Student behaviour

A calm, ordered and under-control classroom is a prerequisite to learning. Achieving these conditions relies on good lesson planning, strong teacher–student relationships, the setting of high expectations, attention to detail and strong skills in behaviour management.

If the students you are teaching are being lazy, argumentative, silly, rude, uncooperative or consistently producing work of a poor standard, it is very likely that this is because you are allowing it to happen, or, at least, not doing much to stop it. By not challenging these behaviours or doing anything about them, you are, in effect, saying: 'This behaviour is okay.' However, I don't believe that many teachers would think that such behaviours are okay. Quite the opposite.

Teachers need to make clear what their expectations and standards are for the students they teach. Before they can do this, they need to decide for themselves what these expectations and standards are. This includes in relation to student behaviour and standards of work. All students need to be clear about what these are – grey areas will more than likely lead to problems.

For example, what do you expect students to do when they arrive at your classroom? Are they allowed to walk in and take a seat, or do you expect them to line up? There can be advantages and disadvantages to both approaches, but you need to decide what you are looking for, make this clear to students and make sure that your expectations are followed. If you expect the full attention of everyone when you are addressing students (as you should), you need to tell your students that this is what you expect, and you need to insist that you get it. Different teachers will go about achieving this in different ways. There is no single right way, but there are plenty of wrong ways.

Managing poor student behaviour

All teachers, no matter how experienced, face the challenge of dealing with poor student behaviour. However, what is seen as challenging behaviour by some teachers often isn't seen in the same way by others. In one school, a student who persistently does not bring a pencil with them to class, or who is often seen chatting with the student they are sitting next to, is perceived by teachers as engaging in challenging behaviour; in a different school, daily challenging behaviour is exemplified by the student who has just stormed out of the room, having sworn at their teacher and kicked over their chair. Regardless of the specifics, the management of 'poor' student behaviour can be one of the most challenging aspects of a teacher's job.

Poor student behaviours can often be avoided by making sure that:

- Lessons have been well-planned
- The classroom is tidy and ordered
- There are clear procedures and routines, which everyone understands
- There are high expectations for student behaviour, which everyone understands
- There are clear consequences for poor student behaviour, which everyone understands and which are applied fairly and consistently
- There are positive interactions between the teacher and all of the students in the class
- The teacher knows all the students by name
- The teacher positions themselves well in the room and moves around, as appropriate
- The teacher uses visual cues and student names to correct low-level misbehaviours, dealing with them in a low-level and subtle way, rather than making a big deal of them
- The teacher varies the pace and volume of their voice to hold the attention of the class

- The teacher uses pauses and silence when waiting for full attention or to break up extended chunks of exposition
- The teacher asks frequent questions during chunks of exposition to help hold the attention of the class and check that students understand what is being said
- The content of the lesson is accessible to all students – it's not so easy that they get bored, but not so difficult that they switch off or give up
- The visuals the teacher is making use of are clear, accessible and interesting
- The lesson is delivered with passion, enthusiasm and confidence

Consequences

Consequences are not a bad thing. Actually, they are a good and necessary thing. Granted, as and when they are applied, teachers don't tend to like using them and students certainly don't like receiving them. However, they are an essential feature of any behaviour management system. They are essential for helping to teach students that their actions and choices have consequences, in all walks of life. I actually believe that we are doing our students an enormous disservice if we are not teaching them this. We are setting them up to fail. Consequences which are proportionate, consistent and appropriately used help teach students how to behave.

For me, the key components of any effective behaviour management system are:

- Recognition of effort, standards of work and good behaviour
- Proportionate consequences for poor behaviour
- Restorative approaches following any consequences

Case study: Struggling with student behaviour

Recently, I was delivering a presentation about what makes great teaching to a group of newly qualified teachers. At various points, I paused to ask if anyone had any questions or anything they would like to say. About halfway through the presentation, one of the teachers put up their hand and said, very politely: 'I really like everything that you've been saying about teaching and learning and I'm finding it very interesting, but the reality is that I don't think I can do any of this, because the standard of student behaviour is so poor.'

I started by thanking them for their point and then agreeing with them: I don't believe that you can deliver great teaching – or anything close to great teaching – if the standard of behaviour in your lessons is poor.

I went on to say that it was important for them to recognise that there were things that they couldn't control and things that they could. Things that they couldn't control were the school's behaviour policy and the students they had in their class. Things that they could control were their own behaviours. I advised that while there was no magic wand to address poor student behaviour, I believed that the most important things for them to concentrate on were:

1. Teaching the class that **when you are talking, you expect everyone's full attention**. That means that they stop talking, they put everything out of their hands and they look at you. When you are talking, students give you their full attention. When they want to say something, they should put up their hand – there should be no shouting out.

2. When addressing the class, give an instruction that you would like attention (perhaps 'Okay, fourth year...') and then **wait for silence**. Follow through on your expectation of full attention. If you don't get it, wait. Adopt an assertive stance close to the class and in a position in the room where everyone can see you. Make eye contact with students. Smile at those students who are giving you what you have asked for. Use names (e.g. 'Imogen...') to remind individual students that you are waiting

for them to stop talking. Avoid provocative phrases like, 'Will you please stop talking!' Instead, stay calm, stay collected and be assertive.

3. **Recognise positive behaviours** and ensure that there are **proportionate consequences** for poor behaviour.

Regarding the final point, all too often I see student behaviour deteriorate in classrooms and schools as a result of a lack of consequences. Somewhere along the line, some teachers and school leaders have come to believe that consequences are archaic and should be *replaced* by restorative approaches. Restorative approaches are important, but they don't replace consequences. Rather, they should *follow* consequences.

I said to the teacher that, while I sympathised with them, I had worked in a number of schools in which student behaviour was a challenge, and that it was possible not only to manage it, but to get behaviour to a place where it was good. In many schools, different teachers who are teaching the same class experience different student behaviours. There is no getting away from it: the only difference is the teacher.

The two factors which make the biggest difference
There are two factors which make the biggest difference in terms of how students behave in lessons:

1. The quality of the teacher's behaviour management skills
2. The quality of teaching

Where there is good behaviour in a class, the chances are that the teacher is getting both of these right. Where there is poor behaviour in a class, the chances are that the teacher is getting one or both of these wrong. Figure 13.1 illustrates this relationship.

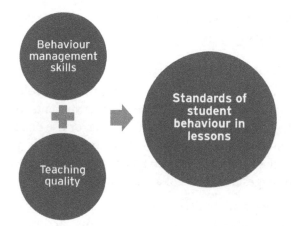

Figure 13.1: The standard of student behaviour in lessons is determined by two factors: a teacher's behaviour management skills and the quality of their teaching.

Whenever a teacher is having issues with behaviour management, these are the two key factors they need to reflect on and, if necessary, do something about.

You get what you give

Students look to their teacher for the lead on how to behave and what to do. The way that students interact with their teacher will, to a large extent, depend on how the teacher interacts with their students. If teachers keep calm and remove emotion from potentially confrontational situations, then students can be taught to do the same. If teachers treat students with respect and demonstrate, through their words and actions, that they care, students will respect this and are far more likely to commit to learning in this subject. Of course, the reverse is also true. I once heard of a situation where a teacher had turned to a colleague who had come into their classroom and, in response to something a student had just asked them regarding something they were struggling with, had said: 'Brain the size of a walnut.' I was told that the student heard this but didn't react – at least visibly. Inside, however, they were likely exploding with a range of emotions, including embarrassment, anger and shock. I am certain that any respect that the student had for this teacher disappeared in that single moment, as the result of a throwaway remark. I am also certain that, as Sir John Jones points out, they will never forget it. Nor will other students in the class.

The importance of modelling

Modelling expected standards can play an important role in the setting of high expectations. For example, if you expect students to underline the headings they write in their jotters with a ruler, or use one when drawing diagrams, then when you are doing these things yourself (perhaps on the whiteboard at the front of the room) it is important that you do the same. Not doing so suggests that it is okay not to.

The same principles apply to the environment that the teacher creates in their classroom. Cluttered classrooms create distractions and negatively impact on learning. They also do nothing to model expected standards to students. While it may seem trivial, having a tidy and uncluttered classroom is an important expression of the standards you expect.

Target setting

Target setting can play a powerful role in helping to motivate students. Targets may be long term or short term, and I believe that both have value. An example of a long-term target might be the grade that a student is aiming to achieve in an exam, perhaps because this is what they need to get into college or university. A short-term target might be to score at least 4/5 in tomorrow's Daily Review because the last three days the student has scored 3/5 and, while the teacher has acknowledged that this is good, they are setting the bar higher – they want the student to do a bit more study at home to improve their learning.

This second scenario is an example of frequent, low-stakes quizzing in action. The student is asked to keep a record of their own scores, so that they can look back on these over a period of time and set targets against them. For one student, this might be to keep getting 5/5 every day; for another student, it might be to get 4/5 for the first time, with their next target being to get this again the next day, and their following target being to achieve this five days in a row.

The recording of scores and the setting of targets in this way creates an opportunity for you to interact with your students and take an interest.

For example, you might say: 'Put up your hand if you got at least 3/5', 'Put up your hand if you hit your target today', 'Put up your hand if you scored better than you did yesterday' or 'Put up your hand if you achieved or matched your best ever score.'

Taking an interest in how students get on in such activities is important. It shows students that you are keeping a careful eye on the progress of all of them. The stakes are low – nothing much is going to be done with this information beyond informing the student and the teacher about how the student got on – but the impact on learning is high because activities like this are about recall. Students may or may not try their best without setting a target, but experience tells me that, for many students, striving to achieve a target is motivating. For those for whom it is not, so long as the stakes are kept low, at the very least, it doesn't do any harm.

A gym analogy
Think about what happens if you go to the gym and start to run on the treadmill. If you haven't set yourself a target, there's a good chance that you will stop running once it starts to become difficult. For the sake of this argument, let's imagine that this point is at 10 minutes. At 10 minutes, because things have got difficult, you decide to hit the stop button and call it a day. You're quite pleased with yourself, because at least you ran for 10 minutes. But what if you had set yourself a target of 11 minutes? Would you have kept running for that extra minute? I suspect that you would. You would likely have thought to yourself, 'Even though I'm now finding this difficult, I'm not too far away from my 11-minute target, so I'm going to push myself, because I think I can make that.' Then you make it! And you feel great. The sense of achievement you get from having reached a target you had set yourself – or perhaps that someone else had set for you – is typically greater than if you simply did something and then stopped when you felt like it.

In this example, the target that you set yourself was one that you felt was achievable, and you achieved it. What if you had set yourself a target of 30 minutes? What might have happened to your motivation then?

In one scenario, you might have kept pushing yourself, battling through the difficulty of the situation and, as a result, achieved your target of running for 30 minutes. Your sense of satisfaction would be enormous, particularly if this was a personal best for you.

But what if you had failed? What if you only made it to 25 minutes and then gave up? Or worse; what if you didn't even get close, making it to only 17 minutes before you gave up? Would this demotivate you? Would this adversely affect your future performance? I suspect that it wouldn't do much damage. Instead, I suspect that it would give you a clear baseline about your current standard of performance and where your limit lay, which you would then aim to improve upon the next time. The next time, or perhaps after a few 'next times', you do end up hitting your 30-minute target, with the initial failure having little or no adverse effect on your ability to achieve it with a bit more hard work and perseverance. Therefore, we shouldn't worry too much about setting targets which are high, so long as people are given enough time and enough of a chance to be able to achieve them. Sometimes, being able to do so will rely on the support of others, with encouragement being incredibly important.

Encouragement

The higher you set targets and expectations, the more important encouragement becomes. If targets and expectations are low, it is unlikely that much encouragement will be needed, because students will meet these without much effort. Encouragement becomes most important when students are having to work hard or do things which are difficult.

Returning to the example of the gym, the chances of you achieving your target are far higher if your personal trainer or a friend gives you encouragement. Imagine that you have been running for 25 minutes and every part of your body is screaming for you to stop. If no one is taking an interest in how you are doing, there's a good chance you might just decide to stop, because you can always have another go the next time you're in. So you give up.

But imagine that your personal trainer or friend starts to tell you how well you are doing, reminding you that you've managed 25 minutes and there are only another 5 to go. They say things like, 'I know you can do this' or 'Keep pushing yourself just a little bit more.' The chance of you giving up is far lower. It might not even be what your personal trainer or friend is saying that is motivating you. Instead, it might simply be because you know that they are watching you, that they care about how you are doing, and that you want your performance to please them. Believing this, you push yourself and you achieve your 30-minute running goal.

The same principles apply in your classroom. Assuming that the learning activities are challenging – as they should be – every student will need encouragement to support them to complete these. While this encouragement might, and often will, come from their peers, it is encouragement from their teacher which typically has the biggest impact.

Praise

In saying this, I will offer a word of caution. Research suggests that 'using praise lavishly' can be detrimental to student learning and progress[105]. Students are quick to work out when teachers don't really mean what they say. Frequently in lesson observations, particularly observations of teachers who are relatively new to the profession, I will hear teachers say things such as 'Brilliant!', 'Fantastic!' and 'That's great!', when actually, what they were praising didn't really merit such extreme positivity. Something gentler would have had a bigger impact. A smile, a 'good answer' or 'I like that' can be just as powerful and motivating as language which goes beyond this. Praise which is 'overdone' loses its meaning and impact quickly. Teachers should use praise, but it is important that students perceive this as genuine and sincere.

At the same time, it is important that teachers let students know when they are less impressed with standards of work or behaviour. Students knowing that you will be honest with them and tell them when standards have fallen short can, in itself, be motivating. An appreciation that substandard work or behaviour won't go unnoticed or unchallenged can motivate students. Constructive criticism is important. So long as it is warranted, students will respect it.

As with praise, criticism should be measured – there is no need to overdo it. Generally, most students will want to please you with their work and behaviour, so there is no need to make too big a deal of things when

---

105. https://www.ibo.org/globalassets/events/aem/conferences/2015/robert-coe.pdf

standards fall short. In fact, there is always the danger that, if you do go over the top with things, it can have a negative effect on the situation or on the professional relationship.

In this chapter, we have concluded our discussion on the typical pedagogy of high-quality lessons. In our final chapter, we shall turn our attention to the type of leadership needed to drive improvements to teaching quality in every classroom in every school: **teaching-centred leadership**.

Chapter 14
Teaching-centred leadership

The importance of leadership

The success or failure of a school is determined by the quality of its leadership. A successful school with ineffective leadership does not exist. While there are many examples of great schools led by great leaders, there are no examples of great schools led by poor leaders. Successful schools – which are *learning schools* – are those in which leaders are committed to learning, by both students and staff.

So, what is leadership? There are a lot of people who talk about its importance, but do all of these people really understand what leadership is or what effective leadership looks like in practice? I don't believe that they do. In our final chapter, we shall explore this.

Leadership styles

Literature is awash with explorations of different leadership styles. In the context of education, these include: 'moral leadership'[106], 'strategic leadership'[107], 'distributed leadership'[108], 'transformational leadership'[109],

---

106. Leithwood, K. *et al.* in Bush, T., Bell, L. and Middlewood, D. ((2009) *The Principles of Educational Leadership and Management*

107. Davies, B. and Davies, B.J. in Davies, B. (2011) *The Essentials of School Leadership*

108. Busher, H. (2006) *Understanding Educational Leadership*

109. Hargreaves, A. and Fullan, M. (2012) *Professional Capital*

'instructional leadership'[110], 'learning-centred leadership'[111] and many more besides. Later in this chapter, I will present a new leadership style to you. This is the leadership style which I believe to be the right one to lead teaching and learning improvement in schools.

But before we get to that, I would like to consider the purpose of leadership.

The purpose of leadership

If we are to understand what leadership is and what effective leadership looks like, then we need to go back to basics and consider the purpose of leadership. For me, the purpose of leadership is to take people with you and 'go somewhere'.

Going somewhere

People can always 'go somewhere' on their own, without leaders. However, without a leader, people will generally go in different directions – many in the wrong direction. Some will not go anywhere at all; they will simply drift.

Rather than allow people to go in different directions or to drift, a leader will:

1. Establish and communicate where they want people to go
2. Orientate people and resources in that direction
3. Support, challenge and motivate people to get there
4. Recognise the success of getting there when they arrive
5. Decide where to go next and restart the process

Leaders are relentless: the 'going somewhere' process never stops. Wherever it is they have got to, they want to go somewhere better. For leaders, the grass *is* always greener.

Leading change

Through the process of getting people to go somewhere, leaders lead *change*. Crucially, this change needs to be *positive change*. Leaders should be judged not just by the change that they make, but by how positive this change is.

---

110. Fullan, M. (2014) *The Principal*
111. Dimmock, C. (2012) *Leadership, Capacity Building and School Improvement*

What are you leading? Where are you going?

People talk a lot about the need to develop and improve leadership in schools. However, they often remain curiously silent on *what exactly* school leaders should be leading. By this, I mean they are unclear about the 'somewhere' they are going.

A useful analogy is driving. Imagine that you are the driver of a car and have three passengers. As the driver, you are the leader. The passengers are the people whom you are leading. The fact that they have got into your car indicates that they want to go with you. Perhaps it was easy to get them into the car, or perhaps it wasn't – maybe they initially wanted to go somewhere else – but you have managed to persuade them to go with you (note: you have *persuaded* them, not kidnapped them). However, you don't tell your passengers where it is that you are going and they are not at all happy. As a result, two of them start to get a bit difficult, muttering something about wanting to stop and turn around (the other one is happy to just go with things for the time being). However, you press on, reassuring them to stick with it and to trust you, because you know where you're going. But the reality is, you actually don't. Instead, what has happened is that you have got into the car, got people to get in with you, and just started to drive. But you didn't have a clue where you were going and you still don't know. You hoped that it might come to you once you started driving, but it hasn't. So, what are you going to do?

My advice would be simple: make a decision about where you are going and go there. In making that decision, make sure that it is a sensible one. If you are not sure, make use of your hands-free and ask someone who is more likely to have a good idea. If you don't know where you are going or how to get there, should you really be driving?

Pointless leadership

Developing leaders purely for the sake of developing leaders is rather pointless. Nobody can lead unless they know what it is that they are leading. Trying to teach people how to lead in the absence of purpose is almost impossible.

I was once asked to give a presentation at a national conference on the theme of 'collaborative leadership'. While I felt honoured to be asked, I must admit that I struggled to get to grips with what it was that I should be talking about. Eventually, I realised that to be able to talk about leading in a collaborative way, I had to be clear about what it was that was being led. While I believe that collaboration is an essential feature of successful leadership, 'collaboration' isn't 'where you are going'. Rather, it is a means to help get you there. Collaboration is part of a process; it isn't an outcome. The same is true of 'distributed leadership'. Distributing leadership is an important principle of effective leadership. However, like collaboration, it is part of a process, not an outcome.

Purposeful leadership

All leadership in a school needs to be aligned with a common purpose. The leadership of an individual is far less powerful than collective leadership aligned with a clear, shared objective. In fragmented schools, different leaders are leading people in different directions. In purposeful schools, leadership is aligned in the same direction.

Some school leaders will tell you that the purpose of their leadership is 'to make the biggest difference that they can', to 'improve experiences and outcomes for young people' or to 'make our school outstanding'. No one can argue with the importance of such sentiments, but does this really tell you anything meaningful about the purpose of their leadership? I'm not convinced that it does. For me, such sentiments are just too vague.

Purpose means *specificity*: *this* is where we are going; *this* is how we are going to get there; *this* is how we will know when we have got there. The principles of effective leadership have a lot in common with the principles of effective teaching.

The best direction

Is there a 'best' direction for leadership in a school to point towards? I believe strongly that there is.

In Chapter 2, I argued that the purpose of school is to support, challenge and inspire students to *learn*. However, leadership in school does not impact directly on student learning – rather, it impacts *indirectly*, via its influence on *teaching*. *Teaching* is what impacts directly on student learning. This is a fundamental point to appreciate. For leadership to make a difference to student learning, it needs to make a difference to teaching quality. Accordingly, leadership in schools needs to **focus on improving teaching quality**.

A new leadership style: teaching-centred leadership

Leadership which focuses on improving teaching quality is teaching-centred leadership. Teaching-centred leadership is key to the continuous improvement of teaching and learning in classrooms, departments and schools.

Figure 14.1 sets out a model for teaching-centred leadership:

Figure 14.1: A teaching-centred model for leadership in schools.

The strength of a school's **professional learning culture** determines its **capacity** for improvement – *teaching capacity* and *leadership capacity*. Weak professional learning cultures won't develop staff capacity; strong professional learning cultures will. As teaching and leadership capacity improve, **teaching quality** will improve. Teaching quality sits at the centre of the teaching-centred leadership model. As the quality of teaching improves, **student learning** will improve. As a result, **student outcomes** will improve, bringing about transformations in students' lives.

Losing sight of the purpose

If we accept that a focus on teaching quality is as important as I am arguing it is, why aren't all school leaders focusing on this? Why aren't all school leaders **teaching-centred leaders**? I believe there are five reasons:

1. They are spending too much time on competing priorities (which are important, but not more important)

2. They are spending too much time 'dealing with things' (such as poor student behaviour), which could either be dealt with by someone else, or which suggests that there is an underlying problem which isn't being addressed (perhaps relating to teaching quality)

3. They don't know how to go about improving teaching quality (so they either try, but don't make any impact, or they don't try)

4. They believe that teaching in their department or school is good enough (but really, it isn't)

5. They believe that teachers, as professionals, will take care of everything to do with teaching improvement themselves – school leaders don't have a role (but they do, and it is a very important one)

None of these are good reasons. Returning to our driving analogy, such leaders are driving in the wrong direction. They need to stop the car and plan their way forward. School leaders who aren't focusing on improving teaching quality need to consider why they aren't and take steps to do something about that. Conversations need to be about teaching and learning, not about litter. School leaders need to stop acting as 'trouble-shooters' and 'highly paid janitors'. Instead, leadership needs to focus on what really matters: teaching and learning.

Focusing on the wrong things

Many school leaders do recognise the importance of teaching and learning. However, scratch beneath the surface and you will often discover that they don't really understand what this means. As a result, they end up focusing on the 'wrong' things. Instead of *pedagogy* – which is the 'right' thing – they focus on things like 'new approaches to lesson planning', 'moderation of assessment evidence' and 'tracking systems'. These all have a place, but that place is relatively small. They are not the key areas which are going to make the big difference to teaching quality and student learning.

New approaches to lesson planning
Careful lesson planning is important to the success of a lesson. However, the best lesson plan in the world does not necessarily make for the best

lesson in the world. Lesson plans might set out very clearly what a teacher *intends* to teach and how they *intend* to teach it, but they don't tell anyone anything about what is *actually* taught, how it is *actually* taught or what is *actually* learned by students. You would have to watch the lesson to get any sort of reliable information about that.

I know of school leaders who insist that teachers forward their lesson plans for the next week to them at the end of each week, so that they can review and check them. Let's be honest here: this is a complete waste of everyone's time. These school leaders would be far better NOT reading these and spending the time saved going into lessons to observe teaching, having a structured discussion about the lesson afterwards and offering supportive feedback. Alternatively, they could spend the time developing their professional knowledge through professional reading on what makes great teaching.

If, at any point, a school leader felt that there were issues with the structure or content of a teacher's lesson, that would be a more appropriate time to ask to see a copy of the teacher's lesson plan. Having read it, they could then have a discussion with the teacher about it. However, I really can't see another reason why a school leader would need to see a teacher's lesson plan, far less *all* the lesson plans of every teacher in their department or school.

Moderation of assessment evidence

Too many teachers and school leaders spend too many hours on activities which have little or no impact on teaching and learning quality. One such activity can be 'moderation of assessment evidence'. In Scotland, over the past decade there has been something close to a national obsession with this. I suspect that a similar situation exists in other countries. To briefly summarise: the national 3–15 curriculum has been organised into five 'levels' – early, first, second, third and fourth. Schools are expected to collect data relating to how many students have achieved a particular level at a particular stage in their education (for example, by the time they leave primary school). As you might expect, to determine if a student has achieved a level or not, teachers need to assess student learning. However, how teachers and schools do this is completely up to them. What this means is that some schools are assessing student learning through use of question-based tests, some by getting students to create presentations and posters, and some by sampling the day-to-day work that students are producing in lessons. There is no standardisation of the assessment.

Whenever the phrase 'standardised assessment' crops up, I know that some teachers and school leaders get a little hot under the collar. To a point, I understand why. Really, standardised assessments are only necessary if the learning of different students in different schools is to be compared, which is what national examinations do. If a comparison isn't going to be made between schools, then they don't need to use the same assessment. However, in the example of the Scottish context we are discussing, the learning of different students in different schools *is* being compared, and therefore assessments *do* need to be standardised. But they aren't. Teachers and school leaders are expected to bring to meetings examples of the different assessment evidence that they have collected, to compare with those from different schools who have collected very different assessment evidence. What ends up happening is that teachers have some discussion about what they are looking at in a professional way, but the impact on teaching and learning is limited at best. Apples are being compared with pears. Had the assessments been standardised, such discussions could have been useful professional learning. As it is, the time is being wasted. Certainly, the time being spent on this is vastly disproportionate to any impact it makes on student learning.

The point of raising this example is not to have a go at specific national policies or to get into a debate about the rights and wrongs of standardised assessments. Rather, the point of bringing this to your attention is because, just as it can be all too easy for teachers to get students to be *busy doing things* in lessons without them learning, the same holds true for teachers and school leaders. It is getting them to be busy doing *the right things* that is key. In the case of teachers, the right things are those which will improve teaching and learning. Time is precious, and teachers don't have enough of it to be wasting.

Tracking systems
Having evidence of how your students are progressing is important. At various times in a school year, teachers are usually asked to report this to parents and discuss it with school leaders. If such reporting and

discussion is to be based on anything more than a best guess, teachers need to assess student learning and have some means to track this.

However, while at one time the terms 'assessment' and 'end-of-topic test' were generally thought of as one and the same, they are not. 'Long-cycle' assessment[112], such as end-of-topic tests, are only one type of assessment. They play an important role because they assess student learning of a broad body of knowledge. However, in the full assessment spectrum, long-cycle assessments are nothing more than a small part. 'Short-cycle' assessment is even more important. This includes continuous use of:

1. Daily, Weekly and Monthly Review
2. 'Pose, Pause, Pounce, Bounce' questioning techniques
3. 'Chat to a partner' moments
4. Show-me boards
5. 'Active assessment' activities (such as true or false, deliberate mistakes and multiple-choice problems)
6. 'Exit Tickets'

Such assessment practices generate the most immediate and useful evidence of student learning. If you want to find out about how effective your teaching has been, the assessment practices listed offer a powerful means to do that. They will give you immediate feedback, which you can act on straight away.

Returning to the topic of tracking systems, so long as they are used proportionately, these do have an important role to play in helping us to understand how students are progressing. However, it is important to appreciate that tracking systems on their own don't do much to improve teaching quality. Instead, their role relates to generating information which can inform reporting, discussion and intervention planning when a student's progress is flagged up as a concern. It is important for school leaders to appreciate that the development and use of departmental and school tracking systems is but a small part of the teaching and learning improvement puzzle. The time spent on developing and using such systems should reflect that.

---

112. Wiliam, D. (2018) *Creating the Schools Our Children Need*

Focus on pedagogy

As we have said many times throughout this book, **a focus on pedagogy is the best way to improve teaching and learning in schools**. It is the key point that all teachers and school leaders need to understand.

A focus on pedagogy means just that: a *focus*. A light touch isn't going to do it. This means that a one-hour twilight session on success criteria which is never revisited or followed up isn't going to do it, no matter how well the session was delivered. Just because something has been taught to teachers doesn't mean it has been learned by teachers. The 'teaching–learning gap' applies as much to teacher professional learning as it does to student learning.

Once, I heard a headteacher say, 'But we did success criteria years ago – we don't need to do them again!' Recently, I heard another say that they didn't think that they needed to do any professional reading on teaching and learning because 'It is all just re-inventing the wheel – the same old fads coming around and around.' Such leaders may understand that improving pedagogy is important, but they don't understand how to lead it.

Influencing people

Earlier in this chapter, I argued that leadership is concerned with leading positive change. However, change – and by that I mean real, sustained change in the mindsets, behaviours and habits of people – is not easy to achieve. But it is achievable. The key to success is to understand how you can *influence* people.

Teachers can't be made to teach in a particular way; leaders can't be made to lead in a particular way. Nor should they. Leadership is about influence, not control.

Influencing people takes great skill. Not everyone is able to do it. If you know someone who has a leadership title but isn't able to influence people, the truth is, they aren't really a leader. Leadership is not about position; it is about influence.

Case study: Influencing people

In 2018, the General Teaching Council for Scotland (GTCS) published an article I had written on the topic of leadership. In it, amongst other things, I discussed the importance of *influence*. I include this article as a part of our discussion on this topic.

What makes a good leader?
The wisdom of continual learning is key to educational leadership

In June 2015, I was interviewed by my local authority for the national *Into Headship* programme. At that time, I had limited experience of educational leadership literature and believed that experience and learning from others were more important. I also believed that many of the principles of good leadership could be learned from the popular television series *Game of Thrones*. This belief formed the basis of my presentation to the interview panel, which included a discussion of the following questions (asked by Tywin Lannister of the young king-to-be, Tommen): 'What makes a good king?' and 'What is a good king's single most important quality?'[113] (To be clear: I wasn't suggesting that the position of headteacher is equivalent to that of king! Rather, I was using this example to consider the qualities of a good leader.)

Returning to the questions, after considering and then dismissing different answers, king-to-be Tommen decided that the single most important quality in a good king is 'wisdom', i.e. recognising what you know and what you don't, where you are strong and where you are less so, and ensuring that you seek advice and support from others. Thinking back to the time of my interview, if I compare myself as a leader now to where I was then, the single most important change as a result of the *Into Headship* programme is that I believe I have become wiser.

Participating in *Into Headship* has changed me – I now think differently and I do things differently. A key change has been in the amount of time that I spend reading. I have never been much of a

---

113. *Game of Thrones*, Series 4, *Episode 3*, 'Breaker of Chains' (2014)

reader, but *Into Headship* has changed that. Over the 18 months of the programme, I read a lot. In fact, it would not be an exaggeration to say that I read more books and journal articles in the 18 months of the programme than I had in the previous 18 years! And the most surprising thing for me? I enjoyed it. Over the course of the programme, I found myself getting up an hour earlier to read (and that is surprising, because I've never been a 'morning person'), and while I've not agreed with everything I've read, I have taken time to think about it and to discuss it with other people. By spending more time reading, I have become more confident in my beliefs about certain things and I have changed my mind about others.

One significant change that has come about through reading relates to my understanding of the purpose of educational leadership. There are many different leadership models out there and *Into Headship* has been very useful in helping me to consider a wide variety of these in detail. From this, I have come to believe that educational leadership is first and foremost about leadership of learning. This is what sets educational leadership apart from leadership in other fields. The key purpose of leadership in schools is to build a culture of learning, with the principal objective of making teaching and learning better (no matter how good it is already).

In leading the organisation, whenever there is a decision to be made, a key question should be: will this support teaching and learning improvement?

However, having come to this conclusion, a challenge for me has been to consider how the actions of the headteacher can make a difference to student learning. Clearly, teachers and students are able to directly affect teaching and learning in lessons but with headteachers typically absent from this environment how are they able to make a difference?

Into Headship has taught me that the key to this is to understand the concept of indirect influence: focusing your own work to ensure that everything about the design of the school and the way that people spend their time is aligned to teaching and learning improvement.

Building teams and developing and motivating staff should be key drivers for a headteacher and it is on these activities that I now strive to spend most of my time.

Returning to my *Into Headship* interview, do I still believe that principles of good leadership can be learned from *Game of Thrones*? As part of that interview, I discussed Jon Snow who (spoiler alert!) knew a lot about what needed to be done, but who forgot to take key people with him, and paid a heavy price for that.

Into Headship has taught me a lot about what needs to be done and, just as importantly, about how to take people with you in order to achieve it. It has taught me to be wise in the widest sense – strategically, politically and emotionally. I believe that I am a better leader for it and that, consequently, teaching and learning in my school is better as a result, which for me is the key measure. But, of course, learning is never-ending, so I'm going to keep on reading, keep on talking and keep on listening. And, yes, I'm going to keep on watching *Game of Thrones*.

Approaches to influencing people

Different people are influenced in different ways. However, there are certain principles relating to influence which should be useful for all school leaders to keep in mind. These are:

- Cup of coffee conversations
- Planting seeds
- Catching bees with honey
- Use of social capital

Briefly, we shall discuss each in turn.

Cup of coffee conversations

In Chapter 11, we discussed a scenario in which a member of staff who was reluctant to get on board with a lesson observation initiative got on board following a 'cup of coffee conversation'. Taking time to sit down with people (perhaps with a cup of coffee) and talk things through is important. Such conversations develop trust and they help ensure that people feel listened to. Making time to engage in such conversations is a key leadership behaviour.

Planting seeds

Effective leaders are people who plant lots of seeds. What I mean by this is that they suggest things, but they don't expect them to happen immediately. Instead, they allow time for people to think about them and talk to other people. They aren't being pushed into a corner. I know that, initially, I can be reluctant to embrace new ideas. However, if given a bit of time, my initial hard reaction tends to soften and I usually come around.

Catching bees with honey

A deputy headteacher with whom I once worked used to say, 'You catch more bees with honey.' What he meant by this is that if someone is proving difficult to persuade to do something, the best way to influence them is by being positive, not by giving them a hard time. Being positive means setting out the positive case for why you would like something to happen. It means saying things like, 'I would really appreciate it if you could…' and 'Please would you take some time to think about this and we'll chat about it again soon', rather than, 'I'm telling you to do this, so you're going to do it.' Sledgehammer approaches rarely work; use of honey does.

Use of social capital

Leaders should never underestimate the power that people have to influence one another. If you ask someone to get on board with something and they don't, consider asking someone else to speak to them. Often, you will find that they end up doing exactly as you were asking; it's just that it took someone else who had a different relationship with them to tap them on the shoulder and persuade them. Authors such as Clive Dimmock, Andy Hargreaves and Michael Fullan discuss this as making use of 'social capital'[114].

---

114. Dimmock, C. (2012) *Leadership, Capacity Building and School Improvement*; Hargreaves, A. and Fullan, M. (2012) *Professional Capital*

Case study: Principal teacher of teaching and learning

In my school, we have appointed a principal teacher of teaching and learning. Beyond their own teaching commitment, this person has played a fundamental role in leading improvements to teaching quality across the school. Key to their success has been the fact that:

1. They have a strong professional knowledge of what makes great teaching
2. They are a great teacher themselves
3. They have strong interpersonal skills
4. Teachers and school leaders value and respect their opinion
5. They are committed to their own professional learning and continuous improvement

One day a week, this person goes into lessons and observes teachers teach. They make time to sit down with teachers afterwards and discuss the lesson, in line with the principles that we discussed in Chapter 11. So valued is this person, that there is usually a waiting list of staff who want them to come to observe their lessons. They are able to influence people in a way that others are sometimes unable to. They are a living embodiment of social capital in action.

Tipping point

When thinking about the principle of influence, a key is idea that of a 'tipping point'. When you reach a tipping point, whatever it was that you were trying to get people to do (or not do) has become 'the norm'. This doesn't mean that you have influenced everyone, but what you have done is influenced enough people so that those who aren't on board are in the clear minority. The momentum that you have created by influencing the majority will carry most of the minority with it.

Middle and senior leadership

Teaching improvement does not just happen by itself – it requires leadership. While teachers can, of course, lead their own improvement, it takes the leadership of middle and senior leaders to truly transform teaching practice across departments and schools. Through their words and actions, leaders need to get across that the continuous improvement of teaching is the number one priority for their department or school.

In terms of driving forward change, middle leaders are the key players. Senior leaders can set direction, but it is middle leaders who drive schools forward. While their leadership role is typically less strategic and more operational than that of senior leaders, it is no less important. Arguably, it is more important. I have seen schools with relatively poor senior leadership teams but with strong middle leadership teams who were able to compensate. That said, this situation is rare, because weak senior leadership and weak middle leadership more often go hand in hand. Without strong senior leaders to help develop middle leaders, there is little chance of the middle leadership team developing as a strong one.

The challenges of middle leadership
The middle leadership role is one of the most challenging in a school. Middle leaders teach students, manage staff and lead change. However, because of the time taken up by teaching and management, they are often limited in the time that they have available to lead. This is a serious issue in many schools. High-quality leadership from headteachers and deputy headteachers won't bring about transformations in practice if there are weaknesses in the middle leadership team or if middle leaders don't have enough time to lead.

The importance of collaboration
In *learning schools*, middle leaders work closely together, supporting each other and learning from each other as much as they can. For example, they might share minutes of their departmental meetings with one another. This can spark ideas and discussion, and share good practice.

Middle leaders also work closely with senior leaders. There isn't an 'us' and 'them' culture. Instead, middle and senior leaders meet regularly, sometimes one to one and sometimes as a team. In doing so, middle leaders influence senior leaders and other middle leaders; senior leaders influence middle leaders and other senior leaders. Making time to talk and listen is one of the best ways to influence.

Case study: Teaching & Learning Calendars

Like all leadership in a school, the focus of middle leadership should be on teaching and learning improvement. Because of the constraints that many middle leaders have on the time available for them to lead, it can be useful for them to develop a calendar of activities which will support this agenda. Doing so will help them to map *what* needs to happen and *when* it should be happening. This helps to make them accountable to themselves and to keep their leadership on track.

In our school, we call such calendars '**Teaching & Learning Calendars**'. Some schools have similar calendars and call them 'Quality Assurance Calendars'. However, calling them this gives too much weight to the role of quality assurance in schools. Quality assurance has a place, but that place isn't more important than professional learning, self-evaluation and improvement planning.

Once a year, heads of department produce a Teaching & Learning Calendar for their department, which they share with their team, line manager and other heads of department, in the spirit of collaboration and learning from each other. They are all given the same list of activities to be included in their calendars, these being:

1. Teacher self-evaluation and discussion of this using the school *Lesson Evaluation Toolkit*
2. Peer lesson observations
3. Middle leader lesson observations
4. Student evaluations
5. Student focus groups
6. Review and discussion of student progress data
7. Review of department Improvement Plan
8. Review of teacher Professional Learning Plans

The finer detail of Teaching and Learning Calendars is determined by the middle leader. They decide how often these activities happen and when they happen. This is an example of a tight–loose balance in action: a senior leader sets out *what* they would like included; the specifics of *how* this looks are up to middle leaders.

Activity	Strength/ weakness	Aug	Sep	Oct	Nov	Dec	Jan	Feb	Mar	Apr	May	Jun
Self-evaluation of lessons using *Lesson Evaluation Toolkit*	A	✓	✓	✓	✓	✓	✓	✓	✓	✓	✓	✓
Peer lesson observations	A		✓		✓		✓		✓		✓	✓
Head of department lesson observations	G			✓			✓			✓		
Student evaluations	A		✓			✓		✓		✓		
Student focus groups	R		✓			✓		✓		✓		
Review and discussion of student progress data	G	✓	✓	✓	✓	✓	✓	✓	✓	✓	✓	✓
Improvement Plan: progress review and discussion	A				✓				✓			✓
Professional Learning Plans: progress review and discussion	A			✓			✓			✓		

In our fortnightly one-to-one meetings, I discuss Teaching & Learning Calendars with middle leaders, including what activities have been happening, what learning has come from these, and what is planned to happen over the coming weeks. Teaching & Learning Calendars are a key resource to support teaching-centred leadership.

The teaching-centred leader

Teaching-centred leadership requires teaching-centred leaders. Teaching-centred leaders are leaders who:

1. Make the continuous improvement of teaching quality their number one priority
2. Focus on developing a shared understanding of what makes great teaching
3. Focus professional learning on teaching and learning, prioritising pedagogy
4. Lead by example
5. Spend a lot of time reading

6. Spend a lot of time observing lessons

7. Support and challenge teachers to continuously improve their practice

8. Make time for people – to listen, coach and mentor

9. Understand that everyone is different and that the way to get the best out of one person is not necessarily the way to get the best out of others

10. Take time to recognise strengths and good practice

11. Have difficult conversations with staff when they need to (but not when they don't really need to)

12. Make teaching and learning the dominant topic of discussion

13. Invest time and resources in collaborative professional learning approaches

14. Plan for continuous teaching improvement, informed by evidence of strengths and weaknesses

Are you a teaching-centred leader? If you are, just how teaching-centred are you? What can you do to become more teaching-centred? These are important questions for all school leaders to reflect on.

Teaching at the centre

Teaching-centred leadership puts teaching at the heart of a school. Schools need to look after their teachers. This means that they need to invest in them and support their learning. They need to challenge and inspire them to continuously improve the quality of their teaching, no matter how experienced they are or how good their teaching is already. An investment in teachers is an investment in teaching. This investment will pay off through improved student learning and outcomes. This is what teaching-centred leadership is all about.

Conclusion

Revisiting key questions

At the start of this book, we recognised that there is a lot of great teaching going on in our classrooms and schools. We also discussed a number of questions in relation to this, which I would like to revisit now.

Regardless of your role in a school – teacher or school leader – I asked you:

1. What makes great teaching?
2. How do we know what makes great teaching?
3. What is the difference between good teaching and great teaching?

Take a moment to think about your answers and whether or not these have changed as a result of reading this book. I hope that they have. As we conclude, there is value in summarising some of the key messages we have discussed in relation to them.

What makes great teaching?

Great teaching is a blend of **Specific Teaching** and **Non-specific Teaching** approaches:

- **Specific Teaching** is about the synergy of high-quality *pedagogical subject knowledge, direct-interactive instruction* and *formative assessment*
- **Non-specific Teaching** is about *student-led learning* – the application of learning, exploration and discovery

Integral to both are high-quality *teacher–student relationships*.

While great teaching involves both Specific and Non-specific Teaching approaches, in the interests of teaching students the knowledge they need to develop skills and attributes and to attain, **a focus on Specific Teaching is key.** *This* is the area on which leadership of teaching and learning needs to focus. As a general rule, Specific Teaching should account for 80–90% of teaching and learning time; 10–20% of time should focus on Non-specific Teaching which enriches teaching and learning.

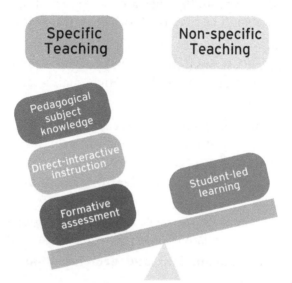

Teacher-student relationships

Great teaching involves a balance of Specific Teaching and Non-specific Teaching approaches. However, in the interests of maximising student learning, this balance needs to favour Specific Teaching.

The teaching–learning gap
Key to understanding great teaching is understanding the **teaching–learning gap**. This relates to the difference between what is taught and what is learned. In great teaching, teachers measure and address this gap on a continuous basis. Use of Specific Teaching is key to this.

Learning and enjoyment
Learning and enjoyment are products of great teaching. It isn't a case of achieving one or the other: in great teaching, it is both.

It is important that students enjoy their learning. However, as important is that they are actually *learning*. When planning lessons, teachers should plan for *high-quality learning* as opposed to enjoyment. Enjoyment will come as a result of high-quality teaching. The risk in letting enjoyment drive lesson planning is that learning gets lost and classrooms become little more than youth clubs. Just because students are busy and enjoying what they are doing doesn't mean that they are learning. Professional teaching should first and foremost be concerned with high-quality student learning.

High-quality lessons

Great teaching manifests itself through the pedagogy of lessons. Lessons are the delivery units of great teaching. High-quality lessons are those which typically include:

1. Activities that require students to **recall knowledge** from previous lessons, which may or may not be relevant to this lesson, but which needs to be learned as part of the course
2. Clear communication and use of **learning intentions and success criteria**
3. Activities that allow the teacher to **find out what students know or can do already** (in relation to what is being taught in this lesson)
4. Clear **teacher explanations and demonstrations** which hold student attention
5. Activities that allow students to **put into practice** what they are being taught
6. Appropriate levels of **support and challenge**
7. Use of **questions** to make students think and to check for understanding
8. Activities that get students to **discuss and learn with other students**
9. Clear **feedback** to individual students and to the class about their learning
10. Activities that **evaluate the impact of lessons**
11. Strong **teacher–student relationships**
12. **High expectations and standards** for student behaviour and quality of work

How do we know what makes great teaching?

Educational literature and research are key. Therefore, professional reading and discussion of this reading are key. Knowing what makes great teaching is fundamental to improving teaching practice. It is empowering.

What is the difference between good teaching and great teaching?

I suggest there are two factors:

1. The extent to which the typical features of high-quality lessons are *regular* features of lessons
2. The *quality* of these features in lessons

Further questions (for teachers)

If you are a teacher, I asked you some further questions:

1. How good is your teaching?
2. How do you know?
3. How would you rate the quality of your teaching out of 10?
4. How confident are you that your teaching is as good as you think it is?
5. Does your teaching need to get better?
6. Do you want to make your teaching better?
7. Do you know how to make your teaching better?

Again, please take a moment to think about your answers to each of these and whether or not they have changed since you started reading this book.

How good is your teaching?

I am afraid I am in no position to answer this. However, as a result of reading this book, I hope you have a clearer idea. What I am able to do is offer you an answer to the next question...

How do you know (how good your teaching is)?

While you can never truly be sure of how good your teaching is (or anyone else's is) there are particular things you can do to help you become clearer:

- **Develop your professional knowledge and understanding** of what makes great teaching by reading and discussing educational literature and research, sharing practice, observing other teachers and participating in other in-school professional learning activities.

- **Self-evaluate your teaching**. The more your professional knowledge and understanding develops, the better your self-evaluation will become. Use your school *Lesson Evaluation Toolkit* to support this.

- **Seek feedback from other professionals** – teachers and school leaders – by inviting them into lessons to observe you teaching and asking them to use your school *Lesson Evaluation Toolkit* to guide feedback discussions with you.

- **Seek student feedback** about the quality of your teaching. This should include the use of evaluations and focus groups.

- **Make use of continuous formative assessment in lessons** ('Short cycle' assessment) to find out the extent to which what you have taught has been learned. 'Daily, Weekly and Monthly Review', 'Pose, Pause, Pounce, Bounce' questioning techniques, 'Chat to a partner' moments, Show-me boards, 'active assessment' activities and 'Exit Tickets' are all excellent for this purpose.

- **Analyse attainment data**, such as from end-of-topic tests and examinations ('Long-cycle' assessment).

By focusing on these, you will become clearer about how good your teaching is and what you need to do to improve it. In doing so, you will break the teaching delusion.

We break the teaching delusion when we focus on activities which helps us to become clearer about how good our teaching is and what we need to do to improve it.

How would you rate the quality of your teaching out of 10?
Again, this is one that I can't help you with, although I am interested to know if this has changed since you started reading this book. Has it gone up? Has it gone down? Has it stayed the same?

How confident are you that your teaching is as good as you think it is?
As a result of reading this book, I hope that the answer is 'a lot more confident'.

Does your teaching need to get better?
Regardless of how good it is already, regardless of your experience or expertise, I hope that the answer to this question is a very firm: 'yes'. If it isn't, I have failed to get across a key message, which is the need for teachers and school leaders to be relentless in their drive for continuous improvement.

Do you want to make your teaching better?

For the reasons I have just given, I hope the answer is another firm: 'yes'.

Further questions (for school leaders)

If you are a school leader, I asked you:

1. Does teaching in your department or school need to get better?
2. Do you want to make teaching in your department or school better?
3. Do you know how to make teaching in your department or school better?

Does teaching in your department or school need to get better?

Yes, it does. Let's move on.

Do you want to make teaching in your department or school better?

Yes, you do. I know you do. If you didn't, you wouldn't have spent time reading this book.

Do you know how to make teaching in your department or school better?

This one is more difficult. As a result of reading this book, I hope that you do.

The solution lies with two areas:

1. Developing a **shared understanding of what makes great teaching**
2. Developing a **strong professional learning culture** (focused on teaching and leadership quality)

If we are to move towards great teaching in every classroom, in every school, the development of a shared understanding of what makes great teaching is key. As important is the development of a strong professional learning culture, which supports, challenges and inspires everyone to learn and improve, regardless of how good things are already. Creating and using a *Lesson Evaluation Toolkit* will help you with both.

Empowering teachers and school leaders

As the teaching profession evolves, it is right that we move towards a teacher-empowered system. However, this does not mean that we abandon teachers to 'get on with it' themselves. True empowerment means ensuring teachers have access to high-quality professional learning. Teachers will always require direction, support and challenge. In an empowered system, where a culture of professional learning has been established, teachers don't resent this – they feel inspired by it. Teaching-centred leaders drive the development of this culture.

Making the job easier

When I was first appointed deputy headteacher, a deputy headteacher in the school I was about to leave said to me, 'Never forget that the job is about making everyone else's easier.' I thought that was great advice, and I still do.

As a senior leader whose leadership draws on the principles of a **teaching-centred leadership** model, I believe that I do make the jobs of others easier. As a result of a focus on developing a shared understanding of what makes great teaching and a strong professional learning culture, every teacher in our school is a better teacher now than they were when I first started, or indeed, than they were this time last year. I am confident that every teacher in our school would agree with that. As a teacher, I include myself.

As a result, our jobs have become easier and more enjoyable. There are fewer behaviour problems from students in lessons because the quality of teaching has improved. As a result, students are more engaged and they are enjoying lessons more. Many teachers have reduced their workload because, instead of taking home 30 jotters to mark to find out what students have learned, they are, instead, using pedagogies such as Daily, Weekly and Monthly Review and Exit Tickets. These are far more effective and efficient.

By encouraging staff to read educational literature and research, by investing in new books for our Professional Reading Library, by encouraging staff to set up professional Twitter accounts, and by establishing a 'Learning from Reading' noticeboard in our staffroom, staff are talking about teaching and learning with excitement and enthusiasm. In the staffroom, the topic of conversation has changed, because staff *want* to talk about teaching practice, to debate it and discuss it. The more they are learning, the more they want to continue. They feel more confident and empowered. Reading and sharing learning from reading has created a real buzz in our school. We have become a *learning school*.

The introduction of a Teaching and Learning Improvement Group and Professional Reading Group has created opportunities for staff to come together and learn with and from each other, and to lead teaching-focused initiatives. Some of the best ideas about what we can do to improve teaching have come from these groups, rather than from one person. These include Peer Observation Programmes, teacher-led workshop programmes and a website to share teaching practice across the school. There are staff who describe participation in these groups as being one of the highlights of their jobs.

Collectively, such initiatives have played a key role in helping to transform the professional learning culture of our school. When asked, however, most staff will tell you that *the* key initiative has been the development and use of our school *Lesson Evaluation Toolkit*. This is the resource which pulls everything and everyone together. This is the resource which has brought about our shared understanding of what makes great teaching. If you want to develop as a learning school with teaching-centred leadership at your core, start by developing your own *Lesson Evaluation Toolkit*. Everything else will follow.

Certainty

David Bowie once sang: 'I don't want knowledge, I want certainty.'[115] In teaching, the certainty we all need is that we are making the biggest difference we can to the lives of every student we teach. We make this difference through the quality of our teaching.

Everyone's teaching can get better; everyone's teaching needs to get better. With a collective focus on the right things, in the right way, everyone's teaching *will* get better. There is no delusion in believing that.

---

115. Bowie, D. (1997) 'Law (Earthlings on Fire)'

Q&A

For teachers

Q: I want to make my teaching better but I'm not sure how to go about doing that. What should I do?

A: The key to developing and improving your practice is developing your knowledge and understanding of what makes great teaching (and what doesn't), informed by educational literature and research. **Professional reading is key.**

Professional reading is concerned with educational theory, which is important. However, it is also important that you consider how theory can be put into practice. To support this, I would suggest that you take advantage of every opportunity to **observe other teachers teaching.** Don't wait for a school leader to tell you to do this; take the initiative and set this up yourself. As you are watching other teachers teach, reflect on what you have learned from reading and how what you are seeing might help develop and improve your practice.

As important as watching other teachers is getting high-quality feedback about your own teaching practice. To do this, **invite other professionals to observe you teach.** This might be other teachers, middle leaders or senior leaders – the role of this person in school is a far less important consideration than the quality of feedback they are likely to give you. If you are to learn from the process and improve as a teacher, you need to receive high-quality feedback. You need to trust the person who is observing you and respect their professional opinions. You need the feedback you receive to be clear and constructive. Don't invite someone to watch you teach and then wait a year before you invite someone back again. If you are to really improve your teaching practice, you need much more regular feedback than that.

A key measure of teaching quality is the size of the teaching–learning gap, that is, the gap between what has been taught and what has been learned. Ideally, you don't want there to be a gap at all. **Use formative assessment strategies** such as Show-me boards and Exit Tickets to get continuous feedback from students about their learning. By finding out the extent to which what has been taught has also been learned, you can take steps to address any gap.

You should also **seek the views of students** on your teaching via evaluations and talking to students. Be brave and ask them what they feel is working well and less well. Is there something that they would like you to do more or less of, or differently? You don't necessarily need to act on it, but seeking this sort of feedback is important.

You should **take advantage of every opportunity that you can to learn with and from other members of staff.** If there is a staff Professional Reading Group, join this. If there are in-school workshop programmes, participate in these. If there are other systems to share practice across the school, engage with these. Collaboration with other professionals is key to developing and improving your teaching practice.

Specifically, I suggest that there are **five 'quick wins'** which can help transform your teaching:

1. Use Show-me boards in every lesson
2. Start lessons with 'Daily Review'
3. End lessons with 'Exit Tickets'
4. Say 'Everyone think about that' and 'Chat to a partner' after you ask questions
5. Build 'active assessment' activities into instruction

Q: I don't feel that my school has a strong culture of professional learning. What can I do about that?

A: Talk to your line manager or another school leader. Share any ideas that you have about initiatives which could help develop the professional learning culture, such as setting up a Professional Reading Group. Don't wait on people coming to you: take the initiative and lead!

For school leaders

Q: There isn't a shared understanding of what makes great teaching across our school. How should we address that?

A: Through the development of your **professional learning culture**. The different components of this culture will interact to develop a shared understanding of what makes great teaching. Key to this is **professional reading** and the development of a school *Lesson Evaluation Toolkit*.

Q: We want to develop the professional learning culture in our school. How do we go about doing that?

A: Professional learning is generally embraced by staff when:

- The purpose of the learning is clear
- Activities are aligned to the purpose
- The activities lead to learning

In order for these conditions to be met, schools need to know themselves well. They need to know where their strengths and development needs are so that they can plan for improvement. The purpose of professional learning is to action planned improvement.

Improvement planning should focus on teaching and learning. By this, I mean the *how* (pedagogy) and the *what* (curriculum). If schools are to do this successfully, they need to **develop a shared understanding of what makes great teaching** across the school. The best way to do that is to involve everyone in the development and use of a school *Lesson Evaluation Toolkit*.

Leading the development of a *Lesson Evaluation Toolkit* should be the school's **Teaching and Learning Improvement Group**. If your school doesn't have such a group, it is imperative that you establish one. This should be a key strategic group in any *learning school*. The role of this group is to plan, co-ordinate and evaluate a school's professional learning programme. The components of such a programme could include:

1. **A Professional Reading Group**
2. **A Peer Observation Programme**
3. **Middle and senior leader lesson observation**
4. **A staff-led workshop programme**
5. **Systems to share practice across the school**
6. **Systems to gather student feedback**

It is important that schools invest in resources which support the development of their professional learning culture. Because professional reading is so important, schools should invest in books for a **Professional Reading Library** for staff. If staff require resources to put theory into practice (such as Show-me boards), then schools need to invest in these too.

Schools also need to invest in their leaders. They should ensure that there is a high-quality in-school **Leadership Development Programme**. They should also consider creating formal teaching- and learning-focused leadership roles, such as a **principal teacher of teaching and learning**.

Teachers and school leaders should be encouraged and supported to lead initiatives which support the development of the school's professional learning culture. This doesn't mean that just anyone should be free to lead just anything – there is always a need to keep an eye on quality. However, ideas should be encouraged and staff should be given the opportunity to try things out. Regardless of their experience and expertise, if they are to be successful they will need to be supported in their leadership through **coaching and mentoring**.

Q: There are a lot of things here. Where should we start?

A: Start by establishing a Teaching and Learning Improvement Group, the first task of which is to lead the development of a school *Lesson Evaluation Toolkit*. Once your school *Lesson Evaluation Toolkit* is in place, start to use it as much as you can.

Bibliography and references

Included in this section are books and articles which have helped influence my thinking. Many of these are referenced as footnotes in chapters.

Angelides, P. and Ainscow, M. (2000) 'Making Sense of the Role of Culture in School Improvement'. *School Effectiveness and School Improvement*, 11(2), pp. 145–163.

Ashman, G. (2019) 'Explicit Teaching'. In A. Boxer (ed.) *The ResearchED Guide to Explicit and Direct Instruction: An Evidenced-Informed Guide for Teachers*. Woodbridge: John Catt Educational Ltd, pp. 29–35.

Barber, M. and Mourshed, M. (2007) *How the World's Best-Performing School Systems Come Out on Top*. London: McKinsey and Company.

Barber, M., Whelan, F. and Clark, M. (2010) *Capturing the Leadership Premium: How the World's Top School Systems Are Building Leadership Capacity for the Future*. London: McKinsey and Company.

Barton, C. (2018) *How I Wish I'd Taught Maths: Lessons Learned from Research, Conversations with Experts, and 12 Years of Mistakes*. Woodbridge: John Catt Educational Ltd.

Bell, L. and Bolam, R. (2009) 'Teacher Professionalism and Continuing Professional Development: Contested Concepts and Their Implications for School Leaders'. In Bush, T., Bell, L. and Middlewood, D. (eds). *The Principles of Educational Leadership and Management* (Second Edition). London: Sage, pp. 89–107.

Bolden, R. (2011) 'Distributed Leadership in Organizations: A Review of Theory and Research'. *International Journal of Management Reviews*, 13, pp. 251–269.

Brundrett, M. (2010) 'Developing Your Leadership Team'. In B. Davies and M. Brundrett (eds). *Developing Successful Leadership*. London: Springer, pp. 99–114.

Bryson, B. (2004) *A Short History of Nearly Everything*. London: Black Swan.

Buck, A. (2016) *Leadership Matters: How Leaders at All Levels Can Create Good Schools*. Woodbridge: John Catt Educational Ltd.

Bush, T., Bell, L. and Middlewood, D. (2009) 'Introduction: New directions in Educational Leadership'. In Bush, T., Bell, L. and Middlewood, D. (eds) *The Principles of Educational Leadership and Management* (Second Edition). Sage, pp. 3–12.

Bush, T. (2011) *Theories of Educational Leadership and Management* (Fourth Edition). London: Sage.

Bush, T. and Glover, D. (2014) 'School Leadership Models: What Do We Know?' *School Leadership and Management*, 34(5), pp. 553–571.

Busher, H. (2006) *Understanding Educational Leadership: People, Power and Culture*. Berkshire: Open University Press.

Campbell, C. (2011) *How to Involve Hard-to-Reach Parents: Encouraging Meaningful Parental Involvement with Schools*. Nottingham: National College for School Leadership.

Christodoulou, D. (2013) *Seven Myths About Education*. Oxon: Routledge.

Christodoulou, D. (2016) *Making Good Progress?: The Future of Assessment for Learning*. Oxford: Oxford University Press.

Clarke, S. (2014) *Outstanding Formative Assessment: Culture and Practice*. Hodder Education.

Coe, R., Aloisi, C., Higgins, S. and Major, L.E. (2014) *What Makes Great Teaching? Review of the Underpinning Research*. The Sutton Trust.

Cole, P. (2012) *Aligning Professional Learning, Performance Management and Effective Teaching.* Centre for Strategic Education, Seminar Series Paper Number 217. September 2012, East Melbourne, Australia.

Cole, P. (2012) *Linking Effective Professional Learning with Effective Teaching Practice.* Melbourne: Australian Institute for Teaching and School Leadership.

Crehan, L. (2016) *Cleverlands: The Secrets Behind the Success of the World's Education Superpowers.* London: Unbound.

Davies, B. and Davies, B.J. (2011) 'Strategic Leadership'. In Davies, B. (ed.) *The Essentials of School Leadership* (Second Edition). London: Sage, pp. 13–36.

Davies, B. and Davies, B.J. (2013) 'The Nature and Dimensions of Strategic Leadership'. In M. Brundrett (ed.) *Principles of School Leadership* (Second Edition). London: Sage, pp. 73–93.

Dimmock, C. (2012) *Leadership, Capacity Building and School Improvement: Concepts, Themes and Impact.* Oxon: Routledge.

Dix, P. (2017) *When the Adults Change, Everything Changes: Seismic Shifts in School Behaviour.* Carmarthen: Independent Thinking Press.

Draper, J. (2016) 'The Changing Face of Leadership Opportunities'. In J. O'Brien (ed.) *School Leadership* (Third Edition). Edinburgh: Dunedin, pp. 88–106.

Earley, P. (2013) *Exploring the School Leadership Landscape: Changing Demands. Changing Realities.* London: Bloomsbury.

Forde, C. (2016) 'Leadership Development'. In J. O'Brien (ed.) *School Leadership* (Third Edition). Edinburgh: Dunedin, pp. 107–132.

Forde, C. (2016) 'Leading Professional Learning'. In J. O'Brien (ed.) *School Leadership* (Third Edition). Edinburgh: Dunedin, pp. 166–191.

Fullan, M. (2008) *What's Worth Fighting for in Headship?* (Second Edition). Maidenhead: Open University Press.

Fullan, M. (2011) *The Six Secrets of Change: What the Best Leaders Do to Help Their Organizations Survive and Thrive.* San Francisco, CA: Jossey-Bass.

Fullan, M. (2014) *The Principal: Three Keys to Maximizing Impact.* San Francisco, CA: Jossey-Bass.

Hargreaves, A. and Fullan, M. (2012) *Professional Capital: Transforming Teaching in Every School.* Oxon: Routledge.

Harris, A. (2009) 'Distributed Leadership: Evidence and Implications'. In Bush, T., Bell, L. and Middlewood, D. (eds) *The Principles of Educational Leadership and Management* (Second Edition). London: Sage, pp. 55–69.

Hattie, J. (2009) *Visible Learning: A Synthesis of Over 800 Meta-Analyses Relating to Achievement.* Oxon: Routledge.

Hattie, J. (2012) *Visible Learning for Teachers: Maximizing Impact on Learning.* New York: Routledge.

Hendrick, C. and Macpherson, R. (2017) *What Does This Look Like in the Classroom? Bridging the Gap Between Research and Practice.* Woodbridge: John Catt Educational Ltd.

Hirsch, E.D. (2016) *Why Knowledge Matters: Rescuing Our Children from Failed Educational Theories.* Cambridge, MA: Harvard Education Press.

Jones, J. (2009) *The Magic Weaving Business: Finding the Heart of Learning and Teaching.* London: Leannta Publishing.

Kirby, J. (2016) 'Knowledge, Memory and Testing'. In Birbalsingh, K. (eds) *Battle Hymn of the Tiger Teachers: The Michaela Way.* Woodbridge: John Catt Educational Ltd, pp. 16–27.

Kirby, J. (2016) 'Homework as Revision'. In Birbalsingh, K. (eds). *Battle Hymn of the Tiger Teachers: The Michaela Way.* Woodbridge: John Catt Educational Ltd, pp. 54–66.

Lambersky, J. (2016) 'Understanding the Human Side of School Leadership: Principals' Impact on Teachers' Morale, Self-Efficacy, Stress, and Commitment'. *Leadership and Policy in Schools,* 15(4), pp. 379–405.

Leithwood, K., Anderson, S.E., Mascall, B. and Strauss, T. (2009) 'School Leaders' Influences on Student Learning: The Four Paths'. In Bush, T., Bell, L. and Middlewood, D. (eds) *The Principles of Educational Leadership and Management* (Second Edition). London: Sage, pp. 13–30.

Lemov, D., Woolway, E. and Yezzi, K. (2012) *Practice Perfect: 42 Rules for Getting Better at Getting Better.* San Francisco, CA: Jossey-Bass.

Lemov, D. (2015) *Teach Like A Champion 2.0: 62 Techniques that Put Students on the Path to College.* San Francisco, CA: Jossey-Bass.

Lumby, J. (2013) 'Distributed Leadership: The Uses and Abuses of Power'. *Educational Management Administration and Leadership,* 41(5), pp. 581–597.

MacBeath, J. (2008) 'Stories of Compliance and Subversion in a Prescriptive Policy Environment'. *Educational Management Administration and Leadership,* 36(1), pp. 123–148.

MacBeath, J., O'Brien, J. and Gronn, P. (2012) 'Drowning or Waving? Coping Strategies among Scottish Head Teachers'. *School Leadership and Management,* 32(5), pp. 421–437.

McMahon, M. (2016) 'Leadership for Learning, Learning for Leadership'. In J. O'Brien (ed.) *School Leadership* (Third Edition). Edinburgh: Dunedin, pp. 133–150.

Middlewood, D. (2009) 'Managing People and Performance'. In Bush, T., Bell, L. and Middlewood, D. (eds) *The Principles of Educational Leadership and Management* (Second Edition). London: Sage, pp. 132–150.

Murphy, D. (2013) *Professional School Leadership: Dealing with Dilemmas.* Edinburgh: Dunedin Academic Press.

Murphy, D. (2016) 'Leadership in a Democratic Society'. In J. O'Brien (ed.) *School Leadership* (Third Edition). Edinburgh: Dunedin, pp. 30–56.

Myatt, M. (2016) *High Challenge, Low Threat: How the Best Leaders Find the Balance.* Woodbridge: John Catt Educational Ltd.

Myatt, M. (2018) *The Curriculum: Gallimaufry to Coherence.* Woodbridge: John Catt Educational Ltd.

National College for School Leadership (2004) *Distributed Leadership in Action: Full report.* Nottingham, UK: NCSL.

Naylor, S., Keogh, B. and Goldsworthy, A. (2004) *Active Assessment in Science: Thinking, Learning and Assessment in Science*. London: David Fulton.

Needham, T. (2019) 'Teaching through Examples'. In A. Boxer (ed.) *The ResearchED Guide to Explicit and Direct Instruction: An Evidenced-Informed Guide for Teachers*. Woodbridge: John Catt Educational Ltd, pp 37–53.

O'Brien, J. and Murphy, D. (2016) 'Leadership, School Leadership and Headship'. In J. O'Brien (ed.) *School Leadership* (Third Edition). Edinburgh: Dunedin, pp. 1–29.

OECD (2015) Part II, Chapter 9 'Implementing School Improvement Reforms'. In *Education Policy Outlook 2015: Making Reforms Happen, OECD Publishing*, pp. 155–170.

Rhodes, C. and Brundrett, M. (2009) 'Leadership for learning'. In Bush, T., Bell, L. and Middlewood, D. (eds). *The Principles of Educational Leadership and Management* (Second Edition). London: Sage, pp. 153–175.

Richard, R., Church, M. and Morrison, K. (2011) *Making Thinking Visible: How to Promote Engagement, Understanding and Independence for All Learners*. San Francisco, CA: Jossey-Bass.

Robinson, M. (2013) *Trivium 21c: Preparing Young People for the Future with Lessons from the Past*. Carmarthen: Independent Thinking Press.

Rosenshine, B. (2012) 'Principles of Instruction: Research-Based Strategies That All Teachers Should Know', *American Educator*, 36(1), Spring 2012, pp. 12–19.

Sherrington, T. (2017) *The Learning Rainforest: Great Teaching in Real Classrooms*. Woodbridge: John Catt Educational Ltd.

Sinek, S. (2011) *Start With Why: How Great Leaders Inspire Everyone To Take Action*. London: Penguin.

Sutton Trust (2015) *Developing Teachers: Improving Professional Development for Teachers*. London: The Sutton Trust.

Torrance, D. and Humes, W. (2015) 'The Shifting Discourses of Educational Leadership: International Trends and Scotland's Response'. *Educational Management Administration and Leadership*, 43(5), pp. 792–810.

Walker, A. (2009) 'Building and Leading Learning Cultures'. In Bush, T., Bell, L. and Middlewood, D. (eds) *The Principles of Educational Leadership and Management* (Second Edition). London: Sage, pp. 176–196.

Ward, S.C., Bagley, C., Lumby, J., Hamilton, T., Woods, P. and Roberts, A. (2016) 'What is "Policy" and What is "Policy Response"? An Illustrative Study of the Implementation of the Leadership Standards for Social Justice in Scotland'. *Educational Management Administration and Leadership*, 44(1), pp. 43–56.

Weinstein, Y. and Sumeracki, M. (2019) *Understanding How We Learn: A Visual Guide*. London: Routledge.

Wiliam, D. (2011) *Embedded Formative Assessment*. Bloomington: Solution Tree Press.

Wiliam, D. and Leahy, S. (2015) *Embedding Formative Assessment*. West Palms Beach, FL: Learning Sciences International.

Wiliam, D. (2018) *Creating the Schools Our Children Need: Why What We're Doing Now Won't Help Much (And What We Can Do Instead)*. West Palms Beach, FL: Learning Sciences International.

Willingham, D. (2010) *Why Don't Students Like School? A Cognitive Scientist Answers Questions About How the Mind Works and What It Means for the Classroom*. San Francisco, CA: Jossey-Bass.

Young, M. and Lambert, D. (2014) *Knowledge and the Future School: Curriculum and Social Justice*. London: Bloomsbury.

Acknowledgements

Teaching is one of the most important jobs in the world. It is also one of the best jobs in the world. The profession has given me a lot. I have written *The Teaching Delusion* to give something back.

Writing it has been both challenging and enjoyable. It has taken a lot of time and it has required a lot of support. I wish to take this opportunity to acknowledge some of the key people who have supported me.

Firstly, I would like to acknowledge the staff and students of Eyemouth High School. While this book is about more than one school, Eyemouth High School has helped shaped it. It is a special school because of the people who are a part of it. These people are the school. Without them, this book would not exist.

I would never have become a teacher without the support and encouragement of my family. My mum, dad, sister and grandparents have supported me throughout my life. No one could wish for a better family. I would not be the person I am today without them.

Choosing teaching as a profession is one of the best decisions I ever made. It was Douglas Buchanan from the University of Edinburgh who saw the potential in me and who gave me my first break by accepting me onto the postgraduate teacher training programme in 2002. Douglas is one of the best teachers I have ever had.

In 2015, I returned to the University of Edinburgh to study educational leadership at Masters level. Deirdre Torrance and Sheila Laing were wonderful course tutors and I credit them with igniting my passion for reading. Without them, I'm not sure I would have that passion.

I started to write *The Teaching Delusion* in 2018. I am tremendously grateful to my colleagues and friends who, over the course of 18 months, have read and reread drafts, offering feedback and suggestions. It would not be the book that it is without them. In particular, I would like to thank Derek Huffman (English teacher at Berwickshire High School), Kelly Fairbairn (former head of English at Eyemouth High School and now deputy headteacher at this school), Ian Yule (head of additional support at Eyemouth High School) and Scott Steele (headteacher at Lochaber High School). The input they have given me has been invaluable.

I am hugely grateful to Alex Sharratt, Jonathan Barnes and everyone else at John Catt Publishing for believing in this book and for all of the support they have given me in writing it. I am also very grateful to Megan Whiting and Gráinne Treanor, who have proof-read this book at various stages in its development, and to Robin Macpherson, who has written a wonderful foreword to it.

Finally, I would like to thank my husband, Jamie. The support and encouragement he has given me has been incredible. Jamie is also a teacher and loves the profession as much as I do. This book is dedicated to him and to every other teacher who believes in using the power of learning to transform lives.